WHEN THERE'S NO PLACE LIKE HOME

An Autobiography of the Homeless

NOAH SNIDER

THOMAS NELSON PUBLISHERS
Nashville

Published in Nashville, Tennessee, by Thomas Nelson, Inc., and
distributed in Canada by Lawson Falle, Ltd., Cambridge, Ontario.

Scripture quotations are from the Holy Bible: New International
Version. Copyright © 1973, 1978, 1984 International Bible Society.
Used by permission of Zondervan Bible Publishers.

Library of Congress Cataloging-in-Publication Data

Snider, Noah.
     When there's no place like home : an autobiography of the homeless
/ Noah Snider.
          p.   cm.
     Includes bibliographical references.
     ISBN 0-8407-3324-0 (pb)
     1. Homelessness—United States.   2. Snider, Noah.   3. Homeless
persons—Oklahoma—Oklahoma City—Biography.   I. Title.
HV4505.S65   1991
305.5′69—dc20   91–23898
                                                            CIP

Printed in the United States of America
1 2 3 4 5 6 7 — 96 95 94 93 92 91

CONTENTS

PART SEVEN
More Help Wanted

PREFACE

Stress and distress are not difficult to find in the world around us and in our own lives. It touches each of us in a private way. Stress comes to some wrapped in the pressure of personal relationships. For others, stress is the battle to succeed financially. For some, distress is the frustration of a cause: Save the Whales, Feed the Children, Cure AIDS, Defend the Earth. For many, it is the investigation into a childhood that may have caused recurring pain and sorrow beyond our understanding, or the battle to change our psychological profile and buried anger. For some, it is aging in a society that worships youth. For others, it is keeping up with the newest style and fashion so we can be accepted.

Tremendous stress also comes from rapid changes in society, our difficulty keeping pace with technology, and the competitive way world business works. Distress for many is born in the change of religion's role in their lives, in the growing lack of respect for once uncontested church doctrines, and in the resulting loss of that once guaranteed security and warranty backed by the Word of God. There is stress in all that we want and do not have in life, and in all that we have yet want more of.

We all seem to be caught up in a maelstrom of change, a world that doesn't remember the luxury of stopping long enough to determine our purpose and position. Any day in any paper, sandwiched between strudel recipes and movie schedules, are the bolder headlines:

SOVIETS FLEX MUSCLE IN LITHUANIA

CZECHS SOLD LIBYA TONS OF EXPLOSIVES

CATHOLICS DROP CHILDREN'S
HOME AS TOO VIOLENT

JAPANESE BUY MORE OF AMERICA

TWELVE MILLION CAIRO RESIDENTS DOWN
SLEEPING PILLS TO ESCAPE NOISE

FIFTEEN THOUSAND AUTO
WORKERS LAID OFF

ISRAELIS KILL PALESTINIANS IN NABLUS

TV MINISTER INVESTIGATED

INTEREST RATES RISE

PRISON POPULATION EXPLODES

STORMS EXPECTED TO INTENSIFY AS
WORLD TEMPERATURE INCREASES

STREET GANGS WELL ARMED

BOY KILLED FOR HIS TENNIS SHOES

EMBARGO ON CONSUMING FISH
FROM THE GREAT LAKES

TENSIONS RISE IN SOUTH AFRICA

SATANIC CULTS INCREASE

COCAINE CARTEL KILLS ANOTHER
PRESIDENTIAL HOPEFUL

600–700 BANKS TO GO BELLY UP

MIDDLE EAST BOILING AGAIN

COMMITTEE SAYS 19 MILLION
MAY BE HOMELESS BY 2000

GOVERNMENT OFFICIAL SAYS
HOMELESSNESS TO END BY 2000

RECESSION TO BE SHORT LIVED
SAYS GOVERNMENT OFFICIAL

RECESSION TO BE EXTENSIVE
SAYS ANALYST.

We need not look far to find the fools, buffoons, and offenders of God and Nature's laws in this life; they are all around us. They are the ones we love and hate, the ones we avoid, the ones we like and dislike, the ones we distrust, and the ones we trust. None of us need look further than our own mirror. For in that reflection we can find the best of all mankind and the very worst, the trusted and the untrustworthy, the loyal and the betrayer, the one who would die for the truth but lies to live.

Ultimately, we all will be judged under God's law, not man's, for we can live according to the law of humankind and yet fall short of obeying the universal law of love. All of us are like the dung beetle. We begin at birth rolling this ball of dung made from the illusion of others. The ball grows and grows until we are of an age to plant our own seed. We then lay our eggs in the ball we have been pushing, so that when the egg is pierced from within and the new soul emerges, it must instantly begin its rolling of the dung remaining from its parent. And so we are a species of creature who by choice, not by design, push our dung balls of illusion through life and onto our young.

But we were designed to be butterflies, taking what we need gently and leaving the color of all things intact. We were designed to light softly on all things, leaving no debris, only ensuring that next year's colors are never duller for our having been there.

Somewhere, somehow we lost our color. Few of us make it through chrysalis now. We are locked by choice into being caterpillars, eating everything in our path.

I know a story of an old man who returns from a journey on which he readjusted his perspective of life. In prose and poetry he answers the questions of a young seeker of truth.

The youth asked the old man, "Did you have a home, and live like the rest of us?"

The old man answered, "Yes, but I have a home now. It is on the inside. Everyone needs a home to go to where they can be safe, secure, where worry must wait outside the door. We all need a place where the voice of our self-created gods cannot touch the ears of our mind. A place where the candles to appease the spirits need never be lighted, and the demons and gods wear no disguise.

"For we are all a little of the virgin and the whore, the law and the lawless, the one who would die to give and kill to keep, the real and the reflection."[1]

In the book you hold in your hands, you will meet some of the butterflies in our world. The ones who, in the bleaching process of life, somehow retained their color. You will also meet some of those who have become gray with desperation, and those who have been blackened by greed. You will find yourself here in these pages. We are all here.

We all live in the tapestries we weave. Tangled in each private tapestry is the warp color of our own limited experience and the weft of our personal being and private belief. We are only what we allow and are allowed. We are all weavers of life, our own and others'. Yet, in the overall larger weaving of the universe, we are but loose threads waiting to be pulled from the system of things. The universe does not need us. We are most important to our own importance. Such are the colors of the poor and the rich. One does not weigh more than the other.

Each of us has met and been touched by butterflies in our lives, for their color sets them aside from those hiding in the sameness of life's gray. They are the ones who gave not from their abundance of things but from their abundance of love. They are the ones who helped in our greatest need and did not abandon us. They are the ones who did not consider us an investment, and upon their judgment of retarded return, sell us short.

No one walks this journey in self-made shoes, but our direction is ultimately our own choice. Choices change as do perspectives and parameters. But only love will expand them.

Stay with the progression of the book, if you will. I will walk you in a retracing of the steps of comfort and despair. I may lead you around what isn't pleasant to step in. We do not have to stand in something to know it is there. I still have enough of that part of life on my shoe for both of us. We will walk into each door of reason, to view the problem of homelessness, and exit to reason its impact on our lives. In your hands of justice we will place both sides of the issue. Hold them if you will. Warm them with your compassion. Then, weighed with your honor, put the conclusion away on the shelves of your heart and do what you are moved to do. Homelessness is a complex and rapidly spreading disease that chicken soup and rest can not cure. I know. I was homeless once.

I thank the editors and Thomas Nelson Publishers for allowing the book to be published as written. The work is a composite of styles and nonstyles, as we all are. It is texture and color—sometimes pleasant sometimes not, as we all are. It is orderly at moments and disorderly at others, as we ourselves are. The book follows the maze of right and wrong turns we all follow in the attempt to alleviate the problem of the homeless and the maze some have followed while living there.

I supplied the editors with a bag of periods and commas, with instructions to put them wherever they wished. It did not matter to me. I believed then and believe now that a portion of the problem in getting help to those in need is the insistence on form and forms. Under and in the paperwork and red tape is a convenient place to hide until we can figure out what we are willing to do about the growing problem. By the time many can qualify for help or we can determine how to help, it will be too late.

I invite you to step up on this paper treadmill. Walk with me and watch the seam of frustration go around and around. The benefit of this written treadmill is that you may get off any time you wish. Hopefully you will stay on for a few turns. The people in the text, for the most part, are unable to choose.

I have used the interview format to expose the reader to the personality, philosophy, and individual methods of helping. The interviews also allow private assessment of the problems and programs related to homelessness. This book has the texture of the homeless tragedy.

Our speech is an ingredient of our personality. We use it as seasoning to our image. Everyone has his or her own recipe of nouns and adjectives and uses them as salt to their conversations. I have not changed much of the flavor of the interviews and quotations. That is a part of their charm you will share. One chapter is transcribed from the tape much as it was recorded. This book has the texture of the homeless tragedy.

I have had absolutely no problem getting interviews with the advocates and front-line volunteers. However, I have not been able to quote one single government policy-maker. I attempted to reach Secretary Kemp and his assistant, Anna Kondratas, for official government response. I was able to speak with a number of staff personnel, regional directors, and analysts. I received information by taped interview, by mail, and in person. Every one of the staff representatives of HUD freely discussed their personal, professional, and official government opinion.

However, without exception, I was asked not to use names. I have done that. I thank each and every one of you for trusting me. There was not one staff member that did not generally support the government's position. There was not one person who said that Secretary Kemp was less than a dedicated and sensitive servant of the people. I wish I could have met him, perhaps one day I will.

There are those who say, "Get involved in the political process for change, contact an elected official, make a phone call, write a letter." To them I say, "This was my first sincere attempt to do so and I never got past the guards. It was easier hitching a ride with my pants off."

We always risk offending some when we publicly thank the ones who have helped us, for invariably we neglect some names. To those who have been the butterflies in my life, I thank you now, though I too often neglected to do so when it would have been most appropriate.

I thank Jay and Ann Davis for the lamp and the love, and Jim Wilson and his wife for supporting me.

I thank all of my friends who offered me a place to rest; Mike and Deborah Scott for the bed and books; Jefferson Spivey, a

"Drinker of the Wind" and one of the finest writers I have ever met.

Jeff and Allison, one day I will be able to help you.

Sondra Threepersons for help with "The American Dream"; George Williams for the job and believing in me again; Chad Ransdell for his integrity unbroken.

Charlie Dry and Anita Bryant for the help, devotion, and support in my writing—I wish you the best of all things honorable in your new life together.

To Lloyd and Carol Allen for a place to stay in Nashville.

Pat Jacobs, the world's greatest woodcarver and friend.

Also thank you to Brian Clark for the strength and the steadying and the many, many, many hours of assistance on this project; one day you will read his amazing book.

Ted Squires and Bill Watkins at Thomas Nelson for believing in an unknown writer. Bill, I am forever in your debt.

To all my new friends at and with TAS, and especially Marie, thank you.

To all those who donated their time and thoughts to this effort, I gratefully acknowledge your help. To Father Jerry Hill, Harry and Bubba Dailey, Marguerite Gras, Congressman Walter Fauntroy, to Sister Ruth Wynne and Sister Betty Adams and all those with the greater wings, I am better for having known you.

I saw her a Friday ago, dressed in her bib overalls and blue hair bandana. She was stooping to dry the tears from the eyes of a small homeless boy. "It's all right," she said. "Jesus loves you." That was the very first thing she ever said to me. She waved good-bye. "See you next week, Noah. Jesus loves you."

Sister Betty Adams died Friday, May 3, 1991. I went to see her that Sunday. She knew I would. The Jesus House will miss her; I already do. But Jesus House and my memory are a whole lot fuller. Jesus loves you, Betty.

IN MEMORY OF
SISTER BETTY ADAMS

HISTORY

I have often wondered why history was important at all; we so seldom learn to avoid old mistakes. The path we take is the path we have already taken. We all seem to exist on a huge wheel and each time the wheel meets the earth the ones on the bottom are squashed. Why is it that after all these centuries of the earth spinning, the ones on the bottom are still being destroyed? Why have a bottom at all if it is assured destruction? Could it be that we simply do not become actively concerned until we personally are nearing the bottom, and the ones on the top who could do something are not yet interested?

Sometimes something is just far, far too big for little people to see it. For instance, the earth was once thought to be flat because it was too big to be seen even when the tallest of us stood on his ignorance and strained his eyes and imagination.

Sometimes when something seems too big, we stop looking for its end and make excuses why we no longer care. That is what maps are for. The distance between New York and Los

Angeles is only two *inches* on the map in my atlas. That doesn't seem very far. Two inches is three hard days' drive in my experience. I know where I am at any given point of that trip because I know where I have been and the time it takes to reach my goal. I have a map, I have a destination, I have a time frame. I know where I am.

The best way to know where we are at any given time in our history is to know where we have been. Where we are, then, is a measure of how sophisticated we have become in our human development. It is the benchmark for assessing our progress or lack of it.

There are a few things we can be reasonably sure of and many things we cannot. One thing we can be sure of is we got here somehow. I am not a historian. History seems so complicated with the varying views of the observers and the experts who have dedicated lifetimes and made their living to supposing what and why things happened. This is what I think might have happened, though I am not sure. One thing I know for sure: Whatever happened had a direct bearing on what is happening and what will happen, and that includes the homeless.

The clouds have been circling the earth greeting the dawn for a considerable time. Some estimate that the universe has given birth to 5,575,000,000,000,000 dawns. It is estimated that the earth has spun to greet the dawn perhaps 1,000,000,000,000 times. Some in the scientific community believe man has opened his eyes to 14,600,000 dawns, give or take a couple million dawns one way or another.

Some who interpret the Bible feel man has watched the dark change to day 2,170,000 times, give or take nothing. I don't know about all that; I was not there. Beyond that I really don't care that much. I could have witnessed about 18,250 dawns myself, but I slept through most of them. I do not miss many now; I wait for them.

One fact that I accept and am very comfortable with is that this elderly and stately earth got along quite well without us. Trees and plants grew and multiplied to cover most of the earth not covered by water. The ocean filled with thousands and thousands of life forms, and the land filled with creatures of all shapes, sizes, and colors. Some had skin, some fur, some scales, some had feathers, some shells. Both on the land and in the water, big things killed and ate smaller things, then died and were eaten by still smaller things. *Then something happened.* . . .

Many of the biggest things were killed off. The biggest things remaining went on killing the smaller things remaining and things continued on about the same. That's just the way it was. *Then something happened.* . . .

The temperature changed and more big things and little things died, but that was all right because what remained kept eating each other in life and death. Someone or something started painting on cave walls and the wearing of fur became stylish. *Then something happened.* . . .

Humans picked up sticks and tied stones to them and started to kill bigger things and little things and each other. Then something happened and they started killing everything.

Here is where I bog down a bit. I think what happened was some early bankers and stockbrokers who did not like to work came up with the concept that stones with holes in them and clam shells and shiny metal were more valuable than just plain old food, like raw meat and grubs. And the amazing thing is they sold the idea to those who worked and had the food.

Somewhere in the trading process a certain animosity developed between the productive people and the fellows with the stones, and that animosity exists even today. The people of the stones thought they were better than others because they were able to get the food they needed with the labor of their minds, not their backs. The people of the ground thought they were better because they worked for their keep and took no advantage of the earth or anyone.

A great deal of things seemed to happen during this time. It appears we divided into groups and called them tribes. The bankers were in one tribe and the farmers were in another and so on. And it seems every tribe had a private god that charged varying amounts to protect the people in that tribe and listen to their prayers. Some of the gods wanted people's hearts cut out with a special stone knife; others wanted people to party. One wanted people to behave. (Is this confusing? Just bear with me, if you please, because I'm struggling with this too.) *Then something happened. . . .*

It seems God was worn to a nub over all the bickering about who was worth what. He became tired of the partying of so many who were interested only in their own enjoyment, and the I-don't-care-about-anyone-else attitude. He despised people killing each other. So he had a man build a boat and told him to warn everyone of what was about to happen. The man also invited everyone on board. They did not listen; it rained and they drowned.

Now some say this did not happen and some say it did. The division remains. However, scientists say the water or the ground rose because they have found shells on the top of some mountains. I have never seen a shell on a mountain because I throw up when I climb a ladder. I'll take their word for it and bypass the entire argument.

Some time passed. Things went on as usual, as they usually do. The different gods made it through the flood along with the spirit of the entrepreneur. So the worker and the work and the division continued in their drying new world.

Somehow people developed different colors and colorful languages and further division ensued. Men drew lines around their towns and things so they could say, "I'm from There," or "This is mine." If you were not from There, There probably was less than safe. So men stayed where they were until they wanted what some others over There had, then they simply went over and took it. *Then something happened. . . .*

God wrote a note on a stone and said, "Don't do that." The people said, "Okay," but continued as usual—finding, selling, or stealing stones and clams and shiny things.

They continued to kill each other and divide and draw more lines of difference. There were considerably more people now with more and better weapons. Some had every possession available and became bored, so they began collecting and owning people. The practice took hold and gave the broker something new to inventory. Trade flourished and more division grew and grew and grew. *Then something happened. . . .*

God sent his Son to tell the people not to do that. Some said, "Okay," and the rest, along with some of the teachers of the words on the stone tablet, killed Him.

Before He died, He said, "Remain apart from all that was not good in the world and continue to love one another. In this way all the world will know you are my disciples." He also said things would get worse. True to all His words, things did. People continued to divide. Even many of the ones who believed in the Man began killing each other, and they could not be told apart from the ones who did not believe in Him.

They continued to kill each other. They kept many enslaved to make themselves rich. They started to kill everything again; this time the trees and the oceans themselves. Even the earth, which had always been an exacting yet gracious landlord, began to complain loudly about the way humans were disrespecting their lease.

Fewer and fewer had everything, and more and more had nothing. Condoms became a convenient replacement for moral value, so, many just pulled a cellophane condom over themselves to keep out all the distraction. And everything went on about the same as always and it was impossible to tell this always from any other. *Then something happened. . . .*

Comic Relief had not happened yet, but Earth Day had. Farm Aid II played to and for many. Some started to separate their plastic bottles from the cans and the glass. Some were frightened, some were angry, and some started riding bikes. But most were still struggling with the changes taking place and began looking at the promises that only seemed to affect fewer and fewer. Hope was slowly replaced by impatience. That terrible hulking apparition, *Revolution,* was pulling back his black hood, knowing that soon, like Barabbas, the people would probably choose him over Reason. Bickering and war, distrust and distraction, hunger and poverty, disease and despair were growing.

Then something happened. . . .

A publisher pulled one who was about to be squashed from under the wheel. They picked him up, dusted him off, adjusted his tilted dignity, and asked him to see if anything might be done for the others about to be crushed. So he gratefully gave up being an impression in the sand of time for the moment and found some on the top that had begun to be very interested in stopping the wheel. And he talked to them. This is their story, mine, and some of the homeless who live among us.

MEET THE
HOMELESS

PART **1**

CHAPTER
ONE

Gutter to Glory

I used to know a girl who liked to lick the sidewalk. I thought by the time she was twenty, she'd have a tongue like the sole of a tennis shoe. My wife told me one of her friends licked concrete when she was young. I don't understand that. There must be a reason for licking concrete. There must be a reason for many of the things we do.

I find, at fifty, there are many things I do not understand. I do not understand how some people seem to have everything and some seem to have little or nothing. I do not understand how many with a lot of things feel they are more important or more valuable than those with less. They seem to have a special relationship with a God that allows them to feel that way. They can do what they want socially and morally, and they pay fairly well for the special position in His or Her eyes (His or Her depends on whom you are talking to).

I do not understand why some of the poor and homeless feel

they have less value than those with more things. But I do know their relationship with their God is more dependent.

I do not understand how I have come to feel both the feelings of those who have and those who have not. It just might be because I have been both. I have lived both lives. Because of the comfort of the having portion of my life, I would like to return to it. Because of the insight of the have-not portion, I cannot return to it totally.

There are things I do understand. I understand greed. I felt its temptation and its pull. I do not, however, understand how I justified owning it. I understand desire, too, and the security money and things seem to ensure. I understand now that money and things can change ownership in a seeming instant, and that their departure takes with them the security, confidence, social position, friends, and at times wives, and the heretofore unappreciated comfort of a home. I have come to believe that their departure can, and may, happen to any of us.

I understand how comfortable I feel at this moment at this typewriter, how good the warm room wrapped around me feels, how safe I feel here with some of my things lying around me. This night I am an egg in a secure nest, high above the street where I lived six months ago. But I am reminded by that indelible experience that nests are occasionally shaken by the winds of change or heartless hands. I know, too, that eggs fall. The best the egg can hope for is a soft landing and small cracks. I know, too, that promises and commitments by even those you love and who profess to love you are seldom kept when you cannot live up to the standards they set for your life. We are living in a time when the bank balance somehow is in direct proportion to the value society places on our value as a person. It is a difficult moment in the history of mankind.

I remember how the street erased most of my options. Perhaps it was sleeping on the street that someone may have licked. Perhaps the humor of that scene brought back some of the options. I remember being hungry, shivering with the cold, and trembling in the wet weakness of the morning. I remember trying to pray my darkness away, wishing the one I loved would somehow love me enough to find me, and say the magic words "I love you for what you are, not for what I would have you be."

4

I realize how the intensity of that short period of my life shaded and shaped my perspective of things, of me and life and love and God, of right and wrong and fairness and money, of commitment and marriage and parenting, of friends and the future, of my size, of the size of the world and the universe, of the way hate is born by breach birth and how it washes in growing waves over reason. I realize, too, how hate can erode the illusion of social control, how its malignancy can grow to consume both its host and target.

This is what I term the ledger of my life—the things I can understand and the things I cannot. I understand we probably all have ledgers, kept on paper or in our souls. In the coming pages, we will examine some ledgers together. I realize we will agree and disagree. That is but a part of your ledger and mine. My ledger concludes that all ledgers will one day be totaled. I understand, too, that we all act out our private ledgers.

How do we make sense of all the dialogue, all the varying facts and figures concerning the homeless? How do we put them into unified motion? How do we mold all of the fractured interests into a homogenous form that will flow through the conduit of the helping heart into the veins and lives of the helpless and homeless?

In the six months since this book began, approximately forty-nine million new souls have arrived on our planet. If you are an average reader, there will be one million more when you finish in four days. Sixty to 70 percent of them will have been born to absolute, abject poverty. Disease and hunger is the very best they can expect. This book addresses one manifestation of this growing and real problem in our world, our country, our state, our cities, and in many of our own families. It is but one symptom of the disease eating at the world's format and structure. It is a visible ulcer of an underlying virus now affecting every man, woman, and child alive. It is the problem of homelessness.

To understand the ramifications and difficulties in solving the homeless issue, we must identify the problems effecting its staggering growth and the growing concern for its existence. One problem is the availability of jobs. This issue of fewer work opportunities, in turn, has its feet in the new technology of today and the ecological concerns now sweeping our planet. The growing aggression in the world to compete for industry and commerce brings global competition to our job markets.

This book is not about condemning or judging. It is simply meant to remove the cataracts covering our eyes and hearts so we can see the possibilities—the possibility of lessening the number of homeless, and the possible consequences for not doing so. The diagnosis is easy: Our society is sick, very sick. Some say terminally. The prognosis, at best, is not optimistic. This mirrors a social, moral, and spiritual problem, which many still refuse to examine. It is the fruit of graft, greed, corruption, lack of love, and lack of faith. It is the product of both poor management and poor planning, by the poor and rich alike. And it is no longer someone else's problem. It is your problem. And it is my problem.

I accept the fact that this book will not be embraced by those with their head in their designer jeans, but I am certain there are millions of Americans who are blessed with resources, who not only want to help, but will rush to help. I am also certain this book will be welcomed by some of the estimated seven hundred thousand to three million homeless, the estimated thirty million souls living at or below the poverty level, and those ten to twenty million Americans nearing the poverty level.

The time for articulate debate and dialogue is past. We can no longer hide the problem under piles of buzz words. The luxury of those living outside the tragedy of poverty is no longer a protection. When the outrage of diverting funds for the sustenance of the poor to the building of golf courses in Palm Springs becomes national shame, the anger of those hungry and hopeless—who have had their children's sandwich pay for the sand- wedge of the greedy wealthy—will turn to hate for all those in the Palm Springs of the country, the very ones who can and in many cases have helped. And when the abuses of some who received have turned off the tap of assistance, the hornet will sting himself.

We all have options. Our option is to add to or remove data from our ledger at will. Our option is to close our doors to sensitivity and pain and distraction or to open them. It is our private option to pay attention to what is happening around us or to ignore the danger signals. But we must remember that our options do not affect only ourselves. They ripple throughout our relationships and their relationships. We are not simply individuals. We are communities, composed of social beings dependent on one another . . . whether we like it or not. If we fail to come to grips with this, we will die a slow, agonizing, lonely death, and thousands upon thousands will die with us. The choice is ours—yours and mine. And it has everything to do with the problem of the homeless, with how we respond to their need, and how they respond to us. This book is about both the haves and the have-nots, and what we can do to help each other.

Who Are We?

That's a fair question. Who are the homeless anyway? There have been hundreds of newspaper and magazine articles covering the plight of the poor, and hundreds of television and radio hours devoted to profiling the homeless. From these "reports" it appears that most people believe the majority of homeless are substance abusers and the severely mentally ill. The best estimate for homeless families with children is 33 to 65 percent of the "homeless population."[1]

Most of the articles I have read contain phrases such as "The facts are" or "In fact." I do not know what the facts are. That is, I have found no way to verify data for myself. I'm sure, however, that the number of actual poor and homeless is staggering, by even the most conservative accounts. My ledger says that if the number was one—especially when I was the one—it would be one too many.

We use a variety of terms to describe the homeless: the *tem-*

porarily dislocated, underhoused, transitory between dwell-ings. A term I particularly dislike is *homeless population.* It is distasteful, disturbing. It tells us more about the homeful than the homeless. It is used by those that have exiled the extremely needy to a nation of their own. A nation without leadership, without resource, without territory. It condemns the homeless to citizenship in a nomadic nation within a narcissistic nation. It fosters an us-and-them mentality, keeping us at arm's length from each other, permitting us to define and segment each other in terms of wealth or the lack of it rather than in terms of intrinsic worth and dignity as human beings. How tragic we are as a nation, moving our social and economical bulk on the lubrication provided by currency inscribed with the motto "IN GOD WE TRUST," But so many of our individual and corporate actions betray the motto we truly believe in: "IN MONEY I TRUST."

In a *U.S. News and World Report* article by David Whitman, Dorian Friedman, and Laura Thomas entitled "The Return of Skid Row," the authors conclude that the growth in the population of homeless substance abusers stems from a number of causes, including the disappearance of the flophouse, looser regulation of public drunkenness, and the popularity of crack cocaine. They argue that the increase in the number of homeless has swelled taxpayer payments for them because their problems are far more intractable than those of the displaced families featured in most media accounts. "Unfortunately few soup kitchens and shelters do anything to help homeless substance abusers break their addiction."

The authors of the article further conclude that the public is more sympathetic to alcoholics and drug abusers who are rich and famous than to those who "tug on the sleeves of passersby for a handout. The conscience-stricken need to understand that addicts need as much help as the celebrities treated at the Betty Ford Clinic."

My ledger has a special feeling of love and respect for authors of articles like this. This assignment apparently was or became more important to them than the payment they received. But it accents the massive complexity of homelessness. Their conclusions are only partially true. The disappearance of flophouses and the looser regulation of public drunkenness did not cause

9

homelessness; rather they made the street people more visible by the lack of places to keep them from view. These conditions do not cause the number of homeless to rise. On the other hand, the increased visibility of substance abusers is due to the growth in the number of users. And the fewer places available to keep them out of sight simply forces awareness.

Moreover, increased public drunkenness does not show a change in the law; rather, it demonstrates our greater tolerance for this offense and the lack of jail space to hold all the offenders. The Oklahoma Department of Corrections reports that there were 755,422 prisoners nationwide as of June 30, 1990, a 12 percent increase over June 1989. At any rate, my ledger cannot equate a jail cell to a home. The chemical abuser or the public drunk remains homeless, even if he does have his cell for the night. We can simply no longer house or hide them all.

The public may also be more tolerant of the celebrity abuser than the poor, staggering, vomiting soul we see on the street. Perhaps it is also true that he or she needs as much help as the celebrity. My ledger says to me the one on the street needs infinitely more. I believe the public simply relates better to one they wish to emulate socially.

The dozens of celebrities who have gone public with their addictions have done so because they were touched by other hearts while in treatment, and they now wish to touch other hearts in need. People such as Betty Ford, Larry Gatlin, and Johnny Cash, now dedicate a great proportion of their time and energy to making a difference. Perhaps they were moved to action because they personally experienced one of the most insidious problems facing human beings. Whatever the reason, one will find few celebrities who have added the same validation to the problem of poverty and homelessness. I am aware of no star who has lived in the street and returned to speak to us of the desperation there. So it seems most of us have a problem relating to it. I could not relate to it either—until I had been there myself.

Perhaps we need to define *home*, for we all live within our definitions. *Webster's Dictionary* defines *home* as: (1.a.) A place where one lives; Residence. (1.b.) An apartment or house. (2.) A household. (3.) A place of origin. (4.) A habitat, as of an animal or plant. (5.) The goal in a game, as baseball. (6.) An institution for those who need help or care.[2]

If we take the definition as stated, there are no homeless. And this book ends here. Everyone lives somewhere; everyone resides somewhere. The homeless live in the street, under bridges, in cars, in condemned buildings, in missions, in back rooms, in alleys and dumpsters, in cardboard boxes, on couches not their own, in back bedrooms of the generous. We have offered them the pillory of society for a pillow.

But the closest some of the homeless will ever get to the luxury of what you and I call home is when they enter our home via the nightly news. In this light, definition 4 above is perhaps the definition of the street person's home: "A habitat, as of an animal or plant." There are other homeless as well: those not yet living in definition 4. They are living with friends. Some have gone back to parents or family. They are homeless, although they are not counted in the statistical computations. These are called the *couch* homeless. They are the next candidates for visibility as homeless. When talking to staff members at HUD, the couch homeless have not been considered in the computations of numerical totals.

That makes sense to me, in that it is impossible to count these people even though the last census form had a provision for gathering that statistic. Although a space was provided for noting anyone other than owner or tenant as occupying the dwelling, by the very mentioning of the additional tenant we somehow make the temporary permanent. That is neither acceptable to the guest nor his or her host. So this couch homeless person is in that lost land of the underhoused, the transitory twilight zone.

My ledger says a home is where your stuff is, where you are safe, where you are comfortable, where your mail is delivered, where you are nurtured and supported, where you reside unconditionally until you decide to take a new home. A home is where the spirits and the demons of the dark street are not welcome and are not provided a key. A home is where God can find you when you can't seem to find Him. It's the space you can mess up or clean up at your option. It's the place you can receive guests or refuse to.

It is true some prefer the brutality of the street to the brutality of an abusive home. Perhaps they were homeless before they left. The problem of runaway children is a particularly distressing one, with the estimated number equalling some total estimates of the homeless. I wonder where they all found a new home. I wonder about a lot of things. I wonder why totals do not add up, why so many assumptions and perceptions and attitudes and causes seem to lack reason.

I watched an HBO special last year, featuring a very talented and socially sensitive comedian named Louie Anderson. A portion of his monologue dealt with the homeless. It went something like this: The homeless, I don't know what to do, they all have nine coats on. No wonder they are bent over, and they have all the best shopping carts. They have all the best carts. Really, they do. No kidding, go into any grocery, you can see the shoppers going around in circles, pushing a cart with a bad front wheel, saying to themselves, "Darn homeless."

He said he would like to say to them: "Hey, what are you doing? Take one of those coats off when I talk to you. By the time I'm done talking I want all those coats off. How come you have all those coats anyway? Don't you know there's a homeless person in China without a coat?"

He worked into his monologue the method by which his father might have handled such a conversation: "Hey, what you need is a good kick in the pants."

The laughter and applause that followed from the audience were not a fitting response to that young man with a truly sensitive soul. For while Lou's voice touched a horror of our time through humor, his face and his eyes said, "I have just told you how you respond to the tragedy of the poor, and by your laughter you condemn the condemned." A fitting response to Lou's monologue might have been silence or the outpouring of a contrite spirit. I have a feeling that is the response Louie Anderson is living for; it is the one he deserves for his insight, courage, and compassion. He is a responsible set of eyes in a world gone blind. In response to the audience, he shook his head, turned and whispered, "I don't know, I just don't know."

If one could enlist a few people from the talented and the wealthy, Louie Anderson, Robin Williams, Gallagher, Billy Crystal, Jonathan Winters, and Whoopi Goldberg would be a part of the comedy team. Sensitive men and women who wrap our condition in pills of humor, hoping that once they are inside of us, the listeners, the medicinal laughter will heal us.

I did not have nine coats, but I did think of the homeless and the poor in China and everywhere. I did not push a shopping cart and cause anyone to go in circles. But out of my experience this book was born, hopefully to repair the wheels on our shopping carts of illusion and pull even one able helper out of his or her circle of denial. This brings us to the original question of this chapter: *Who are the homeless?*

The homeless are those who can be and want to be helped. The ones who wait in lines for a job. The ones who wander with their children hoping to find a home and a place to fit in this great land of the free and the brave. They are also those who may not be helped to any great degree according to our standards, until they want to be. The ones who stumble and mumble to unseen rhythms and unheard voices, and those who are now content to soak their remaining gray cells in 90-proof escape. Some are like you and me; many are not. The homeless are those people you see carrying their small piece of cardboard bed. They are the abusers, the addicts, the ones who lost their jobs. Some are abused wives and their children. Some are the ones society has decided are not mentally ill enough for hospitalization, but are nevertheless carried as the "Mentally Ill" on the statistical data sheet of the homeless. Some are runaways. All are throwaways. Some are retired; all are disabled. Some receive pensions or welfare supplements. Some work, but still cannot afford to rent or buy a wooden shell to call home. One thing is certain: They all need help.

Whoever they are and regardless of their number, they have suffered greatly and still do. The reason may not be obvious . . . indeed it rarely is. But that gives us no reason to withhold help, for in the visibility of the homeless is hidden the invisible underlying cause. Something disastrous happened sometime to each and every one of the souls on the street. It happened before or after birth. It happened by choice or chance. Choice and chance happen to all of us all the time. But for the homeless the consequences were exclusion and banishment from the American

Dream, except by those attempting to stop the crushing social wheel.

Gatlin, keep singing your message; Louie, keep teaching through your humor; and the crowd with greater wings will surely grow.

CHAPTER
THREE

Pantsless

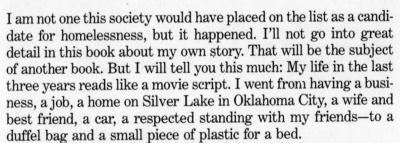

I am not one this society would have placed on the list as a candidate for homelessness, but it happened. I'll not go into great detail in this book about my own story. That will be the subject of another book. But I will tell you this much: My life in the last three years reads like a movie script. I went from having a business, a job, a home on Silver Lake in Oklahoma City, a wife and best friend, a car, a respected standing with my friends—to a duffel bag and a small piece of plastic for a bed.

I remember how I avoided looking into storefront windows. There was a time when I never missed an opportunity to see my reflection. But when I became homeless I did not want to look. I thought, *That isn't me. That can't be me. I don't have that deep wrinkle between my eyes. My shoulders don't stoop like that pitiful creature's. And look, just look, that isn't me! I have arms with muscles like softballs, but that wasted soul hasn't the mus-*

15

cle to move out of the way. I'm not like this. This isn't me . . . this isn't . . .

I realize that we all see ourselves in the windows and mirrors of our mind. But that image is usually distorted. It reflects more of what we want others to see than what we really are. Judging ourselves by that can be so unkind, so unfair. It leads us to become the reflection, to become an alien to our true selves.

My outward circumstances finally caused my inner reflection to fade into oblivion. I dissolved from a 190-pound man with everything to a 145-pound shell who had nothing. Two years before I was the subject of Bill Mitchell's "Sunday Noon" program on Channel 5 in Oklahoma City, profiled as a promising songwriter. Now, however, I was a pitiful waste looking for lunch. I was huddled internally with my helplessness. Looking back, I certainly lost a lot. But of all the things I lost, the most important were my joy and humor. Well, perhaps not all my humor. I remember thinking, *If I went back to Toledo they probably wouldn't give me the key to the city.* In my mind there wasn't any place I could return to be welcomed because the person in the window was not welcome in my mind.

Only a few years earlier, Vic Dunlop, the comedian with the funny eyes, had talked to me about writing for him. I thought about that when I woke the morning after my beating. I remember shouting that morning in a field outside Panama City, Florida: "Vic, there's nothing funny, not even those goofy eyes!" Sitting in that wet grass with no pants on and my shoes gone, I saw my guitar lying next to my feet. Scattered around were parts of a tablet with the songs I had been working on. My duffel bag was empty, a few old clothes lying quietly beside it. I started to laugh. I laughed until the tears burned my swollen eye and the laughing hurt my bruised face. I laughed at the thought that my attackers might have stolen my shoes and my pants, but they didn't steal my dignity. I didn't have any. I cried too. I cried for those poor souls who felt they had to beat me for my pants and shoes. I cried, too, because even in their desperation to find money and clothing, they somehow found the compassion to leave my guitar. I thought of the reality of that moment. The night before I had met some unknown souls who needed my things enough to beat me for them but who cared enough for an unknown beaten soul to leave what they thought was most important to him. I loved them for that. I still do. The morning after, I wrote a song called "Jonah." Perhaps you'll hear it one day. Perhaps, too, I will again meet the couple from Wisconsin, Mark and Judy, who stopped to help a pantsless derelict. They are invited to my home when I get one. They still live in my heart.

Later that morning, while sitting in the restaurant with Mark and Judy, wearing Mark's extra pants and shoes, I thought of all the lost people I had met and been on my journey to despair. I saw their hollow eyes and their tears, long since swallowed by the vast dry desert of the uncaring ones who could cry for their pet but scowled at the poor. That was the last step backward on my walk.

I've lived a lifetime in the two years since Panama City. I've traveled more than miles can measure from the absolute despair of that pantsless morning. Although there is much I still don't understand, there is one thing I understand absolutely: When a person is debilitated with nothingness, he needs a hand out of the bottomless well of hopelessness. And the advice "Take care of yourself," which I so often received from the one who professed to love me, expresses the attitude of many who are in a position to help. One day I am very certain the ones who are able to help themselves will understand the wisdom of those words. And one day, one very bright knowing day, perhaps the ones who say it will understand that everyone cannot take care of himself.

Homelessness, helplessness, hopelessness . . . this triangle of despair is what this book is about. Together they are symptoms of a problem vastly complex and intricately vested in the seniority and the history of man. A problem made even more complex by a large number of other survival issues. A high priority problem that, if not reduced to a workable equation, has the potential to change this country of two hundred and fifty million technologically advanced individuals into a handful of scavenging souls searching for nuts and berries.

This is an example of a possible point of disagreement in our ledgers. Why wait until the middle of the book to disagree? You don't have to agree to make my assumption right. Nor is it necessary that you disagree to make my assumption incorrect. I can accomplish that quite well on my own, thanks. That is a part of my ledger also. The words *high priority* and *complex* are a part of my ledger. I understand that my finding a meal a short time ago was exactly that. So *high priority* and *complex* will be only what your ledger provides.

My good friend Brian Clark wrote, "We are all single actors alone in a world of scripts." I think of that line often when I am adding to my ledger or when I am changing it. For we all live in our own illusion of life, an illusion formed by the fog we have passed through and the fog still remaining. Illusions are neither right nor wrong; they simply are. Illusion gains judgment only from other illusion and reality only in the assumption that is real.

So realities differ in the various colors of illusion. I lived in the illusion that my abilities and my things would forever keep me secure in my illusion of security. That illusion changed in the fear of what may be hiding beyond the streetlight in the darkness of the lonely night. That illusion changed when I could not walk to my refrigerator for a snack. That illusion disappeared along with the word *snack* from my vocabulary. A new vocabulary was formed . . . *fear* . . . *confusion* . . . *hungry* . . . *lost* . . . old words in new meaning.

I became the words to grasp the meaning. You see, when you feel the meaning you have the meaning. When you have the meaning you are, or become, the meaning, like the word *love* and the word *hate*. That is the illusion. And so my illusion changed, as did my certainty that life was not illusion but fact. Now my ledger says that even fact can be mere illusion, for the assumptions of statisticians given here in this book as fact, vary with the illusion of honesty and perception.

I went to see my friend Brian Clark when I received this assignment. I realized the anger within me could impact the potential benefit of this work. I felt a bitter anger toward the greedy rich who could help and have chosen to look away. I felt a growing anger toward those who have taken advantage of the help given them and in so doing have hardened those gracious givers who gave from love. Now, the betrayal by the Greedy Needy might prevent further giving. I felt as though that anger might build a barrier between those who will help and those who can be helped. He gave me another line from his book: *"I am one with all in the world of feelings, the world of love."* I have taped it in my memory. Some anger is good seasoning.

LEDGER

I UNDERSTAND	I DO NOT UNDERSTAND
We may all have our pants down.	Why we only notice the nakedness of others.

I met Marie Hollenbeck, executive director of the Traveler's Aid Society of Oklahoma. I was referred to her by Rick Moore, assistant to Mayor Norick. I was and continue to be amazed at the number of people who want to assist the weak and wobbly ones. Rick told me to talk to Marie, as she was involved in an attempt to count those who did not want to be counted. Marie had overseen the local census campaign and had actually gone to the street with pen and form in hand.

I arrived three days early for our appointment, but still was greeted by a most gracious lady. Marie listened to my story and, before I could ask, she said, "We can help. We are seeing more and more homeless people all the time. What do you need?"

Before I could tell her, she told me. She called the national headquarters and told them about my book project. She received their approval to assist in any way she wished. She culled a list of names and contacts in thirty states. She stayed with the project with patience and grace to completion.

She did one other thing. She advised me to lighten up. I assume I projected some inordinate amount of anger. I believe I looked like a tomato with a shirt on by the time I finished the list of those I was angry with. I do tend to get a touch rosy around the ports when I'm letting off a little steam. Marie was dedicated to the book effort so that it would be a fair and impartial view of the homeless issue. She spent many hours with me simply talking of potentials and frustrations, of successes and failures. I use the word *failure* with great caution. *Failure* is one of the best examples of the words of illusion. I was a failure in the eyes of myself and other illusions for a while. However, in this new illusion it appears that I was not a failure but a student, learning to live and sing and be in another whole new color of illusion.

Marie sent me to Dallas to meet Father Jerry Hill, "the Street Priest." She said Jerry had a different view of the homeless situation, and it would do an immeasurable amount of good to get a large dose of it on Austin Street.

I called Father Hill and told him who I was and what I thought I needed. He agreed to meet with me in Dallas on Monday. That is, for those of you who have not been there, Big-D-little-a-double-l-a-s: Dallas. Everything is big in Texas, including hearts.

Father Hill wasn't there on Monday. Dave, the large man at the door who greeted me, did not know where Father Hill was or when he would return. But he insisted that I please step aside and allow the rescue squad to enter. Someone had had a heart attack and was gravely ill. I gladly returned to wait in my VW Westfalia Vanagon for a little fahrvergnügen. While I sat in the truck looking up at the numerous diamond-shaped glass buildings and the winged horse Pegasus, I must admit I did not feel very whole, very fahrvergnügen. All the old feelings of the street came back to visit with the reality of those with so little existing in the shade of those with so much.

One hundred feet up the street a man was defecating behind and on a parked car. He had a sly smile on his face, as if to say to the car and its owner, "Take that." Two blocks north, people had so much money they did not defecate anywhere; they hired people to do that for them.

I thought, *Good move, Marie. You sent me down here to get rid of some anger and it sure worked.* I was getting rid of some anger all right.

I was unable to get a room close by. It seems Dallas was host to a convention of doctors, and most of the rooms were taken. The closest room I could get in Dallas was one hundred and ten dollars. That was not close enough to my already too close budget. So I went to nearby Arlington, and Ramada'd my remains for thirty-seven dollars.

Arlington was just the place to be because my Volkswagen camper would not fit in the elevated parking of the downtown Fort Worth Days Inn. The horn shouted my arrival when the van roof stuck to the garage roof, and if I had not scraped my way back out of the garage and moved on to Arlington, I feel certain someone would have asked me to. Arlington was also a wise choice in that it was between Father Hill and Nancy Mattox Ulmer, the regional coordinator of the Interagency Council on the Homeless. Since Father Hill was gone, I tried Nancy Ulmer. Unfortunately she was not in either. I began to wonder about my choice to do this kind of book.

I had been on the road since 4:00 A.M., so I laid down. I reasoned I would nap and get up and go home. I did nap but I did not go home.

I got up to get coffee before hitting the road, and then ran in to Crazy Eddie, a friend from Oklahoma City. I don't know why they call him Crazy. He is one of the most sensible people I know. Only a crazy person would turn down an opportunity to earn fifty bucks for tearing a little earring from a fairly giant ear. Crazy isn't crazy, so I call him Eddie. Anyway, I told him what I was doing in Fort Worth. His "encouragement" of my visit was enough to convince me that I should stay until my business was completed.

I tried Father Hill again. He was in and we were on for Tuesday. I reached Nancy Ulmer, and we set an appointment for Wednesday. Suddenly this writing business wasn't all spelling, commas, deadlines, and small advances. More was soon to come.

On Tuesday, I met Dave at the door on Austin Street. This time he allowed me entrance, and I met Father McCord, a gracious gentleman who was talking to a reporter from Channel 8. As I noted the configuration of the line of tables on the far side of the warehouse floor, I noticed that each seat was occupied and each face of the occupant was turned my way. They could have been the judges at the Nuremburg trial instead of the judged, for they all sat on the far side of the table with their hands folded. Like occupants in the primate house at the zoo, there was nothing in front of them on the table to occupy their time and little expression on their faces to indicate that that made any difference.

I noticed, too, how much I hated the word *OCCUPANT*. It's as if when your name is not known you suddenly become the "OCCUPANT": "Dear Occupant," "To the occupant." These people were occupants, but not in my illusion of life anymore. They were occupants of another illusion, but they were welcome guests here at Austin Street. They were the ones who could come in early because they could behave. They still had a portion of their dignity intact, although it hung now from torn clothes and dreams. Some were the ones who lived now in a world of their own but not totally of their own making.

Just as I was feeling comfortable with being angry for all of the old ghosts of discomfort like nothing to do and nowhere to go, I met Reverend Beula "Bubba" Dailey and her husband, Harry E. Dailey. Harry is the codirector of the Austin Street Mission, and Bubba is the administrative assistant. Harry had an errand to attend to and left Bubba as my guide to the Austin Street Mission. I had never met a lady named "Bubba" before, nor a woman reverend. I'm grateful you get to meet her now.

Harry and Bubba

Bubba told me Father Hill was due back soon and proceeded to lead me around the one-story warehouse. It was one room of about twenty thousand square feet of space. Yet this place had sufficient space to contain most of the reasons for places like this. On one end was an office where Father Hill and the Daileys did the things necessary to do the things needed. There was a room for the women who stayed as staff and a room for the men who worked for the Austin Street Shelter. The shelter differed from the Mission. You'll see how later. The men and women who work as staff are recruited from the population using the facility.

In one corner of the warehouse were two or three hundred blue sleeping mats piled and stacked in neat order, an order not available to the souls who would sleep on them that night. The only order in the lives of most of the shelter people was found in

Father Hill, Father McCord, Harry Dailey, Reverend Bubba, and the staff.

Bubba told me of the problem with the city of Dallas and the Central Business District membership, their downtown neighbor. It seems the CBD did not want shelters in their shadow and they wanted to move them all to a location well out of sight.

She said, "We are fighting for our lives. They really just do not want us anywhere. We have no say on the committee. There is a certain mindset down here that if *we* were not here the homeless problem would not exist." I told her I believed the attitude was not unique to Dallas. Every community I have been in would rather move the homeless to another state, or better still, to another planet.

Bubba said they had been in a conference that morning where a new report was released by the Homeless Task Force. She said the report supported the location of the shelters in the areas where they could most easily be accessed by the street people, a conclusion not well received by the CBD and its attorneys. She said they had to move anyway because the Dallas convention center was expanding and the building now home to the shelter would soon be a parking lot.

I have never met anyone from any shelter who did not have some pressure from the community to move. Besides, I thought the Austin Street Mission was already a parking lot of sorts. A lot for the wrecked of humanity. A repair shop where society would like Father Hill to fill and Bondo the dents of the dented and give the rusty ones a thin coat of society's values before sending the newly rehabilitated off to rust quietly somewhere else. Thankfully there are no thin coats of value at Austin Street.

Bubba showed me the room for the staff women, then the staff men's dorm. She pointed out the shower facility for the shelterees and said, "Sometimes you have to get right in there with them and help them clean up." She pointed out that most of the women at Austin Street had some psychological problems and that outside the shelter they were raped and beaten on a regular basis. Only in here were they safe.

Bubba led me into the office so that I might lay down my things and continue on the tour. I noticed a tack board with Polaroid pictures on the wall next to Father Hill's chair. Bubba told me she had started to take pictures of the ones who were brought to the shelter beaten. On the board were various photos of gashed heads and bloody matted hair. Pictures of swollen faces beaten beyond recognition, of eyes gouged to never see again, and mouths that once smiled and held teeth. "The homeless are preyed upon by the punks that don't access shelters," she said. "One of our ladies was beaten this past week, so I decided to start taking pictures."

She told me how much things had changed over the past two years. Now when they get a report about one of their people down, they grab their baseball bats and get in the van, then get as close to the person as possible. When the beating is over, they get out of their van and use the bats as protection so they can retrieve the beaten soul and take him or her to the hospital. It wasn't always this way. "There is so much violence. We used to take our flashlights and look for people under the bridges and in the box cars, and I was never touched. I was threatened a few times but never touched. You can't do that anymore. It isn't safe."

She showed me the area where on Monday and Thursday they had the psychiatric team come to assist those in the shelter. She said 60 percent of the budget for the psychiatric effort came from the McKinney funds. She said, "If they ever cut the Stuart McKinney money, these programs are going to go down the tube." On Tuesday night they have a medical team come to the shelter to treat those in need. During the day, she said, she and Harry have a day program for the older ones, the sick, and the mentally ill.

I asked her if she had noticed an increase in the number of homeless since she started in 1975. "Not only in the number," she answered, "but in the makeup of the population. In the last couple of years, the children have increased 25 percent. There seem to be even more mentally ill on the street. There are more women and children. We have many with no source of income, some on Social Security or welfare. We have the older ones who have no access to the low-income housing or the transitional housing. They did away with the FRO, the old flophouses. We perhaps need some of the single-room facilities back. The home-

24

less population is growing. One day we're going to have to face the fact. The public is going to have to face it."

I told her the book was for those who perhaps had not yet realized the depth of the problem of homelessness. Or to those who feel they somehow exist beyond the virus's touch. I mentioned that I had been speaking to various groups and had discovered that most did not want to hear what I had to say. "That's right, you're right," Bubba replied. "They just seem to have blinders on. It's like they live in this fairyland. We just can't break through that. No matter what you say, it goes right past them."

Her eyes clouded a bit. "These are my friends down here. Harry and I will always be with them. They are our family." She said they had a staff of nine to fourteen, all recruited from the homeless. Among them was a person with a double Ph.D., another was a dentist, and one had been a history teacher. Three had been professional people. All staff members work for a salary. They are required to save 75 percent of their earnings.

Harry Dailey is the drug and alcohol abuse counselor. The staff from the population sign contracts with him that they will follow the Twelve Step program and save their money as agreed, so that when they return to society they will have a financial advantage.

The Mission acts as a banker for those who wish to have their money secured. In that manner they will not lose it to thieves on the street. The Mission will take the checks and release the money as requested during the month.

Reverend Bubba Dailey added that she flips from world to world; she lives an almost schizophrenic existence. She and Harry have a small, two-bedroom apartment but spend most of their lives in the Austin Street Mission. She said that keeps one's priorities straight. It continually reminds her of how blessed she is.

She told of the one old lady that she met on the street in 1975 when she first began to work with the homeless. The old woman still comes to her every day and says, "Bubba, tell me again how I'm special." Bubba said to me, "I tell her, 'Jamie, you're one of a kind. God only made one of you; you're the only one. That's why you're special.' Jamie and her sister both were abused from day one. We tried to count the times she had been in the institutions. We came up with seventeen or eighteen."

What the street people need, believes Bubba, is someone to tell them they are special, they are loved by God, and we care for them. I believe she's right. Perhaps if those on the street had heard that early and often enough, perhaps if they . . . perhaps . . .

The Austin Street Mission has eighty to ninety various groups that prepare and serve meals. Each takes a turn so it is not an undue burden for any one group. In that way the whole community can become involved. Bubba put it best: "It becomes everyone's ministry. This doesn't look like much, but it's home to us.

"We do not impose our values or our expectations on these people. We just want them to feel better than they did when we found them. They consider this their home and each other as family, and that's all we can expect. Our ministry is primarily to those who cannot change and will never go back to society. We want to be the stabilizing influence in their lives that will be here for them no matter what."

We talked a bit more and she showed me the wall where the people hang their paintings and drawings and dreams. Some were paintings of houses where the children who created them would one day live. Some were well-done landscapes of softer friendlier places, places they had been in life before they could only visit them in dreams. One was a figure of a man on a cross with his self-portrait imposed on the face.

Harry returned from his errand and prepared to go on another. I wished I could have spent more time with him. He is the codirector of the mission and conducts many of the programs. Harry told me, "You need to change the behavioral patterns of these people before you can touch their intellectual insights. We help them to learn to get their needs met more appropriately and acquire some skills and how to act, especially if they've been addicts. The drug of choice down here is alcohol. These people usually started out with morals and ethics, but that has deteriorated over the years of chronic drug use. It takes quite a while to bring even a few of these people back. We are not really success-oriented, that is, success as the outside would view it. If we can upgrade and enhance their self-esteem and their overall mental health and give them a shower and a shave and a smile and not have them cuss us, we feel quite successful."

I wanted to ask him many questions, but we entered a conversation about duty to each other, and that evolved into a discussion about Christ. Harry and Bubba felt that Jesus would have been down there with them. Bubba felt people would still think Jesus was crazy, and Harry said at least they would consider him beyond rehabilitating. Our conversation ended when they introduced me to Father Hill. They parted, and went to change from their television clothes into their Mission clothes.

Father Hill looks a bit like me, white beard and mostly gray hair. There we were, two handsome fellows shaking hands and talking like old friends. We sat down in his office. I got the dry chair and Father Jerry sat in the wet one. It seems the roof leaks directly over his desk.

Father Hill mentioned that the concern of the CBD was over the moving of the shelter location. The Mission was given until December 31 to relocate and it was now late November. Bubba had said the Mission would have to appear before the city council and receive nine of the eleven votes before the new location would be approved, but it seemed as if no one wanted the Mission in their vicinity. I understood their frustration and concern and shared that with Father Hill. Then we turned to discuss the homeless problem in general.

I asked him what he thought was the greatest block to repairing the damage caused by homelessness. I wanted to understand the view of one who has spent his life in service to the homeless. This man is greatly respected. And he is a widely traveled and popular speaker on the subject of homelessness.

His answer was a new one. "I believe, by and large, people are being drawn away from concern for their fellow human beings who are less fortunate, especially the poor. Every day they are busy trying to survive and to hold on to their job. They struggle to do the best they can within this economy. All their energy and their thinking is directed in this fashion. That which we fear and have no control of, we tend to put out of sight or will not confront. We suppress it.

"I believe we all fear poverty. Middle-aged people and older

27

have been raised in a type of poverty because of the Great Depression. They may not have recognized it at the time, but subconsciously they never want to go back to it. So they do anything they can to avoid thinking about ending up poor. Even though they read it in the paper, I have people ask me, 'Why didn't I know it was this bad?' They refuse to see or hear about it with any depth because of their phobia of being trapped in it. Politicians know this and can hand-feed the public and tell them what they want to hear. We seem most interested in voting for those issues that provide human comfort rather than human need, because the issue of human need raises too much psychological pain."

Father Hill asked how long I had been homeless. I told him I had been on the street for a relatively short time, but I had been homeless for more than two years. That brought to mind something that had occurred that day. He began, "I walked into the shelter about an hour ago. There was a young man walking down the street—young, in his early twenties. I thought, *I know that walk.* He lived just down the street from me. I was first introduced to him when he was six years old. His mother was an alcoholic; his father spent no time with him. He was a hyperactive child. He would come down and hang around my house with my two boys. He was always getting into trouble and he'd run to me."

Father Hill looked down. He had his hands folded, and his thumbs were busily trying to catch each other as they spun around and around. He was struggling now with the frustration caused by the personal involvement with the young boy's life and with the innocence of the victim. I was moved that even those who work with this problem every day of their lives are still so emotionally touched by its devastation. Then he spoke.

"I worked with his mother, tried to get her into AA, tried to get her to deal with alcoholism. She refused to deal with it and became angry with me for confronting her. So I backed off and left her alone. The boy got into more and more serious problems. I talked to her again and told her the boy was headed for real problems if she didn't get herself together and get help with her drinking."

Father Hill stopped for a while, pointing toward the door until his voice returned and he quietly whispered, "The boy is out there right now. He's on the street. He's someone from my neighborhood that no one would have guessed would wind up on the street. He is out there right now, hungry and completely lost. That really stopped me today."

We spoke for a while longer, dancing away from the emotion of the frustration and complexity of the problem. The Father asked if I had talked to John Fulenwider. He said Mr. Fulenwider was an articulate advocate for the homeless. During a recent gubernatorial election, a candidate spoke on the causes of homelessness. The candidate said something to the effect that the homeless population was growing because the streets were filling up with drug addicts and repeat offenders. When asked for his thoughts on the speech, Fulenwider did not run the candidate down but remarked on many politicians' lack of understanding. The lack of affordable housing causes homelessness. If you do not have a home, you are homeless.

Father Hill added, "Poverty causes homelessness." My experience interested him. He had met other writers who had gone to the street to try to discover what it felt like to be homeless, but he had not met anyone who lived the experience and *then* written about it. In the seminary he attended, they had a program where they would give you two dollars and drop you on the street for two or three days or even a week. You were to come out of that experience knowing how the other person feels. He did not involve himself with that program because he thought it a distortion. You always knew you had an escape. If you were threatened or your life was in danger or you were hungry, you could just start walking in one direction and walk right out of that experience. Father Hill said that the true homeless person has or believes he has no way out. "To be homeless is to have no alternative. This causes tremendous pain. It forces the person to act out the pain in inappropriate ways, which generally offends someone."

We talked about my experience on the street. I told Father Hill I had really wanted to meet him, but I had had a difficult time getting out of the van to come in. I did not want the smells and bruised faces to enter my dreams again. I was afraid my visit would bring back the haunting memories.

He smiled. "It may sound amazing, but do you know what the leading vocations of the homeless professional are? They are journalists and painters, artistic people. I am not artistic, but what only bothers me destroy so many creative people."

The typical mission approach is what Jerry called the "three S therapy": soup, soap, and salvation. He believed it had great success in its history. He even laughed as he said, "There are some terrible preachers in these missions, but it works. Lives have been changed, turned around. People have gained a new life through Christ. I found there are three things a person needs if he or she is ever going to get out of the situation. One, you need food; that's a given. Second, you need a place to clean up and get fresh clothes. Third, you need a safe place where you are not afraid of being stabbed. Shelters should be safe places. Everything we attempt to do here is for that purpose.

"I know what a person needs. I don't believe there is a problem in getting funding or political support if I can show them or at least tell them we are rehabilitating a high rate. I can lie about it, that's what a lot of programs do, telling about all these people who are saved in X amount of time. Those who have been rehabilitated here and those on this floor who can and do want to get out of this life—if they have the ability—will jump at the opportunity and claw their way out if we set the environment for it. But sadly many of the people here have no alternative. They will die on the street. I have focused my life and my ministry on these people. Everything else is icing on the cake.

"They deserve to die in dignity; that's what I am here for. I have fought that battle all my ministry. I guess I'll fight it to the end because people don't want to accept that. We have created a subspecies called human garbage. The problem I have with the city about the shelter location is on a par with the problem of where to put the city waste. The two main areas of disputed land use are Where can you dump the garbage? and Where can you dump these humans? No one wants either, not in their back yard."

Father Hill told me why he was "redirected" to the need to

give dignity to the bottom-rungers. "There was this street guy and he wanted to see me. He was in the hospital dying. I asked him if he was afraid to die. He looked at me and he said, 'I'm not really afraid to die. What I am scared of is dying and no one knowing it.' That's basically what I have been about since then. I've been a thorn in the rear end of Dallas." I told the Father that thorns in the rear end are there to remind people not to sit too long.

"There have always been angles in these people's lives. The homeless know they will have to pay some price for whatever they get. They want to know what that price is immediately. As I said, the three S's have been successful, but I came away from that with the thought that one day these people may have to prostitute their faith to get certain needs met. The only thing they have left is a very thin thread of a relationship with God. That's all they have; they want to protect it. They don't want to prostitute it.

"If I were on the street and it was cold and I had eaten some soup but not enough vegetables, I would know what to do. I would know where to go to make an altar call, give my life to Christ, and get a plate lunch. If I were feverish and felt as though I were coming down with a bad cold or the flu or I was drenched and needed to be by a heater, I know where I could go. I would go to the place where I could make an altar call for the plate lunch and give my personal testimony and get the bunk by the fire. So I wanted to offer something that when you came in, no matter what you said or did to me, you got the same thing as the person before you and after you. Then, if you want anything else, you could ask me. If it's within my power, I'll get it for you. I'll pray with you. If you want to give a confession, reconcile with God, I'll do anything. But you don't get an extra sandwich for that. My approach does not help everybody. The mission has it's place; I have my place."

Father Hill told of his tutoring under George Cooper of Chicago. Mr. Cooper was a deacon in the Episcopal church and ran a day mission on skid row called the Reading Room. Mr. Cooper had a motto that hangs on the wall over Father Hill's desk. In large letters it boldly shouts:

DO SOMETHING
FOR YOUR
FELLOW MAN
TODAY,
IF IT'S ONLY LEAVE HIM ALONE.

Carl Menninger had visited the dayroom one time and commented that was what the people on skid row needed. Father Hill has patterned his mission and ministry on the motto. He says, "This is my frustration. We find people in need, but out of our 'do-gooder' mentality, we not only try to help but we try to make them meet our own expectations. There are some people for whom the best we can do is to leave them alone. Don't hurt them anymore by pushing them. There are people coming in here who do not want to give us their names. That's all right. I'm a behaviorist: As long as a person behaves, that's all that matters. If you come in here and show your rear end, you're out. A person does not have to tell me squat. If they behave, I leave them alone. A person has to have some peace in this life.

"This whole issue of rehabilitation is misguided. We seem to think we have to get everybody back in line. It's phobic. I have this allergy to dust and carpeting, that's why this concrete floor. I have this fear that one day I'll wake up and the whole world will be carpeted. Heck, I can't stand carpet but I can't pull up all the carpet in the world."

The Father touched on perhaps the one most important factor of homelessness, the missing ingredient common to all those in the street.

"I've often said that if heaven were like the old skid row that I was used to, it would not be such a bad place. The only reason I would personally not be on the street is that my family is too important to me. I need the family and what it provides. Some lost their family, not by choice, through death or divorce. My need and enjoyment of the family would be the one thing that would keep me off the street. Otherwise, and I've been part of the gray flannel world, this is the better alternative to being a banker. I would join this crowd before I would join the banking crowd."

Father Hill added that if he had known me when I was on the

street, he would have made my life a little more miserable. He would not have wanted me to get too comfortable with the situation. He told of one man on the street that he had had words with. The man became angry and left the Mission. Today he has a management position with Nieman Marcus. Now and then, the man will wave when he sees Father Hill.

Death is the final act of the play of life. For some it is the ultimate enemy, for others it is the welcomed way out. Father Hill deals with it often in his line of work. I believe he deals fairly with the most important moment of our life.

"When we get someone who is dying and he has X amount of time, I give him an alternative. I don't want him dying on the floor of the shelter if at all possible. So I tell him I'll do whatever he wants. If he wants the hospital, I'll take him. I tell him, 'If you want an apartment, I'll find the money to rent you an apartment.' Whatever they want, Noah, I'll do. And I mean it. Do you know that I have never had anyone take me up on it? Never. They have all told me, 'These are all the friends I have in the world. I am most comfortable here—'and they die here, with us.

"I try to make this my approach to all my ministry. I honestly ask the person what they want me to do for them. They will usually answer honestly, even if they say nothing. It's amazing, absolutely amazing, but most of the time they just want to be left alone. Not that they do not want to talk. We talk. But they have finally found some peace, some small portion of peace. And they do not want me to rock the boat. If I can hear that, I will not rock their boat. Rehabilitation to me doesn't mean to change these people's lives. It means that I can help them find a little peace in their lives. I did not come to that overnight. I was determined to change everybody into the image that I expected. I almost folded in frustration."

My interview with Father Hill is a lesson to all who would give of their time and self to assist the weak and the lost. Everyone who helps will someday feel his frustration. This may help you get through the point at which many quit.

"I worked with a man one time. All the other programs had washed their hands of him. They were all fed up with trying to help any longer. They no longer wanted to work with me on him. So I invested about six months of my life and time on him. I had him working, he was sober, he lived at a halfway house. He was clean, dressed well, had a very lucrative job. One of the ones we hope to get back from the street to that degree. He was a true success story. He was doing so well. Everyone who had tried to help him was impressed.

"Then one day I found him on the street. He was wiped out. He was drunk and dirty, filthy, stinking. He had messed in his pants. He was wasted. I was so angry with him. If it would have saved his soul, I would have beaten him to death. I knew I had to get out of this business. I was so frustrated. I went back to a friend who had told me one time that I had what it takes but I wasn't using it. I told him, 'I don't know what it is you think I have that I'm not using, but either tell me or I'm getting out.'

"He told me he thought God had given me a good heart, a special knowledge, a special intelligence. But he said I always measured success by my own expectations. He said many of these people can never measure up to what you expect. He said if you'll do to the best of your ability with what God has given you, and you allow God to do the changing, you will see success.

"That really took a tremendous load off me. I no longer had to play God. I can only do this day what I've got to do. It isn't much sometimes, but I can see the success if it's just a full stomach. If I had continued to look for my success day by day, I would already have gotten out of it. Now I can measure success by looking back over the last ten years. I can see and remember people who really have been helped through the shelter. But you have to look through a long period of time, and then you can see the changes in some lives."

Another interesting facet of the process of helping was brought out in our interview. Father Hill mentioned that George Cooper of the Chicago Reading Room was not very popular with the other mission heads on the strip. He said he thought it was because Mr. Cooper was so successful.

The problem of competition and professional jealousy or conflict of method between agencies is a reality. The problem of disagreement between the official government position and the advocates and those who are actually working the programs is a real and audible one. The assessment of the numbers and the

34

growth and severity of the homeless population is the greatest difference.

LEDGER

One can buy all the nickel thoughts one wants for a dime. It would seem there is a large and ready client base and always plenty with nickel thoughts to sell. It's the dollar thoughts that are hard to come by, not because they are scarce, but because they are free. Dollar thoughts are the ones that have an ultimate meaning or direction in life, a meaning or direction beyond to-day, beyond tomorrow, beyond this life . . . on the assumption that there is something after this experience. Most of the planet's population postulates in traditional lore or writing, in ru-moring or reasoning that there is more after our journey on this tiny planet. Most cultures have a religious net at the base of their theory of more after life, a religious net that holds up the assumption out of reach of today. It is a promise of perfection and peace and plenty, a promise of abundance unending. It is a promise of love and justice and truth. This is the dollar thought and it is free. One must simply live to, for, and within a perspec-tive and set of rules and then die to receive the faith's end.

Because of the rules and death requirement, it is not surpris-ing that most opt to pay a dime for the nickel thought. Nor is it surprising that people continue to purchase the lesser thoughts once they accept the possibility of the dollar postulate, hoping they will find a part of tomorrow's promise today. And so we all go through life making change with our nickels of assumption and changing . . . or refusing to.

Our perspective changes when we are forced to see that we are not elite, that we will all get wet if it rains, that we are all subject to chance and change—not only our change, but the changes of those around us.

One of the most powerful and controlling nickel thoughts we buy in common and in bulk is that money is not only of worth and value, but the *measure* of worth and value of each individual in the society. Another common nickel thought is that money is the great security. For some money provides protection second only to the great dollar promise. For others it is the great dollar promise. So the quest, possession, and worship of money is the overwhelming motivator of the one who buys the nickel thought.

But the purchaser of the nickel thought is forever an avid and frantic buyer and the holder and owner of only a copy, an imitation. Some buy the nickel thought that drugs will transport them to the dollar thought, and when they come down from the temporary trip, they must buy again and again. Some buy the nickel thought that things can somehow, someday cumulatively add up to the dollar thought, and so they must buy and buy again and again. For, you see, a purchaser of trinkets is never satisfied until he or she possesses the real thing. Somewhere deep within all of us is the knowledge that, in the economics of universal law, nickels never add up to the dollar.

In our homes, our garages, our storage units, our attics, our basements, and our closets are piled our individual inventory and evidence of the nickel thought. In the streets, under bridges, in missions, in old cars, in back rooms, we find piled and warehoused another kind of swelling inventory of the nickel thought. People—young and old, the strong and the sick, hungry people—beaten souls who are paying with their lives for our cumulative nickel chance at a dollar . . . and losing.

DOLLAR THOUGHT	NICKEL THOUGHT
"Working with the needy keeps your priorities straight."—Rev. Bubba Dailey	You enter the nickel thought.
"Poverty causes homelessness."—Father Jerry Hill	The addict and repeat offender cause homelessness.
"Do something for your fellow man today, if it's only leave him alone." —George Cooper	Pick one.

Perhaps we can all remember the first time we became aware of the homeless. The following is my first introduction.

CHAPTER
FOUR

Bay Rum
or Citrate

From time to time I think back to simpler moments in my life.
Lately I've been doing that more and more often. I remember
when cars and the future had wings, when televisions and the
wrongs of our country needed magnifying glasses to be seen.
Radios looked like small wooden cathedrals with a red light in
the window and they transported us to the land of imagination.
A land many of today's children have never visited because
everything is so real and imagination is no longer a great need.
Milton Berle dressed like a woman when it was still funny and
sold gas for a company that still washed your windows with a
fill-up. Movies were a dime. And Hopalong Cassidy cards came
wrapped in some pretty awful gum. The freedom bell was still
ringing after World War II. But the little white war pennies hitting the marble counter top at Mac's Pharmacy in Toledo, Ohio,
didn't ring at all.

It was a tough time after the war and before the next. Korea was in the batter's box and the stands were again filling with workers with a national purpose. It wasn't so tough for a ten-year-old kid with corduroy pants and striped shirt. I had a job! Heck, I had two. Mom bought me a paper route, and the folks in the Detroit and Central area could never again set their clock by the thump of the paper on the porch. In fact, it was probably more like, "Hey Maude, the Snider kid just brought the paper. It must be Thursday."

The little white lead pennies didn't bounce, they just hit the counter and stuck. "Give me a bottle of Bay Rum, son." It was a man who would sometimes come in twice a day for Bay Rum. He had a few friends who must have shaved often, too, because they all liked Bay Rum. I asked Mac about that. I asked Mac about a lot of things. He knew almost as much about stuff as my father, and at ten with two jobs, he must have figured I needed two fathers, because he treated me like a son. Mac said, "they don't shave with it; they drink it."

"They drink it? It's shaving lotion!"

"They drink it!"

"Must taste awful, Mac."

"I don't know. Never tasted it."

"How come they drink it?"

"Makes 'em forget."

"Forget what?"

"Everything. The war, the friends they lost, the wives that didn't wait, the jobs they lost. I don't know what all they try to forget. I've never asked them. They have enough burden. They're homeless hobos. They'll move south in the fall."

Mac McKee was one of the angels. He was a pharmacist, and McKee Pharmacy was where a man on the road could get a bottle of Bay Rum or a free Coke. Mac did not drink and did not like selling Bay Rum for consumption. But he said the Bible said to give the poor man a drink so he could be happy. I didn't know much about the Bible; I was a ten-year-old Methodist. I knew I wasn't supposed to drink or smoke or swear or play with myself, so I didn't drink, smoke, or swear. This was my first time to meet a homeless person or an alcoholic, or I should say, it was the first time an alcoholic or homeless person had been identified for me. Mac was under some pressure to keep these men out of the store. Mrs. McKee felt they frightened the customers. She was probably right. Some of them were a bit wild-eyed and blown away from the paregoric and Bay Rum.

One day when Mac was upstairs taking a nap, Mrs. McKee asked me to get one of these men out of the store. He was resting his head on the white marble counter top and mumbling through the bubbles coming out of his mouth. The bubbles would slide down his chin and sail in the gusty breath of his exhale across the smooth marble until they would disappear in the sound of a tiny "pip."

I woke him by pushing a bleach rag under his chin. I asked him to leave. He didn't want to go. He started shouting, and Mrs. Mac went to the back room to call the police. I remembered Mac saying these men were not bad, just broken. But it was him or me. I had to work for Mrs. Mac, and when she asked you to do something, she expected it to be done. I asked the broken man if he wanted a soda. He bubbled what I took to be yes. So I opened a bottle of citrate of magnesia. It took about three minutes for the tiny little bubbles to get his feet moving, and he never stopped to say good-bye.

The police were just walking up the steps when the man hit the door and ran right into them. The policemen started gagging and coughing. Mrs. Mac came out of the back room and told me she was going to be sick. She started to buckle over. It's funny how fast a chain reaction vomit happens. I had people throwing up inside the store and out. One of the policemen kept saying, "Geeze, Oh Geeze, Oh Geeeeezzzze!" The broken man was definitely experiencing a full-blown case of diarrhea. Every time he doubled over, the policemen would throw up again. And then Mrs. Mac would get sicker. It was awful. It took all afternoon to clean up and hose down the front steps and sidewalk.

I don't know what happened to the broken man. The police let him go because they didn't want him riding in their car. Mac told me not to sell any more Bay Rum to anyone; so I did not see any of the broken ones again. Mrs. Mac said if she ever saw me give anyone else a glass of citrate, I would never see eleven.

The McKees were fine people. They taught me a great deal about working for and with people. They told my mother they would pay for my college education if I wanted to be a pharmacist. But I wanted to be an actor and a writer. I went to college on an art scholarship. It would be thirty-two years before I became half of what I wanted to be.

I visited Toledo over the Christmas holidays last year. My friend Katy and I walked to the corner to see the old store building. Detroit Avenue seemed much closer to the door than I remembered as a boy. The windows were boarded up and graffiti covered the panels and the brick walls. The building was not nearly as large as it was when I had to clean it.

I relived that day with the broken man and could not help but chuckle a bit. But I also could not help being a bit sad for all the ones who still believed, like that ten-year-old boy in my memory, that all the street people needed to remove them from view was a good cathartic. I wished more of us could somehow come to the belief of that beautiful old man with white hair and bad feet, when he said, "They're not bad. They're just broken."

Even broken people can dream. If a man still dreams we have something to grab hold of to pull him out of his broken dream. Grab hold of a dream.

LEDGER

I can remember lying in the grass, looking up to where this all began and dreaming and talking to my dreams. I dreamed that Sam Walton called.

He would say to me, "Noah, are you speaking for these people? What can I do for you folks? What do you need?"

I would say, "Well Sam, we've thought about it and talked it over. What we need is a Sam's card with our own name on it. Sam, we don't need credit as much as credibility. You see, our own card would give us some identity. We'll pay for the things we buy. Most of us don't want a handout. We'd just like to get the same break those with money get. You could put our picture on it like the other people have. Maybe you could say under the picture, 'A friend of Sam's,' and make it a special platinum card for the poor. There probably would be a problem with the address thing since we don't have one, and we'd have to do something about the where-do-you-work part. I'm sure you can figure something out. Thanks for calling, Sam. I've got other dreams to visit. Got to go. I'll get back to you when I get to a phone or one of us is more real."

I used to dream about Willie and Waylon calling. "Hey Noah, it's me, Willie, and me, Waylon. And I'm he-e-e-r-e, too, it's Jo-o-o-ohnny Ca-a-a-sh. While we got you on the speaker phone here, haul your tail on over. We want to do some of your songs, 'The American Dream' and 'Slave Ship America.'"

"Sure boys," I'd say, "but I'm somewhat busy with all this self-rejection and all. I'll get the first ride going your way. By the way, where the heck are you?"

Another recurring dream was that I would wake up in the morning and there would be a mailbox next to me with my name on it. Inside was an envelope, and inside the envelope was a map of Colorado or Idaho or Oregon or Texas around Seguin, with a big X-marks-the-spot. A large skeleton key would drop out and hit my foot. I must have dreamed that dream a hundred times, and yet each time I was so surprised when the key fell out. On the small tag was a note saying "This is the gate key. The 160 acres is yours. Enjoy and take care—A friend."

I'd follow the map and get to the gate. There were wild things all around me. Everywhere was color and clean smells and sunshine. I felt like Uncle Remus. The birds would land on my shoulder. Tiny rabbits and a raccoon pup would run along behind me. They would lead me to a cabin that had a thin spiral of smoke rising from the chimney. Inside, breakfast was cooking on the woodburning stove, just like it did when I was a child. Eggs with lacy edges were basting and bubbling in bacon fat. Coffee in a copper pot perked on the black stovetop and smelled like a late fall morning. Tiny particles of dust swam upward in the magic soft yellow filtered light that colored and blurred everything as it swept through the window and the smoke in the room. In one corner was a bed with a patch quilt turned down and a clean white pillow. And, as I dipped into the wooden pail for a drink of cold clean water, the dream would dissolve. Just as the tin dipper would touch my thirst. . . .

"Noah? Hollywood here! Heard you've wanted to act since you were a boy. Got a fantastic part for you, baby. See you on the set. Ciao."

41

"Forget Hollywood, pal," I'd respond. "Where's the cold water or the newspaper or the coffee or the bathroom?" I always awoke thirsty.

Dreams are what keep us going. Dreams are the vehicle that carry us away from distraction. Dreams nudge us when we can't nudge ourselves. They gently reach down to us and help us stand up one more time and one more time and one more time . . . and one more time. They smile at us softly when no one else will. They guard our secrets safely and never judge us. They hold us and say, "Here, here's some hope, friend. Looks like you can use it."

At times we only have our dreams to keep us from the nightmares we live in. Dreams are free. Yet strangely it's the cost of the cumulative ones that do not come true that one day keep them from the neediest.

Sam hasn't called, nor have Willie or Waylon or Johnny. Maybe they never will. I think they might. I still check the mailbox every day. Hollywood is doing just fine without me on the set. But I'm not sleeping in the weeds anymore, and I could get a Sam's card now if I wanted one. I have a radio again, and I can at least hear Willie and Waylon and Johnny. I have a mailbox with my name on it and the key might still arrive. I eat lacy eggs whenever Katy's not around to watch my cholesterol intake. Hollywood may be calling from right here in my typewriter. Who knows, there may be some dreams in here for those who can't pay for their own anymore. That would be a dream come true, a real dream come true, a real by-golly-zippidy-do-da dream come true.

I'm so lucky to have grown up with the Disney movie *Song of the South* and beautiful old Uncle Remus with his fantastic smile. How much better it was to be a child then rather than now with Elm Street's Freddie Kruger and his hand of knives. I and my dreams were born in a time of promise and goodness and love. They kept me afloat until promise and goodness and love pulled me out. "My, oh my, what a wonderful day!"

A
WORLDWIDE
SYMPTOM

PART **2**

CHAPTER
FIVE

Lemmings
Have Big Shadows

The rain died as quickly as it was born. In one tremendous roar of thunder I was instantly as wet as a carp. I can remember being angry at God for giving me no warning. I shouted to Him, "Hey! How far down does a man have to go before You can see he's had enough?"

Having few people to talk to, or few I wanted to, I did develop a conversational relationship with my belief. Some of the things I said I'm somewhat ashamed of and probably will not share with you. But as I was pasted like a poster to the dryness of the indented shopping center doorway, I watched two shadows follow two slowly moving figures across the wet parking lot. As they approached a light pole, I noticed how rapidly their shadows caught up with them. When they stood directly under the light, the shadows disappeared.

I understood what I had just seen, for I had witnessed it many times before. There in my wet discomfort, giving God a hard time, I realized that our shadows are proportionally longer the farther away from the light we are. As we walk toward the overhead light, the shadows grow small. If we stand directly under the light, the shadows disappear altogether. I realized life's like that, my life at least. Every time I have run from a problem, the shadow following me got bigger and so did the fear. The bigger the shadow, the more to fear. I realized that was what happened to me on the street. I realized, too, that the moments of my life with the fewest shadows were those when I stood directly under and in the light of my faith. I realized that this experience was caused by chasing a light that would not hold still long enough for me to catch up with it. It was a light that changed intensity and location according to its own need, not mine. I realized that a writer trying to catch up to the light of someone who wanted much more than a struggling writer, was a marathon with no finish line. But at that time I still wasn't exhausted enough to stop. I continued to run and my shadow continued to grow.

The two soggy figures stood in the safety of the light for a while, then sat down on the concrete base and held each other. I don't know why I stood up and walked out there, perhaps it was the way they were comforting each other, perhaps I was looking to get some comfort or give some. By now I had learned that caution is wisdom and the lack of it is stupidity.

As I approached the light pole, I realized they were a young couple with the same immediate problem as mine: They were wet and cold and lost. There is a special look to lost eyes. They look at you but don't really see you. I walked up and laid down my guitar case, put my duffel on top, and knelt in front of the pair. There is something disarming about placing one's eyes below another pair of eyes. Something was disarming, maybe it was the guitar or the way I asked, "You two all right?"

"Doing better than you are, it looks," said the young girl. I noticed she was pregnant, and the young man was big enough to thump a stump. "Got a cigarette?" he asked.

"No."

"Want one?"

"Certainly," I said, "and a fine bottle of wine, preferably white on the dry side."

"I can help with the smoke."

Sometimes a man just doesn't know what to say, especially when he has grown to believe it doesn't matter what he says. So we just looked at each other and smoked. But somewhere in the confusion of what to say and how to say it, we talked about each other and it mattered.

I forgot for a time that I was this tremendous potential for making money who was intent on destruction and starvation as a writer. At least, that's what I was led to believe and, in time, believed it myself. I began to believe I was a lemming crushed in the mindless rush to leap off the cliff. Now I am absolutely certain that I have never been a lemming. And a part of the reason for my journey in the street was my refusal to be one.

The couple came from Iowa. They had been living in the young man's car for about a month. They had earned enough money to prevent starvation, but not enough to provide a place to live. That is a common problem with the homeless who will work. But how do you get to the job, and if you can get there, how does one dress and keep clean if one has no place to dress and bathe?

I received a bit of advice from a friend recently, who suggested I go down to Key West and drive a cab. He has known for some time that I am intent on writing. He further offered that since there are so many writers in Key West, he thought I might find someone who would understand me. Meaning, I assume, he could not. I thought about that possibility, I must admit, but I reasoned that Key West did not need another cab-driving writer sleeping in his cab. And I did not need one more night sleeping in a car. When making decisions now, I consult my mirror to see if I am starting to look like a lemming.

I learned that the young man had a promising football career until injury ended it. The couple had conceived a new guest to planet earth and were awaiting the child's arrival. The couple's families were somewhat unhappy with the choices their children had made, so they rejected them just long enough to make them believe they were alone. Then they were.

Now there we were, three people convinced we were not wanted. But somehow we found the words to say "I love you," and we did. I told them I had a stepson just down the street

47

attending Loyola, but I was certain he would not want to see me. So I said good-bye to New Orleans and James and his lady, and hello to tomorrow. It was already here. They went back to their car; I went back to believing there was no place to go back to.

This couple was not typical of the majority of people I met. Most were tied forever to the program, their ledgers long since completed. I met the drunks and many who swore they were Jesus, maybe one of them was, because He certainly found me on my walk. They were not typical in another way. They were still very certain that their lives on the street were temporary and at any moment they could leave. Maybe it was the mobility the car provided, maybe it was their love for each other, the commitment that no matter what happened they would be there for each other. How well I know the importance of that and the helpless feeling of falling through the huge hole the breaking of that commitment leaves.

The young man came from a modest family that had hoped he would attend college on an athletic scholarship. He would have been the first in his family to attend a university. The girl came from a broken home supported mostly by her mother. They had few of the social skills and none of the contacts to ever be asked to join the country club. John Kenneth Galbraith once commented, "If you come from a good family and went to Harvard, you will have a much better chance not to be poor."

Will those who have made a poor choice in their gene pool, or chose to enter life via the birthing table of the underprivileged or the minority mother—will these pay for their choice by being infected by the Hanson's bacteria of the '90s? Will they be banished forever to the leper colony of the poor and poorly educated? Obviously they had no choice. I understand that we all have varying numbers of choices. However, those who are laboring under the weight of obtaining their next meal might, forgivably, not see the choice of becoming a corporate attorney or the next president. Who was the last president to rise from an impoverished home and how many have we had?

The successful and quiet operation of any society depends on balance: a balance of education, opportunity, and resources both human and financial. We haven't seemed to do too well in either area. We have been overtly wasteful in both cases. The shepherd

48

of management is most often social priority. The master of that shepherd is traditionally the politically or financially powerful. My friends in both places, you need to quiet this operation and very quickly, or else deafness is the best you can hope for when the squeaking of these huge wheels of our society increases.

One day history may record that there was more to the twentieth century than good looks, popularity, and credit cards. But too many just could not see it. And, too, historians may conclude that cotton for all, for a while, would have been a better choice than silk for some and polyester for the poor.

My ledger now recognizes that change in our life-style, drastic change, is possible for anyone. None of our illusions of safety or security can control the political and social worms that can at any time attack the veneer of our financial well-being.

In an Associated Press release from Rio De Janeiro,"Economic Woes Send Brazil's Rich to Psychiatrists," I read that President Fernando Collor de Mello's economic plan has Brazilian psychiatrists working overtime to give the nation's wealthy a couch to cry on. Most of us think the only thing that would cause the wealthy to sob would be that Nieman Marcus sold the only platinum-plated suppository inserter.

"I've been working fourteen hours a day since the plan was announced. The rich feel a mixture of panic, astonishment, anger, and depression, and they want to talk about it," said Flavio Gikovate, director of the Institute of Psychotherapy.

One day after Collor took office, he set an eighteen-month freeze on all bank accounts of more than $1,200 dollars. The plan also limits withdrawals from money market funds to $600, or 20 percent, whichever is greater. It was reported that about $115 billion was frozen, or 80 percent of all bank deposits. The poor majority was not affected, for few of them have savings, and many of the poorest reported they were actually better off, as their salary began buying more.

The wealthy are suffering both financially and psychologically. According to the newsweekly *Vega*, at least two deaths have resulted directly from Collor's "New Brazil Plan." One was a San Paulo lawyer, who had his entire life's savings frozen in the bank and was unable to pay debts. He shot himself three weeks after the plan went into effect. Another was a married father of two who had almost all proceeds frozen from the sale of his home and bar. He died of a heart attack. Most of the wealthy have for the moment adjusted, but they are suffering.

The article relates a popular Brazilian joke. It seems a businessman was waiting in a long line at the bank behind a group of irate customers. The businessman finally lost it and screamed, "That's it! I'm going to kill Collor!" An hour later he was back at the bank, explaining to the manager, "The line was longer at the presidential palace."

Gikovate said, "For the poor, money is simply a means of buying things. For the rich, money means status. Many of my patients are depressed because they can no longer afford the life-style they were accustomed to, and feel their social standing has fallen. Brazil's rich are very spoiled. The poor have always paid for the country's difficulties and the wealthy are not used to sacrificing."

Another psychiatrist, Marcelo Sobrinho, said his workload has increased 40 percent since the plan was announced. "I thought I'd lose clients as they would be short on money, but it's just the opposite. Those who can't pay now are begging me to keep them on, with promises that they'll pay as soon as possible. Before the plan it was the usual talk of sex, love, careers, shyness, and insecurities. Now at least 70 percent of my time is spent on talk about the plan."

Jorge Alberto Costa de Silva, an analyst, thought the middle class was perhaps affected more than the rich. Referring to the limit on money market withdrawals, he said 20 percent of $1,000 is virtually nothing, while 20 percent of one million can go a long way toward easing the pain.

Silva, who is the president of the World Association of Psychiatry, feels the Collor plan "orphaned the middle class." He said, "Bank savings gave many people the opportunity to dream, to make plans for the future. That's been taken away from many in the middle class, and their life now means only eating, working, and going to bed."

You may be wondering why my ledger contains information on Brazil, and how it relates to the poor and homeless in America. It isn't so far away, either in miles or possibilities. On a clear day perhaps you might see the smoke from the burning of a fair portion of the earth's oxygen supply. This burning helped make some rich and many poor. And as the resources that backed many of the banks and depositors disappears, the pressure on the economic and banking communities grows. So, too, as our clean and ecologically acceptable energy resources disappear, pressure on our own manufacturing, economic, and banking community will rise. The banking and savings and loan industries are already in some fair difficulty awaiting the government bailout. The estimate is that it will cost each and every citizen $30 per month for the next thirty years. And since our government is the largest nonprofit organization in the world, it depends on your donations. It also has given itself the power to insist that you up your donation any time and any way it wishes.

My ledger has a list of Noah's universal laws, none of them are as profound or as useful as Newton's, but allow me to drop this on you:

Anything That Happens Anywhere
Can Happen Anywhere.

Here is another:

When Anything Goes Wrong,
the First Thing We Do Is Look
for Someone Else to Blame.

The wealthy have dodged another bullet regarding forced reapportionment of wealth with our nation's last budget approval. One day the government will turn to the only ones with any funds left and, unfortunately, more or all of us may be sleeping on cardboard.

Is life in a society like Monopoly? Does the game end when one player accumulates all the property titles and wealth? What happens to the rest of us? What might happen? Read on.

The Ivory Tower

We all live in ivory towers or tunnels. The continued disparity in distribution of wealth is certainly a part of the problem, not only within this country, but in the world arena. We have watched America become a debtor nation in little more than a decade, with the shift in world wealth moving to Japan and Europe. We can no longer afford to win wars such as the recent arms race with the Soviet Union. In some respect we won. The Soviet Union is on the verge of bankruptcy, hence, the massive swing in social direction. But now we are posturing to help bail them out. We do seem to live in "The Mouse That Roared" script. To some who are suffering, it appears we care more for the poor elsewhere then we do for our own hungry and homeless.

We are all global citizens, and complex international priorities dictate many of our policies. However, they cannot be our *only* consideration. For instance, if a marriage counselor were to dedicate more time to his clients than to his own marriage, he would certainly lose his position with his wife and, if his priority did not change, he would soon find himself seeking help from one of his professional peers. I do not believe in the ultimate profit of healing others at the sacrifice of your own family. There are many like Thomas R. Malthus[1] who postulate that all societies reach the point of numbers which ensure great distress. Perhaps this life is but a experiment, and the experience of life has been only to prove that the world tends to move toward disorder.

Other social factors are common to all past societies that have failed. Most of history supports the conclusion that the death of past societies was caused either by outside forces who wanted their natural resources, or they were destroyed by internal revolution of the poor, led by the repressed middle class. The government and the wealthy were destroyed by force to redistribute the wealth and power.

In the recent past, official government spokesmen have denied economic inequities until they were absolutely forced to recognize them. It is no different today. The Congressional Budget Office predicted that 600–700 banks would fail over the next three years, yet the official government assessment was that we may have been entering a slight downturn. Four months later government officials reported that we had been in a recession for four months.

Ken Skopec, President of Mid-Citco Inc., predicted that bank failures, mergers, and acquisitions would cut the nation's number of banks from 14,000 to 7,000 by the end of the decade. "I truly do not believe the sky is falling," he said, "but there's going to be some pain."

There is a vast difference between the pain discussed over the car phone and that being experienced by the poor and the panicked. It used to amuse me when I heard a politician say people would have to tighten their belts, as he climbed into his chauffeured limo. I am not amused anymore. The one without pants doesn't worry about their falling down.

Anger has never required a deserving target. Anger attacks whatever is visible or convenient. The hungry need food, a simple statement both your ledger and mine will accept. A man who is hungry and without a home will perhaps suffer longer more passively. But the parents who witness the suffering of their children will justify actions for the children's benefit that they would not for themselves. The man who cannot buy food for his wife is not charmed by the man who buys furs for his wife.

We are living in the most heavily armed country in the world. Unlike most other nations, we in America live in an armed camp. Sophisticated weapons are in the hands of many frustrated groups and individuals. Our living standard moves on and depends upon a very highly developed yet frightfully fragile axle of technology. We have seen a small glitch in the phone system paralyze long distance service. The entire financial system, with millions of daily transactions, depends upon transmittal over phone lines. Just think of the tiny squirrel that knocks out electricity in a whole neighborhood by simply choosing a transformer for a nap.

Tens of millions of people living east of the Mississippi receive their food via 34,000 trucks traveling across seven bridges on the Mississippi. The food they eat on Thursday was processed, in most cases, less than a week before. Any disruption to that thin-walled conduit would result in panic. The record-keeping system of the nation is rapidly being transferred to computer disk for storage and transmittal once again by phone.

Our entire system hangs from the filigree threads of electric lines. Any disruption to that umbilical membrane would cause catastrophic consequences. If it were to happen in the winter, we would have no heat. Many in the colder climates would face the certainty of freezing and starvation. Think about it. All the appliances in our homes, both necessary and otherwise, somewhere depend on the plasma of electricity. Most of our communication for dispersing peacekeeping and relief services depend on an uninterrupted phone or satellite system. Most of us have a minimum of food stock in our personal larder, for many of us stop at the store only to pick up the nightly microwave meal or eat out. We are no longer a hardy, independent society. Even on the international scale we are no longer the leading world's manufacturing nation. Instead we depend on the goods and fuel of other nations to survive. Our greatest indebtedness is to former and present enemies: Japan, China, Germany, and the Middle East. Economically they could crush us. We are like baby birds in a nest, mouth agape.

It is time for those perched in their ivory towers to come down. Before more Americans lose their jobs to international trade, we must get our house in order. We must prepare to feed and house the ones in need today and the greater numbers yet to come. There will be more. You may be next. We are not living in a society that will placidly and peaceably stand in bread lines waiting for the great hand of government to create a committee to study the problem. We are no longer a patient and trusting people.

The media have made the difference, both television and radio. They have made and are making available the knowledge of how we arrived where we are, and they no longer have any great concern or respect for the responsible parties. So now the ones suffering know that we as a country literally have given our strength and resources away. And they are just as certain they had little to do with it.

If a small squirrel can knock out a neighborhood's electricity, and a computer glitch or virus can disable our national phone system, what could possibly happen if social violence broke out in many or all cities at the same time? What would happen if Watts, the Detroit and Miami riots, the New York black- and brown-outs, the Atlanta disruption, the Shreveport riot, the Washington camp-in by the poor, the strikes by the truckers or the city workers or the rail and transportation unions, the squirrel, and the glitch were to happen at the same time? What would happen if it happened at a time when our peacekeeping forces were in another country?

If we think it cannot happen, if we are not aware of the boiling anger of the have-nots, the blacks, the worker who just lost his job to a robot or foreign competition, the farmer who lost his land, the poor who lost personal possibilities to pay for that golf course in Palm Springs . . . if we are not aware, we are not paying attention. We need to recognize that pressure is building from the friction of class conflict and privilege in this great melting pot. This pot is coming to a boil.

The threat from forces outside our nation pales in comparison to the potential consequence of the frustration of our growing poor population. The moral and spiritual resolve that once kept our people hopeful and patient has been dimmed by the shadow of survival. But the lessening of moral and spiritual self-control is not unique to the poor or the young. This is evident in the huge divorce rate and the me-ism of our time. Our music and movies reflect our preferences, or at least the preferences of those who pay for the entertainment. If anyone cares enough or there is a need to write a history of this era, I believe it would be entitled *The Decade of the Self* or, instead of the information age, *The Misinformation Age*. If we don't do something about our present course . . . if we let it keep running headlong into greater and greater economic, educational, and social disparity, the book recording our history may be called *The Last Chapter*. Who would write it? Perhaps a former have-not; perhaps a former foreign owner who called the note and now has foreclosed on the mortgage we owed but could not pay. *The Misinformation Age* may be the fairest title. If we really knew where we were, we would have a better chance of getting back to where we would like to be.

LEDGER

The next chapter may be the shortest chapter ever. However, my ledger says that one loud blast may get more attention than any long whiny wail. Truth will birth solutions.

This is not an economic primer, but the wonderings of one who had faith in the promises of past and present leaders. Now I know that official figures do not add up to actual totals, and credit buys nothing if you do not have it. Credit and credibility, perhaps, are the cause and the cure of our distress.

CHAPTER
SEVEN

The Credit Dragon

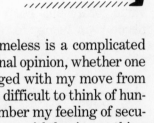

Again I repeat: The problem of the homeless is a complicated study. It is filled with emotion and personal opinion, whether one is poor or prosperous. My opinion changed with my move from one stratum of society to another. It was difficult to think of hunger when my belly was full. I well remember my feeling of security when I had things, but my experience with having nothing is still close enough behind me to cast that big black shadow on each new day.

I will never need a photograph to remind me of the street, I only need to close my eyes. I need no recording of the sounds of loneliness and the pitiful monotone of hopeless voices. The sound of that loneliest moment of my life can be heard in my songs and in my post-journey writing. The smells of bad food, bad breath, body odor, garbage and dirt and filth, unknown to me before, still blow through my mind. I will never forget the mixed emotions of love and hate and fright in the reflection of my face in a window. The pleading screamed from my eyes, "Help Me!"

I never needed help prior to three years ago and did not know how to ask for it. I had always been able to take care of all those around me. As a voluntary parole advisor at McAlester and Joseph Harp prisons, I was able to make house payments and car payments, buy medication and clothing and food for many who needed it. One day I could not do the same for myself and my wife. My step into the street certainly was not instant; it was insidious. It passed through the possibilities of jobs that did not happen, through deals that never closed. It wound its way between promises I could not keep, through financial security I could not provide. It followed the changes in love caused by the lack of money and trust. Then one day the change picked up speed. With a hardy "take care of yourself," it quickened to a succession of couches, back bedrooms, job interviews, a blur of rejections, sleeping in the car, sleeping in a friend's office, back home a few days, back to the couches, more rejections, more rejections, more rejections . . . until I rejected myself.

A person can wear out his welcome rapidly, if not on the generosity of others, on his own abrasive illusion that he has no value to anyone. For a time I believed the illusion that all I needed was money to remove me from my condition, to replace the love I thought lost for lack of funds. But money will not buy true love, and money will not provide purpose. True love is unconditional commitment; purpose is the commitment to a condition. I was committed to a pitiful condition.

One of the real difficulties the government has in working harder to solve homelessness is the spending priority for available funds. We spend about 2.5 trillion dollars on defense in a five-year period. We will spend about 2.8 percent of that amount on social programs. For every 1,000 billion dollars on the war machine, we will spend 28 billion dollars on the rusting engine.

The truth is we have little funding to work with. We as a nation are now living on borrowed money. We are not earning enough as a nation to support our management structure. A great portion of our working public uses its credit cards to the limit, so too with our government, so too with all world governments. To say we are living in a bankrupt world is not sensationalism. Even the Catholic church is closing parishes and selling property because it is in financial chaos. The Japanese are finding themselves overextended and have withdrawn much of their world investment plans to shore up their own shores. The entire world economy is based on paper asset and rumor, and that value is only as valid as the belief in it. If there was one peanut butter sandwich left in the world and no other food, the owner of that sandwich would not trade it for all the money in all the world. In that extreme scenario all the money of the world would not be worth two pieces of bread and a smear of Skippy.

Most governments believe they can keep the people happy and productive by withholding the news that they have social cancer. But one day the patients will find out. They'll probably be furious, saying, "Why didn't you tell us? We would have done things differently." Maybe the intensity of economic and ecological problems looming ahead seems just too ominous to those who see it coming to announce publicly that the family of man has messed in his composite shoe. My ledger says not so. Tell us, tell me, but tell me the truth. The key word is *truth*.

I know, too, my ledger says I don't always know what is true. But sometimes I do. Sometimes I thought I was telling the truth; sometimes I knew I wasn't. But my ledger says the truth is always better in the long run, even if I can't see or understand it. This, too, is another head of the Credit Dragon. We must have faith and confidence in the credibility of the words from those who lead us. I am sure there is a poll somewhere that indicates our national trust in the political leadership. I have seen the "Throw the bums out" signs. We have all seen the incumbent editorial cartoons that are just too true to be funny. The tragedy of that generalization is that the public servants who have conducted themselves in an honorable manner are maligned by association, and those who deserve the rap are not affected by the honorable in the least.

Credit and credibility, then, are two major problems in the homeless issue. The homeless have no credit, the leaders have little credibility. Advocates discount most government statistics. Government spokesmen discount advocate claims. Caught in the middle are the ones who have moved through confusion to desperation.

Who does an unemployed man believe? Who should he listen to? Should he listen to a government official who says things are better because there are only seven million out of work this month instead of 7.1 million? Or does he listen to his wife crying because they are about to lose the house or apartment? Does he listen to his child crying to the rhythm of anger between its parents? Who does he listen to when the one on the other end of the phone doesn't care if the man has no money to pay the phone bill or the electric bill or the gas bill? When the shut-off comes, the man and his family are just as cold, just as hungry, just as hopeless and homeless whether there are seven million or 7.1 million out of work. It does not matter how many people are working to the one who cannot find work to pay for a sufficient life-style for himself and his family.

CHAPTER
EIGHT

Life in the
Garbage Can

To some degree, the wealthy and the poor eat from the same garbage can. We all get our food and drink from the same polluted waters and eat the same produce from the same chemically contaminated ground.

This chapter is the most difficult to follow, for it is about the problem that equals the problem of the poor. It relates directly to global poverty because pollution requires us to change the way we live and produce, if we wish to continue to live. The problem of poverty is mute in a world with no people. Maybe the end of pollution will solve poverty. Perhaps social disaster is the method by which this earth will be relieved from further destruction. My ledger gives that possibility great weight.

Perhaps, too, we can use the wasted human resources of the poor and homeless to repair and heal our nest as much as possible. For we can do much with two million hands and one million hearts with purpose, direction, and fair pay. And in so doing, we can replace the dignity and purpose that this rejected group, to a large degree, has never had.

For years, the traditional inscriptant in the army of poor and homeless was a spoke in the poverty wheel that had been rolling and growing since their first ancestors stepped on American soil. The slave to the system is not greatly different from the slave of the system. The blacks, who were released from one kind of slavery without the tools to dig out of another kind of slavery, and the whites from the traditionally poor Appalachian areas are no longer the only social groups now being drafted into the army of the unproductive. The newer poor and homeless, in growing numbers, come from farm community and factory families, middle-class families migrating downward, and a few upper-class youth who once, in a simpler world, believed and lived and produced as if they and their children were assured a better and grander future. That belief perhaps began with the promise of two chickens in every pot, but perhaps will die in the reality of two Mercedes in a few driveways. That dream is already dying for those who have worked and trained to perform tasks in industries that are now obsolete.

Perhaps one day we will all wake in a cumulative massive myogenic jerk and all eyes will see with fairness, compassion, and love. That will never happen until we break the mirror that stands between the reality of our own faces and the reality of the other person standing beyond the mirror. That will only happen when and if we peer through the mirage of secure class privilege. For the assumption that, because we have more things or the grace of a better beginning, our soul is of more value in the eyes of God or the eyes of man largely perpetuates the unbroken motion and growth of the wheel of poverty. That wheel could grow and gain speed until it crushes this society as it has past societies.

I do not support the New Age belief that we are all gods; obviously a growing number of people support it. I have great difficulty understanding or justifying or respecting a god or gods who by choice become a part of the slush of moral and social decay. My ledger cannot fathom God destroying His own creation without purpose. But if I were God, I wouldn't put the leaves back on this spring. I'd get someone's attention.

The following is data from the Worldwatch Institute Report on progress toward a sustainable society.[1]

- Forests are shrinking, deserts are expanding, and soils are eroding at increasing rates. Each year thousands of plant and animal species disappear, many before they are recognized or recorded.

- Some life-support systems appear to be deteriorating at a faster rate.

- Europe (not including the Soviet Union) now has about 31 million hectares of damaged forest, an area the size of what used to be West Germany.

- In 1986 half the forests in the Netherlands, Switzerland, and West Germany showed signs of damage.

- A dramatic depletion of ozone occurs over Antarctica each September, scientists have discovered, and each year since 1979 it has grown worse. By 1987 what had become known as the ozone "hole" had grown to twice the size of the continental United States. Though the hole involves a series of chemical reactions scientists don't yet fully understand, it could cause a very rapid ozone depletion around the world. That would lower crop output and increase the incidence of skin cancer and eye damage as more ultraviolet radiation reaches the earth.

- When India was photographed by satellite, scientists there discovered a far more rapid forest loss than had been previously estimated. Between 1972 and 1982, the country lost nine million hectares of tree cover, roughly 1.3 million hectares per year. At this rate, India will lose most of its remaining 31 million hectares of forest by the end of the century.

- As the world population increases, it will increase the stress on local life-support systems, create food shortages, and fodder and fuel will become scarce almost overnight.

- Any increase in energy needs will add to the dangerous chemistry experiment we are conducting on the earth's atmosphere. Lakes, estuaries, forests, human health, and the climate itself are now at risk.

- China, which has the world's largest coal reserves and recently passed the Soviet Union as the world's largest coal producer, has plans to double coal consumption by the year 2000. Due to its limited oil resources and a population of more than one billion, growth in China's coal use could well rank as the largest added source of sulfur dioxide and carbon emissions in the world.

- Some 140 acidified lakes were devoid of fish in Ontario, Canada, in 1980, with thousands experiencing biological change. One-half of the pollutants causing the destruction come from their neighbor to the south. Nine thousand lakes in the eastern United States were threatened; 3,000 lakes east of the Mississippi River were acid altered, as of 1980; 212 lakes in the Adirondack Mountains were devoid of fish.

It would appear that the rest of the world has a very grave problem at hand. But the sobering fact is that this is *your* problem and *my* problem too.

We are at the door of a new world system. Even the President speaks of one. We cannot build the new with rusty pieces of the old. If you have studied recent history you will agree that the old system is flawed for most of us and completely out of commission for hundreds of millions of others. We have a choice in the matter: Either we change it voluntarily and at once, or it will be changed for us. We can either continue to destroy or begin to restore. If we keep on our present path, our future—or better, our lack of one—will cost us all infinitely more than we care to pay.

Perhaps you are wondering how this applies to the problem of the poor and homeless. Simply this: Stopping the destruction of our planet will mean we must not produce, manufacture, create power, dump our trash, waste our resources, live, or work the way we have. And although that will help our planet, it will disrupt and displace countless millions of people. For in making the changes required for life on this planet we will further displace workers in the highest pollutant-causing segments of our society—the coal workers, chemical workers, paper mill workers—anyone that works for or in a company that dumps its contamination in the air, in the ocean, in streams, or in or on the ground. If the infringing corporations, by law of the land or by the law of love, decide to change for the planet's sake, the resulting efficiency will mean far fewer people will be needed in those industries.

By the way, many of the facts above are old, not old perhaps on the scale of history, but old in the scope of urgency. I used them so that we might be aware of how long the world has been aware it would have to change, and how little we have actually done.[2]

LEDGER

My ledger says that the whole world is crazy. We're acting like drunks at a free bash, trying to drink the last of the bubbly before the party is over. At that party we have been dancing to the beat of cause.

Division has causes, perhaps many. Some are valid; some are not. But division also is a cause. It is one cause for judgment and difference. The dividing of peoples by any set of standards or grading system tends to cover the simple fact that we all have the same basic needs. The dividing of society into those who have and those who want can cloud the fact that we are all chasing the same dollar and dream.

MERRY-GO-ROUND OF PAIN

PART **3**

CHAPTER
NINE

Chasing the Same
Dollar and Dream

> ## JOBS—JOBS—JOBS—JOBS
> We have many jobs available. $4–4.50
> PER HOUR. Must have transporta-
> tion and HOME phone. Need work?
> Start today. 634-0001 or 721-1110

We are chasing the same dollar and dream. Those who have the
dollar and live the dream wish to keep them. Most of those who
are removed from the dollar and dream it buys still search for it.
The advertisement above indicates the lack of comprehension of
many of the working public to the problems of the poor or homeless. I have heard many wealthy and well-to-do tell me there are
an abundance of jobs available if only the lazy so-and-so's would
get off their back ends and work them.

If a homeless person applied for one of the many reported

69

positions in the ad, he or she would not qualify. First, he would have no transportation; secondly, no home phone. And even if he could somehow get the job at the top pay of $4.50 per hour, the resulting $720.00 per month would be well below the poverty level. A family head certainly could never afford to take the job. He or she can do better on welfare. It is a catch-22 in every sense of the term.

My ledger says that welfare in many cases should be "work-fair." Those who are able to work would be on work-fair; those who are unable to work would remain on welfare.

According to the estimates of living expense by the Low-Income Housing Information Service, after rent, (which consti-tutes 70 percent of income for 33 percent of our poor population, and 50 percent of income for the remainder of the poor), there is only $360 to provide the worker with the remainder of life's ne-cessities. The cost of car repairs for those able to own a vehicle is also disproportionately high, as the automobiles are for the most part old and worn out. Car insurance is required by law in most states. If the worker buys the car, he pays a minimum of $100 per month. His operating cost with insurance would be a monthly minimum of $100. He now has $160 remaining to spend for food, clothing, medical insurance, phone (which is required to keep the job), and any other emergency that may arise. Oh yes, before we forget, the average poor family pays 35 percent of in-come for utilities and fuel. That would amount to over $200, and nothing has been deducted for state or federal taxes. Their monthly budget would look something like this:

RENT	$360
LOAN	100
CAR EXPENSES	100
UTILITIES	200
FOOD	?
PHONE	?
CLOTHING	?
INSURANCE	?
MEDICINE	?
FUN	Out of the question!
	$760

INCOME $720   Oops! Sorry, no food or fun this
                        month. You owe an additional
                        $40. Pay up or it's welfare for
                        you.

It quickly becomes obvious that a worker cannot afford to earn such low wages and maintain the basic requirements of life or his job. The situation is far worse for the worker with children. The fact is we do not live real lives in the cut-and-dried world of statistics and fact. The poor family who must fit their lives into the fact of $720 per month finds a way to do it. They divorce for financial expediency. They do not pay the rent and move out only when evicted. They do not pay as agreed for their car, and they walk more than ride. They do not go to the doctor or the dentist regularly. They do *not* have fun!

- The typical poor homeowner household—like the typical poor renter household—has an income of less than $5,000 per year. It pays 47 percent of its income for housing. Housing is considered unaffordable at that rate. (Financial planners recommend spending about 26 percent of income—or less—on housing.)

- There were 13.3 million households living below the poverty level in 1985. (The poverty level was $8,573.) The figure is estimated to be much higher now.

- The poverty level was $11,611 for a family of four in 1987. Now it is $12,000.

- From 1977 through 1980, HUD committed to provide federal rental assistance to an average of 316,000 additional households per year. From 1981 through 1988, however, the number of such additional households dropped precipitously—to an average of only 82,000 per year. In other words, the number of additional low-income renters receiving housing assistance each year fell by nearly three-quarters.

- If the number of additional low-income renters aided in the 1980s had continued at the same rate as in the late 1970s, there would now be commitments for assistance to an additional 1.8 million low-income households.

- Congressional Budget Office data show that the total number of renter households receiving federal housing assistance did grow from 2.4 million in 1978 to 4.3 million in 1988, and that the proportion of poor renter households being assisted climbed from 22 percent in 1979 to 29 percent in 1987.

- The National Low-Income Housing Coalition estimates that an additional seven million eligible for aid do not receive it because housing assistance programs are underfunded.[1]

- The sheer growth in the number of renter households who fall below the poverty line was greater than the increase in the number of households receiving housing assistance. As a result, the number of poor renter households not receiving any housing assistance rose substantially.

- In 1979, some four million poor renter households received no housing assistance. By 1987, the number without housing assistance had climbed to 5.4 million—an increase of more than one-third.

- Also from 1979 to 1987 the number of additional low-income households who were promised help from the federal government dropped by an average of more than two hundred thousand households per year.

In contrast to the decline in federal low-income housing assistance, there has been a substantial increase in a form of federal assistance that primarily benefits middle- and upper-class families. Each year the federal government provides billions of dollars in benefits to homeowners by allowing them deductions—primarily mortgage interest and property tax deductions—from the amount of income that is otherwise taxable by the federal government. These deductions reduce the total amount of federal income taxes paid by homeowners and thus become an indirect form of federal housing subsidy for homeowners. Such subsidies resulting from tax deductions, credits, or other tax breaks are technically termed "tax expenditures," since they essentially entail government spending through tax code.

- In 1987 roughly 75 percent of the benefits from housing-related tax expenditures went to 15 percent of homeowners.

- The wide disparity between the amount of government housing assistance provided through tax expenditures and the amount provided through housing programs results in a subsidy system strongly tilted toward those who are already more affluent. Data published by the Congressional Joint Committee on Taxation indicate that the benefits from housing-related tax expenditures accrue much more quickly for those at the top end of the spectrum.

Home ownership has a great bearing on the financial burdens of the elderly. If home ownership continues to be out of reach for more and more people, we will build an ever-growing army of elderly renters who suffer inordinately.

- Elderly homeowners were much less likely than elderly renters to be poor or to bear high housing cost burdens.

- The typical elderly homeowner spends 19 percent of his or her income on housing expenses.

- Three out of five elderly renters spent 30 percent or more of their income for rent and utilities.

If the data are examined another way and all young households are considered, including single-parent families and single individuals, the picture remains troubling. All such categories of households where the head is under age 25 have experienced increased housing costs in recent years, and fewer young households are homeowners today than 15 years ago. Housing problems are greater for households headed by a person under age 25 than for any other age group.

- According to a recent national study prepared by the Joint Center for Housing Studies of Harvard, in 1974 the typical

73

young renter household spent 24 percent of its income for housing. By 1987 the rent for such a household had climbed by half, to 36 percent of income.

- During the same period, the income of the typical young household fell 29 percent, after adjusting for inflation.

- In 1987 the typical young household had an income of $13,486.

- According to the study, some 23 percent of young households owned their homes in 1974. By 1987 only 16 percent of young households did.

I contacted Barry Zigas, who is the Executive Secretary of the Low-Income Housing Information Service in Washington, D.C. He was most helpful with his time and comments. He supplied the above information in a booklet titled "A Place to Call Home—the Crisis in Housing For the Poor." It was written by Paul A. Leonard, Cushing N. Dolbeare, and Edward B. Lazere. The information is not the latest. The new figures are even more disturbing.[2]

The authors further make the following conclusion: For most low-income households, housing has become an increasingly unaffordable commodity. With nearly two-thirds of all poor renters and nearly half of all poor homeowners paying more than 50 percent of their incomes for housing, and with substantial numbers of the poor paying more than 70 percent, little money is left for other necessities. As noted earlier, these figures can be regarded as a conservative estimate of the housing problems of the poor households since they do not include most of those people who are homeless.

Unlike expenditures for food or clothing, rent or mortgage payments cannot readily be reduced. Most low-income households cannot easily choose to buy less housing in a given month to free up funds for other basic expenses. Rather, a fixed rent or mortgage payment typically is paid in one lump sum each month.

The extremely high housing costs faced by most poor households have serious implications. The severe shortage of housing that is affordable to poor households probably contributed substantially to the growing problem of homelessness in the 1980s.

In addition, these extraordinary burdens probably have intensified related problems such as the incidence of hunger. The likelihood that a poor household will be without adequate food for part of a month is made considerably greater when rent consumes so much of the household's income that it has too little money left to buy food for the month.

High housing costs also leave poor families especially vulnerable to economic surprises. A delay in a monthly welfare check, an unexpected medical expense, or a job layoff can lead to a missed rent payment, an unpaid utility bill, or a shortage of groceries toward the end of the month. All of these can have significant consequences for poor households.

Behind the growing low-income housing squeeze lie both increasing housing costs and declining purchasing power among low-income households. As noted, the number of low-income households increased sharply between 1970 and 1987, at the same time that the number of low-income housing units declined.

Government commitments to assist poor households with their housing needs have been limited. Currently, fewer than one in three poor renter households receives assistance through a federal, state, or local public or subsidized housing program. While developments in the private economy have created an increased need for government housing assistance in the 1980s (as a result of increases in poverty and decreases in the low rent housing stock), the federal government has retrenched instead. Had the number of units added to the subsidized housing stock in the 1980s continued at the same rate as in the 1970s, commitments to assist an additional 1.8 million low-income households would have been made.

The future now looks ominous for affordable housing. Projections of national trends suggest that, just as affordable housing problems grew sharply for low-income households between the mid-'70s and the mid-'80s, so too are they likely to deteriorate further in the years ahead unless the government makes major policy changes and the private sector takes some positive steps.

We are all chasing the same dollar. With the growth in international competition for jobs, services, products, and resources worldwide, what will be our investment in ourselves? And how will it come about?

Perhaps the world needs a good cry, not in just the raising of voice to purpose, for that volume is growing now, but a good old-fashioned outpouring of tears, an emotional tearing of our garments, a weeping to exhaustion for the plight of this portion of mankind now being ground by the pestle of poverty in the mortar of moral value.

The following speech addresses this question powerfully. But when it was first given none of our political leaders heard it. They left for recess. I watched as the speaker on the house floor emotionally pleaded to empty chairs and eloquently and lovingly spoke to ears that had chosen not to hear. It will be heard here, and I pray it will echo forever.

Not all politicians are myopic. The real tragedy is that our elected officials are aware of the problems and the very real probability that limited partisan views will forever keep us from the panorama of possibilities. That same partisan view will keep many from the promise of "equality for all and the Great American Dream." Congressman Walter Fauntroy knew this when he gave the following speech to Congress:

Mr. Speaker, as the nation prepares to receive the State of the Union Address from our beloved President, I want to share with the American people some thoughts on the golden opportunity that we have in the decade of the nineties to resolve the backlog of problems built up over the past decade of neglect in our nation and our world in education, housing and homelessness, drug control, AIDS research, infrastructure repair, and environmental rehabilitation. This opportunity flows from the fact that the winding down of the East-West conflict in our world may release billions of dollars in money, manpower, and research which for decades have been devoted to military uses to concentrate now on pressing human and environmental needs that are getting out of hand in our world today.

It is for that reason that I want to speak to the American people on the subject: *East-West Tension and North-South Need*.

Mr. Speaker, there is a fierce wind blowing in our world today. It is blowing with hurricane force; tearing down old systems, sweeping away a crumbling order and ushering in a new day. If you listen with your spiritual ears, you can hear the wind blowing the rumbling chords of freedom in Angola, and Namibia and throughout South Africa. The echo of the wind is heard from Tiananmen Square in China and throughout Asia. The sound of the wind is heard from Poland, Czechoslovakia, Romania and throughout Eastern Europe. It rises from the huddled masses who yearn to breath free in Haiti and throughout Central and South America. It is the wind of freedom; it's a wind of change.

These winds of change that are sweeping the globe today have profound significance for improving the quality of life for those who suffered most during the decade of the eighties because of decisions made by both our President and Congress and by the developed, industrialized nations of the northern hemisphere. It is, therefore, my hope and prayer that in the decade of the nineties, East-West tension will yield to North-South need.

Military Expenditures and Social Need

President Dwight David Eisenhower said in 1953 that:

Every gun that is made, every warship that is launched, every rocket that is fired, signifies a theft from those who are hungry and are not fed, those who are cold and are not clothed. This world in arms is not spending money alone. It is spending the sweat of its laborers, the genius of its scientists, the hopes of its children!

We are only now beginning to understand how the political obsession with military force, which has dominated national priorities on our planet since World War II, has drained the world's vitality and wealth, and has robbed us of the ability to meet pressing human need.

In the thirteenth edition of *World Military and Social Expenditures* released last fall, Ruth Leger Sivard again documents the fact that in the decade of the eighties global spending on the military has been one trillion dollars a year. Half of that spending has been by the United States and the Soviet Union. In contrast, global spending on human need and development assistance has been only 2.8 percent of that amount; twenty-eight billion dollars. One thousand billion for defense, only twenty-eight billion for development. The costs of that social neglect have been tremendous.

In a table documenting the victims of war over the past forty-five years and the victims of social neglect, Ms. Sivard points out that the chances of dying from social neglect (from malnutrition and preventable disease) are thirty-three times greater than the chances of dying in war. Look at the annual toll of victims of the 127 wars we have had in the world since 1945 compared to the annual toll of victims of social neglect over the past forty-five years.

- A total of 525,000 people have been killed annually in war, but 3.5 million children have died a year of dehydration, preventable by oral therapy at a cost of one dollar per child.

- 525,000 died annually in wars, but four million children died a year of six diseases, preventable by immunization at a cost of ten dollars per child.

- 525,000 died annually in wars, but ten million children a year did not survive their first birthday; fourteen million a year died before their fifth birthday; and 500,000 mothers still die in childbirth annually in our world today.

- The study shows that 1.2 million people were wounded a year in the 127 wars fought since 1945, but compare that to the walking wounded victims of social neglect in our world today.

- 1.2 million people are wounded in wars a year, but 600 million women in childbearing years suffer from nutritional anemia.

- 1.2 million people are wounded in wars a year, but 250,000 children are paralyzed by polio and another 700,000 go blind a year due to vitamin A deficiency.

- 1.2 million people are wounded in wars a year, but each year ten million mothers who are themselves malnourished bear malnourished children.

Our world's neglect of human needs causes an appalling number of lives to be lost to hunger and killer diseases that are preventable at the cost of a few dollars a piece. A trillion dollars a year spent on military uses and only 2.8 percent of that amount on human need. The greater tragedy is that only half of the development assistance offered by the industrialized nations of the North goes to the underdeveloped, low-income nations of the South; 14 billion annually or only 1.4 percent of what the world spends on military uses.

If only a fraction of the money, manpower and research devoted to military uses were diverted to development, we could not only end the health and education woes of the Third World nations of the South but also invigorate their market economies as to provide the millions of people of the Caribbean and South and Central American economies alternatives to the wretched illicit drug industry that threatens to destroy civilization from within. For example:

- A mere 5 percent reduction in current military outlays of 1 trillion dollars a year, if allocated instead to health care, could double public expenditures for the health care of four billion people in the Third World, providing enough resources to immunize every baby and to bring fresh water and basic sanitation within 10 years to every village.

- The World Health Organization declares that with a modest contribution from the nations of the world of 450 million dollars, less than one-thousandth of the world's annual military spending, they could wipe malaria from the face of the globe at a time when millions die needlessly from this disease every year in the Southern hemisphere.

- The cost of a ten-year program to provide essential food and health needs in developing countries is less than half of one year's military spending.

- For the price of one jet fighter, 20 million dollars, 40,000 village-based pharmacies could be established.

- One-half of one percent of one year's world military expenditures, 5 billion dollars, would pay for all the farm equipment needed to increase food production and approach food self-sufficiency in all of the food deficit low-income countries of the world over the next five years.

President Dwight David Eisenhower was right:

Every gun that is made, every warship that is launched, every rocket that is fired, signifies a theft from those who are hungry and are not fed, those who are cold and are not clothed. This world in arms is not spending money alone. It is spending the sweat of its laborers, the genius of its scientists, the hopes of its children!

To bring it home to America, let me remind members of what Senator Mark Hatfield and Congressman Howard Berman of our Arms Control and Foreign Policy Caucus told us in sending us the Sivard report. They said:

At a time when the U.S. is facing unprecedented competitive pressure from Japan and the European community, the U.S. government allocates only 25 percent of our Research and Development budget to civilian technology and 75 percent to the military, compared to European community nations which spend 70 percent on civilian and only 30 percent on military technology.

Those kinds of misplaced priorities are reflected in our neglect of human need during the decade of the eighties in almost every category, whether it be housing or health care or education or infrastructure and environmental rehabilitation. In the decade of the eighties we cut housing programs by 77 percent, throwing three million people homeless on the streets of America. Cuts in Medicaid funding in the eighties reduced the number of poor people covered by the program from 64 percent to 46 percent at a time when medical costs have doubled from 248 billion dollars to 496.6 billion dollars. We cut training of health care professions by 39 percent, exacerbating the national shortfall of qualified nurses and doctors. We caused 37 million people in our country to have no health care insurance of any kind now.

In the area of education in the decade of the eighties, poor children receiving federally supported basic skills training fell from 7 million in 1981 to 5.7 million in 1988; this, during a decade when the number of poor children increased to 8.5 million. American children's report care of September 1989—computed by the National Association of Secondary School Principals—gave our children C+ when compared to South Korean children who got A− and West German children who got B+.

While we are losing jobs in the labor-intensive, smokestack, auto, rubber, steel, and textile industries which used to be the means of upward mobility for millions of the American people, we are cutting the very programs that would prepare our children for the capital-intensive, information-based, service-oriented jobs of the present and future.

Please forgive me if I have assaulted you with so many facts documenting the social costs of our world's preoccupation with military expenditures, but as the Reverend Jesse Jackson has so eloquently put it, "We must have information to gain the inspiration to reach our destination." And if our destination is a world free of the barbarism of a war, the decadence of racism and the scourge of poverty, then the decade of the nineties must be one in which we change direction. East-West conflict must yield to North-South need. We must change a situation in which the poorest fifth of the world's population has had to attempt to survive on 2 percent of the global national product, whereas the wealthiest fifth absorbs 78 percent of the global pie. On a per capita basis this works out to an annual income of $238 for those in the poorest fifth and $12,286 for those in the upper fifth. It means a life expectancy of fifty-seven years in the South versus seventy-five years in the North and an infant mortality rate of 110 per 1,000 in the South versus fourteen per 1000 in the North.

Dwight Eisenhower was right:

Every gun that is made, every warship that is launched, every rocket that is fired, signifies a theft from those who are hungry and are not fed, those who are cold and are not clothed. This world in arms is not spending money alone. It is spending the sweat of its laborers, the genius of its scientists, the hopes of its children!

Ah, but as we stand today in this the first month of the first year of this the last decade of the last century of this millennium, there is good news tonight! The good news is that the military giants of the North seem now poised to release billions of dollars a year from their forty-five-year wasteful spending binge on military uses. The good news is that Secretary of Defense Richard Cheney and Budget Director Richard Dauman are seeking ways to cut our nation's enormous spending on military uses. The good news is that the Soviet Union has already begun a unilateral reduction of its large forces in Europe. The good news is that both superpowers are lending more support to nonviolent resolutions of regional hostilities.

The winds of change that are sweeping the globe are blowing the world a golden opportunity to make long overdue investments in human need and infrastructure and environmental rehabilitation!

The question of the decade of the nineties is "will this peace dividend that will flow from the winding down of East-West conflict be invested in human resources and economic development to close the gap between 'the haves and have-nots' of our nation and world, or will it serve to widen the gap between the North and the South, between the one-third of the world's population that lives primarily in the developed, industrialized nations of the Northern hemisphere and the two-thirds of the world's population that lives primarily in the Southern hemisphere: Central and South America, Africa, the Caribbean, India and parts of Asia?" That is the question of the nineties!

North-South Need

As Chairman of the Subcommittee on International Development, Finance, Trade and Monetary Policy, I am as concerned as leaders of the economically embattled developing countries of the South about several things:

- First, that financial support for Eastern Europe will mean less for a developing world already beset by reduced official and private flows. That fear is not without foundation. Acting Aid Director, Mark Edleman, told the Financial Times that "ensuring the triumph of democracy and peace in Europe may become our top priority. American resources are limited and money for Eastern Europe will come out of what would otherwise go to Africa, Central America, and the Middle East."

- My fear is that it will also come out of the desperately needed initiatives to restore the 77 percent cuts that were made in domestic housing programs in the decade of the eighties, throwing three million people homeless on the streets of America. My fear is that it will also come out of critical education and training programs that were severely cut in the eighties and that have crippled our efforts to prepare our young people for the capital-intensive, information-based, service-oriented jobs of America's present and future.

- My fear is that it will come out of programs that must be developed and expanded to deal with the most serious internal security problem confronting our nation today; illicit drug traffic. Should we not invest substantial amounts of the peace dividend in drug education, drug treatment and drug enforcement programs if we are to avoid entering the twenty-first century as a nation crippled by drug addicted zombies unable to compete in the world economy, thereby forcing those who live in the ghettoes and barrios of America, like those farmers in the Andean countries of South America whence come the drugs, to sink deeper into the underground drug economy because there are no alternative means of economic survival available to them? That's my concern!

The Third World nations of the South, afflicted with heavy debt burdens and net capital outflows, urgently need increasing quantities of aid, grants and soft money. The inner city and rural poverty-stricken populations of our nation need much of the peace dividend to flow to them in terms of government programs to assist them in becoming productive citizens. My fear is that those official resources will not flow to them but rather to Eastern Europe or to pay off our nation's three trillion dollar Reagan national debt to those who benefited most from the enormous tax breaks of the eighties and who then loaned the money back to the country at 10 percent interest to pay for its military spending binge.

Acting U.S. Aid Director, Mark Edleman, also points out that "Savings from the defense budget will not mean more aid for anyone but it will mean less reductions for current aid recipients." The Gramm-Rudman budget cuts, he points out, now demand this. Savings from the defense budget are likely to be used to reduce the budget deficit. That's my concern!

My concern is that the benefits of the peace dividend will not flow from North to South, from the haves to the have-nots. But I also have a second concern as well.

My second concern is that financial support for Eastern Europe will not only mean less flow of economic assistance from official government institutions, but that it may also mean less flow of private capital investment to the lesser developed communities of our nation. Such private investment is essential if the "have-nots" of our nation and world are to become active participants in the world economy to the mutual benefit of both North and South, East and West.

The *Financial Times* article that I quoted earlier also pointed out that:

> Developing countries hoping to attract foreign private investment are also likely to lose out to an Eastern Europe with market economies. The competitive edge in production costs which many developing countries have used to attract foreign business may not now be considered the best bargain by investors.

In other words, the changes in Eastern Europe may well have an effect on flows of private investment capital to the low-income countries of the South. If the nova rich companies of the Far East (Japan, Taiwan, and Korea), for example, which are contemplating investments, feel they can get a better deal by going into Eastern Europe, then they will. My fear is that Eastern Europe will be more attractive for direct investment and capital flows than poor nations with high potential and great need like Mozambique and Zambia, Haiti, Jamaica and Namibia.

Yes, my fear is that the "peace dividend" will not flow North to South, from "the haves to the have-nots", but West to East with reduced flows of both official aid and private investment capital to the debt-burdened lesser developed nations of the Third World.

A Balanced Public and Private Agenda for the Nineties

The final question, then, is "what public and private initiatives must we pursue in the decade of the nineties to assure that both official government aid and private capital investment function to close the gap between the 'haves and the have-nots'? What must we do to ensure that flows of public and private trade not all go West to East further dividing our planet, whites from non-whites, highly developed nations from lesser developed countries, the North from the South?"

In my view, the watchword of our public policy agenda for the decade of the nineties must be *balance:* balance in addressing the needs of the haves and the have-nots; balance in addressing the needs of eastern Europe and those of the poorer nations of the southern hemisphere; balance between our need to reduce the three-trillion-dollar Reagan national debt and our need to fund adequately the housing, education, and human services programs that were so severely cut in the decade of the eighties, which cuts threw three million people homeless in the streets of America, reduced the quality of public education in our country to levels far below that of our economic competitors in the Far East and Western Europe and crippled our efforts to meet the health care needs of our nation's poor.

Balance Domestically

Such a balanced approach will mean that, domestically, all of our savings from defense reductions should not go to deficit reduction but that adequate amounts will go to restoring the 77 percent cuts to our housing programs that were made in the de-

85

cade of the eighties. It means that all of our peace dividend should not be invested in further "tax relief" for the wealthy few, but in education, urban and rural development and the War on Drugs for the benefit of the unmonied many. As the second ranking member of the House Banking, Finance and Urban Affairs Committee, and as a member of the Select Committee on Narcotics Abuse and Control, that will be my agenda for the second session of the 101st Congress and the decade of the nineties.

You may expect me to pursue, therefore, full funding of our nation's housing and community development programs including the passage of H.R. 1180, the Omnibus Housing Act of 1990. You may expect me to oppose further tax breaks for the rich, indeed, to pursue the restoration of at least a portion of the taxation levels that we shamefully reduced in the decade of the '80s for the exclusive benefit of the top 5 percent income earners of our nation. You may expect me as a member of the Select Committee on Narcotics Abuse and Control to pursue full funding of a comprehensive War on Drugs that provides adequate resources for not only the criminal justice system but also for drug education, drug treatment, and skill training to provide the "have-nots" of our nation an alternative to the illicit drug industry that too many feel is their only means of economic survival.

"Balance" should be the watchword in our initiatives to distribute the "peace dividend" in the decade of the nineties.

Balance Internationally

Internationally, a balanced approach means that not all of our foreign aid and trade initiatives will flow to Eastern Europe and the Middle East, but that we will achieve a far better balance in our foreign relations budget between the developed nations of the Mediterranean Sea and above, and the lesser developed nations of Africa, the Caribbean, Central and South America.

Accordingly, you may expect me as Chairman of the Banking Subcommittee on International Development, Finance, Trade and Monetary Policy to pursue the following public policy initiatives in the second session of the 101st Congress and beyond:

(1) An adequate replenishment for the International Development Association (IDA), with a proviso that at least 45 per-

cent of the replenishment be lent to Africa. (14 billion dollars, of which 3 billion dollars is the expected U.S. contribution.)

(2) A quota increase in the IMF (about 50 billion dollars, of which about 7 billion dollars is the expected U.S. share).

(3) Ongoing efforts to fashion means for reducing the burdensome overhand of commercial and official debt owed by the poor countries.

(4) Trade initiatives to reduce the barriers which developing countries face in selling their goods in America.

How we achieve the desired "balance" will be the most hotly debated "peace dividend" issue of the 1990s.

Black America's Role

Let me say this to my African-American brothers and sisters: We dare not find ourselves on the sidelines in this debate. Our very survival and future advancement toward freedom depend on our being active participants in shaping this debate.

As President of the National Black Leadership Roundtable, and a member of the Congressional Black Caucus, I will recommend that the CBC Foundation sponsor over the next two years, a National Commission on Post-Cold War Priorities as a vehicle for gathering together our best minds to sort out the balancing of the "peace dividend."

The findings and recommendations of such a Commission would establish a truly African-American imprint on the "peace dividend" debate. They would form the basis for interaction with both the Democratic and Republican parties, our Congressional leadership and the administration.

Our Youth Are Our Future

In the meantime, as African-Americans, we have a responsibility, as never before, to get our own house in order; to devise effective self-help means of strengthening the social fiber of our threatened communities. Here, the bottom line is our youth. They are our future. We owe it to them, as our leaders of tomorrow—and to ourselves—to inspire them toward a new sense of commitment and sacrifice for the future betterment of our communities. Toward this end, we must actively enlist their participation in a movement of voluntary community service. Otherwise, more and more inner city communities risk becoming bloody battlegrounds in drug trafficking, violent crime, and social chaos.

I am of the firm belief that the recruitment of African-American youth into a national network on voluntary community service—service specifically tailored to the urgent needs of black America—may offer us the best hope for transforming the peer group environment in our communities and around the country, away from the path of youth self-destruction.

Again, in my capacity as a member of the Black Caucus and President of the National Black Leadership Roundtable, I will seek to stimulate a dialogue among my colleagues on the need for creative self-help approaches that rescue the future for our youth, especially our young black men, thereby ensuring the future vitality and stability of our communities.

"Balance" should be the watchword of our initiatives to distribute the "peace dividend" internationally in the decade of the nineties.

A Nation with a Heart

Dr. Tony Campolo, Chairman of the Department of Sociology at Eastern College in St. Davids, Pennsylvania, tells this story about a schoolteacher friend of his that I think sets the right tone for our nation and our world as we move boldly into the decade of the nineties. He says:

I have a friend, he said. Her name's Jean Thompson. It was the first day of school, she said what school teachers always say the first day of school. "Boys and girls, she said, I love you all the same."

Teachers lie. I was one of those boys that teachers didn't like. How about you? Little Teddy Stollard was a boy that Jean Thompson did not like. He sat slouched in his chair. He didn't pay attention. His mouth hung open in a stupor. His eyes were always unfocused. His clothes were mussed, his hair unkept. He never bathed often enough to get rid of an unpleasant odor. He was an unattractive boy and Jean Thompson did not like him.

When she spoke to him, he answered in monosyllables: "Yeah . . . nahh . . . yeah." When she marked his paper, she got a perverse delight out of putting X's next to the wrong answers. And when she put the "F" at the top of the paper, she always did it with a flair; and she should have known better.

Teachers have records. And she had records. She had records on Teddy Stollard. "First grade: Teddy's a good boy. He shows promise in work and attitude. But poor home situation. Second grade: Teddy is a good boy. He does what he is told. But he is too serious. His mother is terminally ill. Third grade: Teddy is falling behind in his work; he needs help. His mother died this year. His father shows no interest. Fourth grade: Teddy is in deep waters; he is in need of psychiatric help. He is totally withdrawn."

She had records, she should have known better.

Christmas came, and the boys and girls brought their presents and piled them on the desk. They were all in brightly colored paper except for Teddy's present. His was wrapped in brown paper and held together with scotch tape. And on it, scribbled in crayon, were the words, "For Miss Thompson from Teddy." She tore open the brown paper and out fell a rhinestone bracelet with most of the stones missing, and a bottle of cheap perfume that was almost empty. The other boys and girls began to giggle, but she had enough sense to put some of the perfume on her wrist, put on the bracelet and then holding her wrist up to the other children said, "Doesn't it smell lovely? Isn't the bracelet lovely?" And taking their cue from the teacher, they all agreed.

At the end of the day, when all the children had left, Teddy lingered behind. And he came over to the desk and he said, "Miss Thompson, all day long, you smelled just like my mother. And her bracelet, that's her bracelet, it looks real nice on you too. I'm really glad you like my presents." And when he left, she got down on her knees and buried her head in the chair and she begged God to forgive her.

And the next day, when the children came, she was a different teacher. She was a teacher with a heart. She was a teacher whose heart had been broken by the things that break the heart of God. That's what it means to be a decent human being. To let your heart be broken by the things that break the heart of God. And she cared for all the children, but especially those who needed help.

Especially Teddy. She tutored him, she put herself out for him, for she had a heart for God. A heart for God.

By the end of that year, Teddy had caught up with a lot of the children. He was even ahead of some.

Several years later, Jean Thompson got this note:

Dear Miss Thompson:
I'm graduating and I'm second in my high school
class. I wanted you to be the first to know. Love, Teddy.

Four years later she got another note:

Dear Miss Thompson:
I wanted you to be the first to know, I'm the first in my
class. The university has not been easy, but I liked it.
Love, Teddy Stollard.

Four years later there was another note:

Dear Miss Thompson:
As of today, I am Theodore J. Stollard, M.D. How
about that? I wanted you to be the first to know. I'm
going to be married in July, the 27th to be exact. I want
you to come and sit where my mother would have sat,
because you're the only family I have. Dad died last year.

And she went and she sat where that mother should have sat because she deserved to be there. She had become a decent human being. Do you have such a heart of gold? Do you care so much for those who hurt? Then, join me and freedom loving people across this nation and around the world in the noble quest in the decade of the nineties to have East-West resources flow to meet North-South need.

Don't tell me it cannot be done. That's what they told Joshua and Caleb. "You can't enter the land of Canaan. There are giants over there and we are like grasshoppers in their sight." But Joshua and Caleb said, "Oh, no, with God's help we shall overcome." And they merely walked about the walled city of Jericho and the walls came tumbling down.

That's what they told Martin Luther King, Jr., in Birmingham, Alabama, in 1963. They said, "You can't change America; they'll never take down the 'For White Only' signs; it will never happen!"

But Martin said, "Oh, no, with God's help, we shall overcome."

I shall never forget how he led our people out of the 16th Street Baptist Church on a Sunday afternoon. We stood before Bull Connor with his bullwhips and fire hoses and biting dogs like David before Goliath, saying, "You come before us with a sword and a shield but we come in the name of God. We're going to be free. You can beat us with your billy clubs, but we'll keep on marching. You can knock us down with your fire hoses, but we'll get up and keep on marching. You can bomb our churches and kill our children, Bull Connor, and we'll keep on marching. Because there is something within us that fire can't burn out and water can't drown out and billy clubs can't beat out and bombs can't bomb out. It is our belief in ourselves."

And we marched! We marched until the patter of our feet became the thunder of the marching men of Joshua and the world rocked beneath our tread, rocked until I could sit in the East Room of the White House with Martin Luther King, Jr., and watch President Lyndon Johnson sign a piece of paper that declared, "Make the man's dream a living reality!" Don't tell me it can't be done.

If you believe, join people of goodwill all over the world in the noble quest to meet human development needs in the decade of the nineties. Join us with the determination of Dr. Charles Adams of the Hartford Memorial Baptist church of Detroit, Michigan:

Don't let anything paralyze your mind, tie your hands or break your spirit. If you have a hard way to go, walk it by faith. If you face a mean problem, work with it until you work through it. If you have a misunderstanding, settle it. If you have a grudge, drop it. If you have hatred or resentment, shake it off. If you have a high mountain, move it by faith or climb it by works. If you have a battle, fight it. If you have a handicap, rise above it. If you have race prejudice, overcome it. If you have a temptation, conquer it. If you have an evil, destroy it. If you have challenge, face it. If you have trouble, take it. If you have a cross, bear it. If they knock you down, get up. If they push you against the ropes, come out swinging. If they laugh at you, keep smiling at them. If they talk about you, keep praying for them. If they hate you, keep loving them; and if they kill you, just rise again.

Ain't no power on earth that can stop a people with a heart of gold who are determined to see East-West resources flow to meet North-South need in the decade of the nineties.

Congressman Walter Fauntroy

LEDGER

My ledger says we will cry if we wish or care if we will. But from the high plains of Texas to the back streets and barrios of our major cities, from the elevated bars of our legal system to the most pitiful vomit-filled bars of skid row. From the multimillion dollar homes of Palm Springs to the windowless hovels of Harlem, regardless of our rich furs or our filthy rags, from our educated to our ignorant, from the color of our conscience to the shade of our skin, from the new leather seats of those who ride to the worn leather shoes of those who must walk to those unable to do either, from the assumed top of our society to the assumed dregs, there is no difference except that of the illusion of value and worth. From the highest mountain, once pristine, now putrefying in our own waste, to the cesspool lakes from which the majority draw their drinking water, to the bottled water of the rich; from the landscaped yards watered from the last remaining pure water of our aquifers to the grassless playgrounds of the poor; we are all passengers on this earth. The only difference is the price we pay for our ticket, in money, in available resources, in pain or its lack, in concern or contempt. And that price will be proportionally charged to each of us.

The one fact that I am sure of is that the eventual destination for all on board is the same. Whether we crash or land depends on the cumulative pilots guiding this flight. The outcome depends on the skill and wisdom and compassion of those in the cockpit. Pilots, check our compass, assess our fuel supply, define our destination, for we are descending rapidly. Passengers, check your tickets; there is no free ride.

Phone interviews can be frustrating or rewarding. A portion of the latter follows. I conducted it in an attempt to speak with Congressman Fauntroy:

I have yet to have one single phone call returned by anyone of position. Not one single person, from Anna Kondratas to Jack Kemp, to all the rest of them, to Pat Carlisle, to everyone involved, to congressmen, senators, no one, not one single person, has talked to me. Isn't that strange?

Uh-huh.

And, of course, we hear, "Get involved, make a phone call, write a letter, become involved in your government and things will change." Isn't this strange, we get nothing? It's going in the book. I talked to the publisher; he said, put it in. Let's have the truth about what's happening, you know . . . who's saying what and where and why, and who isn't. But it's amazing to me.

Well, hold it, maybe someone else can help, hold it just a minute—

Hello, this is Marguerite Gras.

Yes, Marguerite, this is Noah Snider calling from Oklahoma City. How are—

I'm sure that the congressman would be pleased to have you use this in your book [referring to the speech quoted above], but my recommendation to you, if you're doing a book, is to send us the routine request for permission to release form.

All right. (I thought Oh No, I'm not going anywhere with this. The heck with Washington. No one there cares. How wrong, how wrong, how wrong. This lady cared.)

"It's a routine form. If you don't have it developed right now for the material you're using in your book, you need to get it. And if you will send it to us, we will even send you a copy of the congressman's speech.

Well, that's what I'll need before I do it. I didn't record the whole thing. It came on CNN and, of course, I was typing and busy working on the book, and then I heard part of it and I poked on the recorder—

Right.

—and got a portion of it. It was a very powerful speech.

Yes, it was. Your book is very timely. I don't know how much you intend to include in it, but, you know, the problems for the homeless also include the deinstitutionalization of our mentally retarded—

Absolutely.

—and our mentally ill into group homes, where they have no way of maintaining, particularly the large number of schizophrenic people who are able to maintain a normal life-style and normal performances, if they stay on medication. And when they go off the medication, all their old symptoms return, so that we have a high percentage of that, too. The statistics on that vary from time to time. There is no doubt that the institutions from which these people have been released, by and large, are very grim settings.

Uh-huh.

They are also very destructive in terms of their maintaining a normal life-style. So this is a coming crisis that everyone will have to face, because the homeless who are ill, on the street, still retain their power of determining whether or not they will receive medication and assistance.

Yes.

As a result, they are subject to the most tragic kind of circumstances in their conditions. So there are quite a number of very tough questions facing us.

There certainly are. It just isn't a simple problem so that we can be very selective, you know, and bore into one little difficult vein. Another problem of the homeless is the fact that the American economic patterns have shifted.

Robert Reich. You might be interested in reading Robert Reich, R-e-i-c-h, of Harvard, who did a very fine study on the loss of the blue collar industries in this country. And then, of course, everybody was very glib in the way they said, "Well, never mind, it's bad to lose it but nevertheless we have such an expansion of the service industries that we needn't really worry. We just are seeing a realignment of the economy." However, this weekend's financial pages gave diagrams showing that the service industry has not only stopped growing, but is now beginning to—

Shrink. Yes.

—deteriorate.

Well, it is true, you know. We can't, we can't get everyone computer friendly in time to put them in a position of—

Well, also too, I came out of an early sociological preparation in which the Great American Dream was class and economic mobility. And in those days, if you were blue collar, you were held very punitively as a failure if your child didn't become white collar, if his child didn't become a member of the professions, etc., and I began, as did many people, to notice that there were many people unhappy. We had this revolution in the sixties—

Yes, I was a party to that.

—in which people went back to using their hands, because they felt that this was very important. This gave them a feeling of satisfaction. And I call it the tyranny of class mobility, which is still with us in America. Instead of . . . well, we suddenly wound up with too many chiefs and no Indians.

Absolutely.

And we never give any recognition to the people who really make our country work. And those are the blue collar people who enjoy the work they're doing and should not be penalized for remaining in their particular category.

I agree.

Part of this is due to the heritage of all of the people who came from Europe, where you were fixed by birth in the profession that you could choose. My husband, for example, is a professor, but his family had twenty-nine generations of master carpenters, and I swear, it finally got into their blood, because both he and his concert cellist uncle who came here and moved up the ladder, they still enjoyed carpentry.

Yeah, isn't it amazing? It seems to—it's entered their gene pool somewhere. The sawdust is now in their gene pool.

Yes, I think so.

Interesting. Your name, please?

I'm Marguerite, M-a-r-g-u-e-r-i-t-e. Gras, G-r-a-s. And our address, be sure to send it to my attention—

I will.

—because life is lively here, and we're trying to close out the Congressman's offices, and so I'll be one of the . . . I'll be here because I am one of his committee people and that committee goes on.

Right. Would you mind, Marguerite, if I quoted some of the things that you've mentioned to me?

That's perfectly all right. And if there's anything else you think you need on the homeless that we might have, I would be happy to send you some of that.

You know, we have a challenge before us, and this is the thing that Americans do the best. If we really face the problem—

But even worse is the problem of when we pass a law, it is then handed over to the Executive Branch and it is translated into a series of federal regulations. Now I have dealt—indirectly because we have to be very careful; they don't welcome interfering—but I have had contact with people who write these federal regulations, and many of them are even more removed from the reality of life than we are. Because we at least have constituents, reams of letters keep us informed. So, you know, you have this public policy of "whatever" document that comes to us, and we hold something called an oversight hearing, which questions how our laws are being served by the Executive Branch. And we really pull their tail feathers out, as I often describe it. We bring them up to the Hill, and they have to—it's a great ordeal for them—they have to explain why certain things didn't happen.

Now, some of these documents, government prose and these hearings are printed almost in the style, printing style of the seventeenth, eighteenth, nineteenth century, but nevertheless, there are extremely important public policy statements in these hearings. Because here is where you find the heads of the departments of the Executive Branch making their commitments.

Uh-huh.

Those should help you with the public policy.

Oh, I'm sure it will. It truly will. I'll get the letter off today, and I'll call, if you don't mind, I'll call next week—

All right.

—and once again, I do appreciate your time.

Good luck.

Thank you. Good-bye.

What a treat! Though I did not reach the one I assumed I needed; I contacted the one who was able and willing to help.

So many of the people I contacted had a command of the problem. Many of the contacts had suggestions for solution. Most of them had an abiding compassion. Many of them wanted to help. Marguerite Gras did.

Mrs. Gras mentioned that college graduates were waiting in line to get a clerk's job at a hotel in northern Virginia. That's what the next chapter is about.

CHAPTER TEN

The Pac Man
of Change

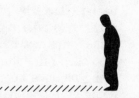

The world we woke to this morning was not at all the one we said goodnight to last night. Changes were born that we may not be aware of for some time to come. New technology stretched its abilities and appetite this morning, and looked for something to sink its teeth into. Yesterday businessmen all over the world met to negotiate contracts for goods not yet produced. Price was negotiated on products and services and the bottom line will determine where the product will be produced.

In a previous chapter, we covered how far the minimum wage would go toward the budget of a family living below the poverty level. It did not quite stretch over the expenses. Our minimum wage is now about eight cents per minute. I wonder how many eight-cents-per-minute-sub-poverty-level American jobs will be existing after today's contracts are signed based on the two cents per minute earned by the Mexican or Taiwanese or Korean or the other third world country's workers. The problem is even greater than the loss of manufacturing jobs.

Many of the men I met on the street had no defined skill. Some had been carpenters, some dug holes and filled them up, some never had a steady job. Some were Vietnam vets who felt they never had a home. A percentage could not read or write, some had a college degree, many had a high school education. Many hung around the spot labor office. Perhaps you have seen these places in your hometown. They are the beat-up buildings, usually within the slum area, from which this inventory of workers is drawn. The manufacturing company may use this resource when they have a particularly distasteful clean-up job. The men are paid each day in cash. The jobs, however, may only come once a week, and hunger visits each and every day. Hunger usually finds the homeless man or woman at the mission, where food and hunger meet to save muscle but not face.

Muscle is not as great an attribute any longer, muscle has been replaced by machine. Those with only muscle have little or nothing to offer our society. Those who mastered specific machinery are now being replaced by computer-run machines. Men who once ran milling, stamping, and piece-work production are being or have been replaced by machines that are capable of doing all the above, plus inspect the parts they made, thus replacing the men once filling *that* need. Many of these factories are, of course, not in this country. That same machine will inventory the parts by number and pass the part to another machine, controlled by computer that will warehouse the part by robot and further ship the part by computer direction, therefore doing away with the need for warehouse and shipping muscle. "The times they are a-changing."

The building trades are changing too. We now use nail guns that nail at machine-gun pace, nailing more in an hour than a man with a hammer can pound out in a day. There is not room enough in the shrinking home-building sector to employ the displaced hand with the hammer. The latest census report states that we have ten million vacant homes and apartments. We as a nation and as a world are displacing human hands with computer chips. We are replacing even the hands making computer chips. We are entering a most marvelous world bearing amazing gifts that fewer and fewer people will be able to purchase. A hand without a job cannot purchase gloves. Our manufacturing sector has had to mechanize and economize to meet world competition and in many cases, labor deintensify to exist. Fewer people equal more profit. This isn't the cry of some heartless industrialist. Modernization is a fact of survival for some, yet certain death to many.

A staggering statistic issued by the U.S. Department of Labor is that one job in five will not exist in five years. Will yours? Another is that we have entered the computer age with one American in five not able to read or write. It is perhaps fantasy to expect to teach the illiterate to read and become computer-friendly before he or she starves. Further, if technology and development within the computer world continues at their present speed, we can expect the sophistication to further replace the need for human hands, making obsolete the newer muscle of the mind.

If one wonders what this all has to do with the issue of the homeless, it is from this group of displaced or replaced workers that a new candidacy for homelessness and poverty is formed. And as the contributing segment of our population is reduced, so too are the numbers of those in service positions, pushing even more toward unemployed status.

We have seen machine replace muscle, and we are now witnessing machines replacing minds. Most of us are simply a combination of both. And the impact of being no longer needed can hit most of us, either now or later, directly or indirectly. Most of us are in the same waiting line. If we now have jobs, we may be waiting to be replaced by someone more skilled or some machine more efficient. The only difference between us is when. We are living in a world of buzz words and rhetoric, waiting to be replaced. We are caught in a cacophony of personal survival issues that drowns out the cries for help from the helpless.

A further drain on those working to support those not able to work is the aging of our population. This group for the great part worked hard and long hours to exist and prosper. Some only worked long and hard, some prospered. Many of these workers have supported their own families for years, and now are ready to retire or have already retired, counting on financial assistance through pension funds and social security. The Labor Department reported that in 1973 there were six workers for each retired person. In 1992, there will be 3.5 workers for every one retired person. And it is estimated that by 2020 there will be only two working for each retired person. How many riders can fit on a horse before they fall off, or the horse breaks down? This is one of those times when I wonder where the color will come from in the rosy future the government officials paint for us. If one in five jobs will not exist in the next few years, that is an additional 25 percent of the public unemployed. Who will pay the taxes for the management fee of this complex America? And who will pay for the retirement benefits, and who will pay for the welfare programs and health care, and who will pay for the further bank failures and who will pay for the . . .

A recent *Wall Street Journal* survey states that only 50 percent of American workers now have a pension, yet 70 percent of those polled expect to when they retire. What are their expectations founded on? When companies fold or fail, even the promise of pension is lost, and the most recent projections indicate that more and more individuals will have to provide for their own retirement. How will that be accomplished when today's earnings do not satisfy today's expenses for most people.

Do you feel as though we are trying to fry a frozen egg?

Change has always been a threat to some and welcomed by others. Change is the great cultural sieve through which the tiny grains of the many are continually separated from the larger few. During the industrial revolution (the machine age), writers formed skirmish lines on both sides of the event. For its value or vexation, they postulated its strengths or weaknesses. Ruskin, Morris, Engels, Marx, Carlyle, and others noted the living standard of the working class and questioned the overall long-term value to society. Spencer, on the other hand, thought that perfection of the state of man was a certainty guaranteed by the new technology. Thomas Macaulay, a supporter of the industrial changes occurring in England in 1830, wrote optimistically:

History is full of this natural progress of society. We see in almost every part of the annals of mankind how the industry of individuals, struggling up against wars, taxes, famines, conflagrations, mischievous prohibitions, and more mischievous protections, creates faster than the government can squander, and repairs whatever invaders can destroy. We see the wealth of nations increasing, and all the arts of life approaching nearer and nearer to perfection, in spite of the grossest corruption and the wildest profusion on the part of rulers.

The present moment is one of great distress. But how small will that distress appear when we think over the history of the last forty years; a war, compared with which all other wars sink into insignificance; taxation, such as the most heavily taxed people of former times could not have conceived; a debt larger than all the public debts that ever existed in the world added together; the food of the people studiously rendered dear; the currency imprudently debased and imprudently restored. Yet is the country poorer than in 1790? We firmly believe that, in spite of all the misgovernment of her rulers, she has been almost constantly becoming richer and richer. Now and then there has been a stoppage; now and then a short retrogression; but as to the general tendency there can be no doubt. A single breaker may recede, but the tide is evidently coming in.[1]

Macaulay, like all of us, saw his day through that day's eyes, but if he had had the advantage of today's eyes he would have seen his country lose most of her outside holdings. He would have witnessed wars that reduced the war he wrote about to a schoolyard disagreement. The debt of his day probably would not pay one year's interest on today's debt. There may be more poor people in England now than all the population of his day. The tide to which he referred never brought the promise; it carried the debris of greed that still washes onto the world's beaches.

He further said, "We cannot absolutely prove that those are in error who tell us that society has reached a turning point, that we have seen our best days. But so said all who came before us, and with just as much apparent reason."

I believe most socially conscious writers hold the well-being of those they write about in the highest priority. There is an "apparent" reason for concern at the moments of greatest change in society. Though our eyes cannot see forward except by assumption, they can see today and the past with some assurance. To determine where we are on our journey to wholeness, we must

101

be aware of where we came from, then use today as an overlay and plot our progress. If we refer to the brief history in the beginning of the book, we can perhaps see that things have not changed very much in attitude and altitude of social equality. We rubbed the lamp, and when the genie gave us one wish, we wished for another lamp instead of a lamp for every one.

Friedrich Engels wrote:

Industry and commerce attain their highest state of development in the big towns, so it is here that the effects of industrialization on the wage earners can be most clearly seen. It is in these big towns that the concentration of property has reached its highest point. Here, the manners and the customs of the good old days have been most effectively destroyed.

In these towns there are only the rich and the poor, because the lower middle classes are fast disappearing. At one time this section of the middle classes was the most stable social group, but now it has become the least stable. It is represented in the big factory towns today partly by a few survivors from a bygone age, and partly by a group of people who are anxious to get rich as quickly as possible.[2]

It is only when he has visited the slums of this great city that it dawns upon him that the inhabitants have had to sacrifice so much that is best in human nature, in order to create those wonders of civilization with which their city teems. The vast majority have had to let so many of their potential creative faculties lie dormant, stunted, and unused, in order that a small, closely-knit group of their fellow citizens could develop to the full the qualities with which nature has endowed them. The restless and noisy activity of the crowded streets is highly distasteful, and it is surely abhorrent to human nature itself. Hundreds of thousands of men and women drawn from all classes and ranks of society pack the streets. Are they not all human beings with the same innate characteristics and potentialities? Are they not all equally interested in the pursuit of happiness? And do they not all aim at happiness by following similar methods? Yet they rush past each other as if they had nothing in common. They are tacitly agreed on one thing only: that everyone should keep to the right of the pavement so as not to collide with the stream of people moving in the opposite direction. No one thinks of sparing a glance for his neighbor in the streets. The more they are

packed into a tiny space, the more repulsive and disgraceful becomes the brutal indifference with which they ignore their
neighbors and selfishly concentrate upon their private affairs.
We know well enough that this isolation of the individual—this
narrow-minded egotism—is everywhere the fundamental prin-
ciple of modern society. But nowhere is this selfish egotism so
blatantly evident as in the frantic bustle of the great city. The
disintegration of society into individuals, each guided by his private principles and each pursuing his own aims has been
pushed to its furthest limits in London. Here, indeed, human
society has been split into its component atoms.

Here, men regard their fellows not as human beings, but as
pawns in the struggle for existence. Everyone exploits his
neighbor, with the result that the stronger tramples the weaker
under foot. The strongest of all, a tiny group of capitalists, mo-
nopolize everything, while the weakest, who are the vast majority, succumb to the most abject poverty.[3]

Engels wrote this in 1845. The great city was London. But it
could be any of our great cities. The people on those streets
could be the people on any street in America or anywhere in the
world. For in the streets and alleys of our mind we all rush past
the needs of others on our private journey to find our purpose,
our wholeness, and in so doing perhaps pass up that purpose.

Engels and others wrote of the condition of the poor and de-
scribed in great detail the depth of their deprivation. The writings were no more popular with those able to effect change than
they seem to be now. For the writings were not widely published
or promoted. But unlike the wealthy classes before, the wealthy
of today are beginning to understand that their wealth is no protection from the horrendous possibilities looming just ahead.

Engels went on to say:

Every great town has one or more slum areas into which the
working classes are packed. Sometimes, of course, poverty is to
be found hidden away in alleys close to the stately homes of the
wealthy. Generally, however, the workers are segregated in separate districts where they struggle through life as best they
can, out of sight of the more fortunate classes of society. . . .

The upper class enjoy healthy country air and live in luxurious and comfortable dwellings which are linked to the center of Manchester by omnibuses which run every fifteen or thirty minutes. To such an extent has the convenience of the rich been considered in the planning of Manchester, that these plutocrats can travel from their houses to their places of business in the center of town by the shortest routes, which run entirely through working-class districts, without even realizing how close they are to the misery and the filth which lie on both sides of the road. The houses are packed very closely together, and since the bank of the river is very steep it is possible to see a part of every house. All of them are blackened with soot, all of them are crumbling with age and all have broken window panes and window frames. In the background there are old factory buildings which look like barracks. Several of these houses, as far as I could see, were completely empty, although the door was open and the inhabitants were leaning against the door post. In front of the doors filth and garbage abounded. I could not see the pavement, but from time to time, I felt it was there because my feet scraped it. The dirtiness of the interiors of these premises is fully in keeping with the filth that surrounds them. How can people dwelling in such places keep clean? There are not even adequate facilities for satisfying the most natural daily needs. . . . Indeed, no one can blame these helots of modern civilization if their homes are no cleaner than the occasional pig styes which are a feature of these slums. There are actually some property owners who are not ashamed to let dwellings such as these exist.[4]

Today of course we all live in the same garbage can, as we have already covered. The rich may be in the countryside but the brown air and dirty rain fall on all of us. Money cannot buy the way out of the dirt and dust of our greed. We need to fix it.

Charles Kingsley, a clergyman in London who was appalled by the suffering of the poor in 1850, wrote:

We went on through a back street or two, and then into a huge, miserable house which, a hundred years ago perhaps, had witnessed the luxury, and rung to the laughter of some one great fashionable family, alone there in their glory. Now every room of it held its family, or its group of families—a phalanstery of all the fiends—its grand staircase, with the carved balustrades rotting and crumbling away piecemeal, converted into a common sewer for all its inmates. Up stair after stair we went, whiles of children, and curses of men, steamed out upon the hot stifling rush of air from every doorway, till at the topmost story, we knocked at a great door. We entered. Bare it was of furniture, comfortless, and freezing cold; but with the exception of the plaster dropping from the roof, and the broken windows, patched with rags and paper, there was a scrupulous neatness about the whole, which contrasted strangely with the filth and slovenliness outside. There was no bed in the room—no table. On a broken chair by the chimney sat a miserable old woman, fancying that she was warming her hands over embers which had long been cold, shaking her head, and muttering to herself, with palsied lips, about the guardians and the workhouse; while upon a few rags on the floor lay a girl, ugly, small, pox-marked, hollowed eyed, emaciated, her only bedclothes the skirt of a large new riding habit, at which two other girls, wan and tawdry, were stitching busily as they sat right and left of her on the floor.

The old women took no notice of us as we entered. But one of the girls looked up, and, with a pleased gesture of recognition, put her finger up to her lips, and whispered, "Ellen's asleep."

"I'm not asleep, dears," answered a faint unearthly voice. "I was only praying. Is that Mr. Mackaye?"

"Aye, my lassies; but ha' ye gotten na fire the nicht?"

"No," said one of them, bitterly. "We've earned no fire tonight, by fair trade or foul either."[5]

There are many who postulate that the poor are a lazy lot who would not work if the opportunity existed, and that they are where they want to be or where their genetic makeup allows. We must remember the poor of England were not the blacks. They were the Irish immigrant and the working class English. I wonder how many of us who believe genetic makeup controls our social status, adaptability, and ability are direct decendants of some of those poorly educated, poverty-stricken souls who came to America to find opportunity. And upon arriving these castoffs took advantage of the opportunity to ensure a better future for themselves and their children.

There perhaps isn't a great deal of difference in the England that our relatives left and the conditions of our cities today. Worldwide, the reports of poverty and hunger, recession and unrest are growing. We see the Russians and the Polish lining up

105

for loaves of bread. We watch as thousands of starving, bloated-bellied Ethiopian children die on camera. Six million Mexican souls are reported to be living on the dumps surrounding Mexico City. In India and Bangladesh, in Hungary and other Slavic countries, mistrust and confusion are changing to violence and bloodshed, and a volume of craziness never before experienced in the history of mankind is growing to a deafening level.

We are watching a renewal of anti-Semitism, a growing racial hatred and prejudice. People are starving all over the world, and a few right here in our own country, and we hear of a report that says the government has 250,000,000 tons of butter stored somewhere. That's one ton for every man, woman, and child in the country. I don't know what to do with my ton. I'd like to give it away as I eat so little butter. What we might do, in the light of the report that too much butter may be bad for the heart, is use it for national defense. We can dismantle all the bombs and chemical warheads and fill them with butter. Then we can use the massive warehouses, where the butter was stored, to shelter the homeless. Even the calmest of level heads is tempted to occasionally jump up on the table and shout, "What the heck's going on here?!"

This chapter is about change, change in our position and our perception. As we have read, the problem of poverty and the homeless is not new. What is new is the extent to which the situation has permeated the body of mankind. It is a virus that could have been controlled by good hygiene, by washing our society of the pollutants. Instead, some of the ones we hired to protect and guard us against infection became the worst of our social tumors. The problem has now metastasized and radical surgery is imminent, though perhaps too late.

One of the greatest changes is the speed with which the media can now report current events. The media, whether motivated by profit or competition or moral drive, keep us instantly aware of happenings in every remote spot in the world. The media no longer protect the privacy of the high official from the eye of the public. Once many of us did not know that our President could not stand, that he was by disease forced to sit in a wheelchair. The media made no reference to the assumed weakness and further only photographed him seated behind a desk. The media now not only reveal what chair our President sits in, but who is in the President's bed. I am sure that not all media personalities are always truthful, but the media now, in sufficient numbers, would not and will not assist in the cover-up of fact or perpetuate the lie that elected officials are somehow beyond reproach.

The sophistication of the media has attracted many to its advantage as the broad stage that reaches the masses. Everyone has a place to dance as social issues and movements are given extensive coverage, both by advocates and by programs and sitcoms that incorporate the issues into realistic story form. The women's movement has had great coverage and made profound changes in the lives of women and the rest of our society. Women have gained much recognition and independence in recent years. Some of those changes, while perhaps long overdue, have arrived at men's door like annoying relatives. In the next chapter we will cover some of the impact of social independence.

Man Overboard

The cause of homelessness cannot readily be identified. It is not one huge fire that can be doused by compassion or a few dollars, or it would already be but a wisp of smoke in man's history. It is three hundred thousand to three million separate fires that had different combustion points. One of the most common catalysts in the homelessness of men is their perception of manhood and the woman-in-their-life's perception of manhood. It is a study in itself, and this will be but the briefest of treatments.

Robert Bly, a compassionate, accomplished American poet, has spoken to the growing displacement of the American male from a traditional role dictated by gender and historical social molding. He speaks about the changes in traditional gender roles and their impact on relationships, men to men and men to women. The pressure men feel is an uncomfortable one, threatened by the women's movement. Women's liberation, growing now from centuries of confinement, has forced men to revalue

108

themselves. Most men, it appears, are ill-prepared or unwilling to do that. Perhaps if we men could accept the fact that because a woman wishes to be all she can be in this life, and works to fulfill that which is actually her right, we can never be anything less.

My ledger says the women's movement is a freeing of men as well as women. I, too, grew with the belief that because my mate needed my protection, it somehow validated my worth and value in our relationship. When I could not provide financial security, which she equated with protection, I lost value in her eyes. More important to me, I lost value in my own eyes. Perhaps if there is time, our new relationships will begin with the covenant that whoever is able to provide will do so. A number of homeless men I have met are the products of lost jobs and careers. Their wives were not able to continue loving a man with no position. Intent on finding a better provider, they chose divorce. Convinced he had little value, he became his belief. One such man named John in Oklahoma City shared the following paper he had written at age twelve. While he had not been to the street (he was living with his mother), he was homeless. He told me his mother had saved the paper and had recently given it to him.

Even though I honestly don't know much about the secret of success, I'll give you my opinion. I think a person who wishes about what he is going to be almost always becomes what he wants and is a success at it. A person should first learn what he wants to be, such as going through high school and then to college to learn more about what he wants. I think a very good personality is the key to a good salesman, and I think some people are naturally gifted with the art of a good personality.

My goal in life is like many others. I plan to finish high school, go to college and become a cardiologist or, in other words, a heart specialist. My dad has succeeded just as well. I figure that the only one at fault if you fail is your own. If you fail, the only one you can blame is yourself. It means that you just did not try hard enough to become what you wanted to become. If you should fail, you should try to start over again, of course, unless it is too late. If so, I'd hate to be the person who did fail. For me, I often wonder what it would be like to be an old bum walking along the street looking for cigarette butts, wearing old shaggy clothes with rips and having people stare at me when I walk by. This is not my idea of success. My idea is having a well-paid job and, of course, getting married. I would have six children. We would have a nice modern house, and make sure every one of our children got a good education, and being able to buy cigarettes instead of having to find them on a street curb. This is the kind of man I would like to be, and pray to God that I become this man.

John wrote this paper in 1963. He believed what he wrote then, and I would imagine still does to a great degree. For it is the job of the male, or was, to be successful, provide a nice home, and make sure your kids did not have to smoke butts from the curb. But in the real process of casting clay boys into bronze men, the process on occasion is ruined in the kiln. The casting is not always perfect. Perhaps too much heat or too little, too much pressure to be perfect. When the bronze man looks into the mirror of his wife's eyes and discovers his imperfections, he blames himself, and so does she. Perhaps in her paper of 1963 she wrote: "I want to go to college and become all I can be. I want to be successful and have a life free of worry. I want to marry a man who will take care of my children, and make sure they do not have to smoke butts from the curb. If he can't, he's not the right man, because he did not try hard enough."

We all live in gender assumptions inscribed in our lives and expectations long before we must live in them. Unlike the sculptures of Remington depicting a rugged horseman fighting a bear, we no longer have bears to contend with. We have killed most of them. Women no longer need the protection of men who would face a bear. Many women would now prefer a man with a platinum card to a Bowie knife. My ledger says the newer bears are coming, and a platinum card will be no defense.

The absolute worthless, helpless feeling of not being able to support my wife, and her insistence that I do so, combined to produce the feeling that I deserved the street. An interesting statistic is that the homeless are those with the smallest support system, usually those without family in their city.

LEDGER

My ledger now says that ledgers are difficult enough, and that we have no right or authority to live within the ledger of others unless by invitation, and then we must conduct ourselves as guests. As I mentioned the issue is a difficult one. It contains many psychological sub-issues that exist in all of us to varying degrees: the need for outside validation of our value and the assumption that we must perform our role to maintain our worth.

All role-playing and its value in our lives does not stem from gender or genetics. Some is but rumor, and that is what we are painfully working through, like cowboys don't wear shorts and real men don't eat quiche and men don't cry and most homeless people are there because they want to be. We will talk about rumor in the next chapter, its assumed value and its potential or real harm.

WHO'S
RESPONSIBLE?

PART **4**

CHAPTER
TWELVE

Rumor

CHANGE HAS BEGUN SAID THE SEED
CHANGE IS COMPLETE SAID THE FRUIT
YOU ARE BOTH WRONG SAID THE WIND
FOR I HAVE SEEN YOUR BEGINNING
AND YOUR END TO BE THE SAME
YOUR PERCEPTION HAS BEEN BLANCHED
BY YOUR OWN DARKNESS
YOUR ASSUMPTION BY
YOUR OWN REGRET
YOU NEED BECOME THE OTHER
AS YOU BOTH HAVE BEEN
FOR IN ONE OF YOU
IS THE OTHER
THAT IS THE SIMPLICITY OF ALL THINGS
THAT IS WHERE PEACE LIVES
IN THE SIMPLE THINGS

THE THINGS UNNOTICED
WHERE FEW VISIT
BUT ALL ARE
WELCOMED
I WELCOME YOU INTO MY SIMPLE PLACE
WHERE WE WILL TALK
NOT OF THE SEEN
WHICH IS THE FRUIT PASSING
BUT OF THE UNSEEN
WHOSE SEED WILL PROVIDE US PEACE
WHEN ALL THAT IS SEEN HAS PASSED
IN THESE MOMENTS
WHEN YOUR NEWNESS IS GUARDED
YOU WILL GROW
UNTHREATENED
UNTIL YOU ARE SMALL ENOUGH
TO BE FRIGHTENED OF NOTHING LARGE
FOR EVEN THE LARGEST
IS BUILT OF THE SMALLEST
AND EXISTS ONLY
AS LONG AS THE SMALL
ARE BONDED BY RUMOR
COME LET ME WHISPER
TO THE STOREHOUSE OF YOUR RUMOR[1]

CHAPTER
THIRTEEN

The Shepherds

All of us must bear responsibility, the poor and the homeless, the wealthy, the ones who are not quite either. The poor and the homeless have a responsibility to be good stewards of the assistance given. The rest have a responsibility to give as their means allow. We all have a duty and obligation to each other to pay fairly for work done, and to work fairly for payment received. If corporations only feel obligated to the stockholder to build profits, regardless of the workers displaced, unemployment will rise, and eventually fewer will be able to afford the product. This lowers profits. The value of stock will fall, for it is only an arbitrary value set by those who have little or no regard for price to earnings ratios.

We are all tied one to the other by an invisible line woven of fine threads of rumor. Two hundred and fifty million people all laced like mountain climbers scaling this huge mountain of problems. We now have thirty or forty million bodies attached to the rope, with no hold on the mountain. The cumulative weight pulls loose a certain number of the dangling ones each day. At what point will the dangling ones pull the rest of us off the mountain? Who falls farther? My ledger says it is advisable to provide a toehold to the ones below.

The shepherds of mankind have been many, they come to the role usually by choice, carrying their varied priorities in golden, jewel-encrusted cases or leather pouches. Some shepherd for profit, some for pleasure, some for truly pure purposes, some for popularity, some out of love, some out of need, some for power, some good shepherds, some not. All shepherds, good or otherwise, understand the use of rumor, its benefits, and its dangers.

I remember as a young boy sitting on the fence at the slaughterhouse, watching lambs being led by a Judas goat. The large black goat would enter the herd of lambs, walking among them, gaining their confidence. He would nuzzle them, play with them, talk goat or whatever goats talk, all the while smiling that perpetual goat smile. He chased them playfully, they chased him. Lambs must understand goat, for he would signal them and they started to follow him. He would lead them up the ramp to the door behind which lambs became lamb chops. Just before the goat would reach the door, he would duck out of the fenced ramp through a small gate guarded by a large man with a rubber apron and a piece of pipe in his hand. The happy, unsuspecting lambs wiggled their way up the ramp and one at a time entered the door where they were greeted by the large man with the apron and the pipe. The rhythm of the metallic muffled ringing still sounds in my mind. I still remember how I hated that black goat, or perhaps the smile with which he earned his keep.

World history, present and past, is full of Judas goats. Some we were and are aware of, some we failed and still fail to recognize. But they still lead the flock of mankind to the ringing of the pipe, all the while smiling that goat smile, saying to all, "All is well."

The problem of the poor and homeless is not new. It is a recurring and consistent theme in our written history, both in secular and religious ledgers. All of the advocates of the plight of the poor for the past three thousand years, with all their impassioned pleas, have done seemingly little to lessen the imbalance between the haves and the have-nots. In flowing dialogue, in prose and poetry, in novels that tear at the heart of the reader, writers for centuries have tried to prod those with the means to help the unfortunate. The question and the debate of man's basic nature has been the focus of philosophers from the moment of the first debate. But is our nature a reflection of our nurturing or of our free will?

We have had thousands of years to become a fair and caring species, thousands of years to evolve beyond the animal that science credits as parent. It is obvious that advanced culture is not determined by the technology present; Jean Valjean and Tiny Tim still live in every city and town and province of the world, and Scrooge still must dream or die to change. Cain still kills Abel and human sacrifice remains. Raid will not chase the fly from the eyes of the poor dying child, nor will reason reduce the bloating of the selfish who allow the swelling bellies of the starving children. The effort of the philosopher and the theologian might have been better spent in the search for the method by which compassion is instilled in those with the capacity for compassion.

I have found that some, least able but most willing, leap to the aid of the needy. And some, most able but least willing, run from the opportunity. My ledger says I have also witnessed the opposite of the above statement. The possession of things or the lack does not determine compassion.

My ledger provides that compassion must be taught and the learning rewarded. And compassion must be acted upon when felt. It is an emotion that only expands with use. My ledger also believes that the loudest opponents of compassion are those who have very little capacity remaining.

We cannot blame most of today's rich for the plight of most of today's poor, for the root of the greatest disease of mankind is a virus beginning long ago. However, the wealthy with the capacity for compassion can do a great deal and a great deed. By using their resources for the benefit of equalizing opportunity and option for all, they may ultimately do more for themselves than those they have helped.

Education, the teaching of necessary life skills, is imperative to the successful workings of any society. Life skills is the body

119

of knowledge necessary to exist and sustain and prosper in a defined time in the history of any culture. If we as a nation, or we as a member of the greater world body of humankind, continue to neglect to learn or teach those skills that form the basic building blocks of a successful life, we will ensure the continued growth in the disparity between the haves and have-nots.

Moral, social, and economic knowledge is not simply taught by word. The greatest teacher is example. The shepherd who leads the people by mandate of the people, must also by example live in wisdom. In so doing, he teaches the value of truth. In his leadership must be found genuine concern and compassion for those for whom he has assumed responsibility. No society can survive if its leadership is self-serving or can be persuaded to give advantages only to the wealthy. This latter policy serves to ensure next season's litter of poor or persecuted, and it will one day add the final motivating militant warrior to the next army of revolutionary change.

In 1868 Thomas Henry Huxley delivered an address to the South London Working Men's College. The address was titled "A Game of Chess." Huxley compared life to a game and posed some interesting questions:

> Suppose it were perfectly certain that the life and the fortune of everyone of us would, one day or other, depend upon his winning or losing a game of chess. Don't you think that we should all consider it to be a primary duty to learn at least the names and the moves of the pieces; to have a notion of a gambit and a keen eye for all the means of giving and getting out of check? Do you not think that we should look with a disprobation amounting to scorn, upon the father who allowed his son, or the state which allowed its members, to grow up without knowing a pawn from a knight?
>
> Yet it is a very plain and elementary truth that the life, the fortune, and the happiness of every one of us, and, more or less, of those who are connected with us, do depend upon our knowing something of the rules of a game infinitely more difficult and complicated than chess. It is a game which has been played for untold ages, every man and woman of us being one of the two players in a game of his or her own. The chessboard is the world, the pieces are the phenomena of the universe, the rules of the

game are what we call the laws of nature. The player on the other side is hidden from us. We know that his play is always fair, just, and patient. But also we know, to our cost, that he never overlooks a mistake, or makes the smallest allowance for ignorance. To the man who plays well, the highest stakes are paid, with that sort of overflowing generosity with which the strong shows delight in strength. And one who plays ill is check-mated without haste, but without remorse.

Huxley concluded his address with unapologetic firmness:

Those who take honors in Nature's university, who learn the laws which govern man and things and obey them, are the really great and successful men in this world. The great mass of man-kind are the "Poll," who pick up just enough to get through without much discredit. Those who won't learn at all are plucked; and then you can't come up again. Nature's pluck means extermination.

Thus the question of compulsory education is settled as far as Nature is concerned. Her bill on that question was framed and passed long ago. But like all compulsory legislation, that of na-ture is harsh and wasteful in its operation. Ignorance is visited as sharply as willful disobedience—incapacity meets with the same punishment as crime. Nature's discipline is not even a word and a blow, and the blow first; but the blow without the word. It is left to you to find out why your ears are boxed.

The object of what we commonly call education—that educa-tion in which man intervenes and which I shall distinguish as artificial education—is to make good these defects in Nature's methods; to prepare the child to receive Nature's education, nei-ther incapably nor ignorantly, nor with willful disobedience; and to understand the preliminary symptoms of her pleasure, with-out waiting for the box on the ear. In short, all artificial educa-tion ought to be an anticipation of natural education. And a liberal education is an artificial education which has not only prepared a man to escape the great evils of disobedience to nat-ural laws, but has trained him to appreciate and to seize upon the rewards which Nature scatters with a free hand as her pen-alties.

That man, I think, has had a liberal education who has been so trained in youth that his body is the ready servant of his will, and does with ease and pleasure all the work that, as a mechanism, it is capable of; whose intellect is a clear, cold, logic engine, with all its parts of equal strength, and in smooth working order; ready, like a steam engine, to be turned to any kind of work, and spin the gossamers as well as forge the anchors of the mind; whose mind is stored with a knowledge of the great and fundamental truths of Nature and of the laws of her operation; one who, no stunted ascetic, is full of life and fire, but whose passions are trained to come to heel by a vigorous will, the servant of a tender conscience; who has learned to love all beauty, whether of Nature or of art, to hate all vileness, and to respect all others as himself.

Such a one and no other, I conceive, has had a liberal education; for he is, as completely as a man can be, in harmony with Nature. He will make the best of her, and she of him. They will get on together rarely; she as his ever beneficent mother; he as her mouthpiece, her conscious self, her minister and interpreter.[1]

Huxley proposes that a successful and happy life depends on knowing the rules to this chess game of life and being educated to its workings and working in it. Authors and advocates again line up on opposing sides. This time on the debate of long-term benefits of the computer age to the masses. But we as a world community no longer have the benefit of seemingly inexhaustible resources or new countries or frontiers to conquer and rape. We no longer have the luxury of dumping our refuse of progress on the earth or in the water or air. The tailings of the human experiment, its unwanted waste of unneeded people, are growing to the danger point, and the toxic effect of their anger is every bit as real and threatening to civilization as atomic waste.

Throughout human history war has provided the common bond within the ranks and populace of both sides of conflict that momentarily quieted individual differences. War has never been waged for strictly political ideology, it has and will be the method to gain control over peoples or control of existing or remaining resources.

War is the absolute consequence of individual interest. There is only one political, social, and moral platform that will end war, provide justice for all, dissolve racial and economic differences, make relationships and families whole, bridge all conflict and disparity: Though it was given long ago and we have had centuries to evaluate its value, we seem not yet ready to accept it: "You must love your neighbor as yourself." Or are we?

We have just come from a war that may prove to men that war provides a slippery grip on things and peoples. The cost of that war could retard the relief of those waiting in line to eat from the great rumor that "all will be well." Some of us are the shepherds of how we control our time. Some, however, shepherd the time of others. I pray that we can move to remove the waiting from the want of the homeless.

We who feel no great urgency in our own lives must come to realize that time is not the great healer when taken in small doses. One hundred years from now, none of those suffering today will be around. That is an overdose of time. However, many who are suffering will be here tomorrow and most will still suffer next week and next month, and more may join them in suffering next year. For the shepherd and the flock alike, waiting is frustrating for most of us. For the homeless person, waiting for something to happen is a painful exercise. It is the not knowing what we are waiting for that adds so to the distress. Are we waiting for relief or death?

I now keep a log of my days for three reasons. The first is that a log is a safe place and method to dispose of or deposit frustration. The second is that on occasion the log reveals the hidden thoughts, those spontaneous revelations of cerebral insight, or lack of it, that we are often better off forgetting but better for getting off of. The third is that it grants perspective on how long I have actually distressed over a thought. I have many stories and interviews not used because of time or space. The following is part of the book log which will share my frustrations, and the sometimes unrealistic assumptions that waiting can parent. The rambling is part of the frustration of waiting. If I could impress one thing on those who would help, it would be the need to move from dialog to action. This is how I talked to myself when I thought no one could understand. This is the actual ledger.

LEDGER

12th and Villa

I am an impatient person. I have great difficulty waiting. Waiting in line, waiting my turn, never bothered me. However, waiting for answers, waiting for direction, waiting for correction, waiting for the other shoe to fall drives me crazy. This is the tenth of March, 7:05, It's been the 10th of March for about a month. This feeling is not entirely unlike the feeling of dying. That cancer could have cured all this, here I am still here I-am-ing. I remember now how I finally did not labor anymore over how someone perceived me. It did not matter. It was comfortable, weightless. It did not matter how I perceived anyone else. It did not matter; they were stewards of themselves. My responsibility for their good and comfortable feeling was relieved. It was but illusion. It was comfortable, weightless. I could dance with the weightlessness of the coming day of death. However, I was impatient for the moment to arrive. Hurry up black tunnel, no reason to continue being cruel. I was secure in my readiness. Readiness is a flexed muscle; it is subject to the failure of fatigue. Come on, I can't hang here forever.

It's raining for the second day. It has hailed or snowed or rained each time I have visited the Jesus House. The sun has yet to accompany me through the double doors of hope. I am sitting waiting for the call from Thomas Nelson Publishers giving me the go-ahead on this project and indicating the amount of advance involved. They asked me to send an expanded outline. I mailed fifty-five pages in February. March eleven, Bill Watkins, senior editor, asked me to send a profile on myself. I will send the profile and an additional fifty-three pages.

PROFILE

Bill, it's difficult talking about myself. I don't know if it's false modesty or otherwise, but I find the need to rush through this part.

I was born May 9, 1940, in Toledo, Ohio. It seemed as if I

immediately attended the University of Toledo on an art scholarship, but I cannot be sure of that. It could have been some time later. I married young, and continued to do so, two more times. The last time I married young was four years ago. You met her by voice, her name is Kay. She decided she cannot live with me and then she could not live without me and so did I. That's one reason I am writing this book. The other reason, of course, is that you and Ted Squires asked me to.

Somewhere between the reality of the arts and the rumor of the world, I followed the rumor and became involved in business. I owned a successful realty company in Ohio and later in Oklahoma. We were trapped here in Oklahoma in the early eighties because the rest of the country needed a butt for jokes. Oklahoma seemed to have plenty of butts in the banking and oil business, so we rightfully got the part. But alas, the play was not funny, and when the curtain came down on Penn Square Bank, all of the extras and innocents were without lines, so to speak.

I noticed that the people who were really responsible for the crash were still out at the club chipping and putting, acting just as important as they never were. And that some poor underling who had the sufficient number of public food fights to appear the buffoon, went to jail.

I noticed, too, that my wife was no longer amused by the potential of my potential and soon traded my paste for other pudding. With a hearty "Write if you get work" ringing in my hollow head and the memory of the doctor saying four years before, "Let me put it this way, three months and you're mulch," I took a walk.

I did not believe in myself nor anyone else, and for the next two and a half years I was in and out of homelessness and hopelessness. I wrote songs at Studio Seven in Oklahoma City, sang in bars, slept in the back rooms. I cleaned offices, and slept in one, Charlie Dry's. Charlie was an astronaut buddy of mine from Oklahoma, he used to come out to the lake to hear me sing. I walked from Oklahoma City to Panama City , Florida. Charlie found me, cleaned me up, and took me to Nashville. He introduced me to Anita Bryant and she introduced me to you.

I hated the soup kitchen on my journey every bit as much as I hated school in my youth, and found very little of value in the curriculum of either, in that neither one addressed nor recognized or respected the interest of the captive.

My anger still exists. However, it is tempered somewhat by great salads and my own bed and a light to read by and socks, and cold water when I'm thirsty and someone to rub my feet and tell me "It's Okay." It is tempered too by your enthusiasm for the project and for me.

Also, the six figure advance ALL writers get, where is it?

Well, Bill, this is by fax on me, so it is by budget brief. Give Ted Squires my regards. Hope to see you soon, my friend. This is a very brief bio and I promise more for the promotion of the book. Sometimes there is a pure cleanness to brevity.

Call me; you've got the Wats line.

Noah

Today's report from Bill Watkins was more than positive, it was go, waiting for the official go. I am an impatient person. Where is my go?

Today I met with the committee from Chapel Hill Methodist Church and Ruth and Betty from the Jesus House. The committee decided they would adopt a family. Ruth suggested the Starts. We met with Aaron, at twelve the oldest of the eight Start children. Aaron is in special ed. The Starts have moved ten times in the last three years. It's tough to fight the battles required for the new kid in school once, let alone ten times. Aaron is polite, sensitive, vulnerable, very worthy but tough as an old shoe. Suddenly I'm not impatient for the call from the publisher. I'm impatient for the committee to approve the Starts as their adopted family.

NOAH 1:1 It is here and forever after decreed that any committee given the responsibility for a decision shall not adjourn for the purpose of eating or sleeping or rest or use of the restroom or any other excuse, and no member of any committee shall be excused for any reason prior to vote of yea or nay other than death, and even then each committee member is hereby ordered to die with his or her thumb in the up or down position. No one eats until everyone eats; no one rests until everyone rests; no one is warm until no one is cold.

What a selfish family we have become.

Still Sunday, 9:30. C.B. Foster just called. He and his wife live in their van. She cut her hand severely and they found help hard to find. They called the church she used to attend. They were advised the church had no social services and could not help, then hung up.

I am meeting the Fosters on Tuesday, March 13. Mrs. Foster was Employee of the Month at Grandy's last month. They are holding her job for her. C.B. said they had contacted welfare. They were told that since they had no children they could not help. They were told to contact SSI, however that takes six months for approval.

Monday the 12th. Angry today, I did not write yesterday, spent the day with Tennyson, Matthew Arnold, and William Morris. I feel the anger I have felt from many of the poor. They seem to bury it for fear of losing the assistance from some of the willing. That same anger boils after relief, and on occasion sabotages the helping hand. This anger strikes out at the closest target. I always feel it when I think of the street or go to the Jesus House. The heck with further worry about what people will think of my opinion. If they ask, from here on out I'll say what I believe. I'll relate what I have seen and what I feel about it. If they are offended, It's their strain not mine.

I am in the process of dying, they are in the process of believing they will not. That's what is wrong with life. We have no required curriculum that deals with the fact that we are all dying. Think how a class in death awareness might be conducted. "Well, students we are gathered here together to share our death experience and to make life a little easier for each other while we are waiting." Wouldn't that be a healer.

Joe across the street slept on his porch again last night. He told me yesterday that he was Choctaw. Guess he still is today. What a rip, he doesn't have a chance, yet his belief keeps him off the warpath. He believes the computer is a part of the Antichrist weapon. I think it is religion. Joe's a good man. I enjoy talking to him. I wonder how he will get all his clothes out of that tree.

I heard from Jay last night. The Sunday school did not vote yesterday on the adoption of the Starts. They do have a lead on a car for them. However, the class does not want to meet the Start family until they can present the car keys. Start needs a car as they live several miles from his work. He now has a bike, but he used to walk to work. Start does not read. Chapel Hill has a group of volunteers to teach the illiterate to read. I am sure God and I hate the word Illiterate. This seems a match between the Starts and Chapel Hill Methodist Church. I must keep waving my arms.

Met with Richard Angel of God Life church today, a long time brother. I told him I had three of the forty from the Chapel Hill class at the Jesus House on Saturday. He said three of forty was a better than average number of volunteers. This feels like pushing a rope. I must give the borrowed car back Wednesday. Feet don't fail me and start walking away again or there will be these two feet all by themselves walking down I-35 because I'm not going with you this time.

Wednesday, 14th. Still no call from Bill Watkins. I left a message yesterday. C.B. called; he and his wife are quite low. He wanted to see me Friday. I think I am bogging down in an urgency of my own making. It's affecting my writing. Maybe I am not supposed to do this.

Friday. I will call another publisher. Jay's brother-in-law left Simon and Schuster to start his own company. Called, left a message for Bill Watkins. Everyone out of pocket, call Monday. It seems the whole world is an empty pocket.

Saturday, 17th. St. Pat's Day, daughter Kelli's birthday, writing day, no need to wait for Thomas Nelson, too much to do. Jay called, the class invited me to church tomorrow. They wanted some direction in their giving. What a conditional web we live in. Control rules almost all of our lives, not our own control, but the attempt to control others. The class would like to give the car to Start on a conditional basis, keys first then the title in six months. They are just being cautious. I have not heard the conditions Start must meet to gain title. I wonder if any of us ever gain title to our own life. I am certain Start will meet them, just as certain the conditions will be fair. The class wants to teach Start to read. They also want to fix Easter baskets for the children and invite the Start family to the annual Easter egg hunt.

A sadness, all this junk that sifted into the our belief, another example of the frantic scramble to control each other. Santa

128

Claus, the Easter Bunny, Halloween, have no beginning or belonging with the gospel of Christ and they did not come to save anyone. Some of us waste so much effort and funds in these things. No wonder many have become so conditional in their private doctrines, and so judgmental of who is worthy of God's promises. Many believe that their belief is the only way to the reward of life. I seem to recall Paul saying, "There is but one mediator between man and God, a man, Jesus."

I cannot understand how some feel they have the divine mandate to usurp that authority, or judge someone unworthy to receive the love and promise of the gospel of love because they refuse to be a part of the twisted teachings and priorities of their personal leavened doctrine.

In the beginning all belief was pure and simple. It was only love. The schematic for a safe, rewarding, and fair life were given out of love. Perhaps it changed with the first whisper promising man could have the wisdom of God which changed to the belief that man is God. Perhaps it changed further when the first brother was introduced to man's deity by a rock held by his own brother. But brothers have been bashing each other's heads ever since. They are still doing it in Ireland. They are still doing it in Africa. They are still doing it in America's churches divided by color, and doctrine. They did it in Germany and Russia, bashing skulls by the tens of millions. In every country on earth brothers are bashing each other, for discipline or control, for profit or duty. Neither political doctrine nor religious doctrine provide safety from man's belief in his own god-ship or the power of the rock.

This errant belief that peace is at hand because the world heads toward democracy is an example of our own imperfect reasoning. The greatest example of democracy has failed at equality for its people. The choice of preference in voting on social and moral issues is for the most part dependant upon the insignia of the elephant or the ass worn by the voter. How can we reasonably expect a whole world of elephants and asses to do any better? In a world that has written an abominable record of brotherhood in it's common belief in God, how can we expect a better ledger in the common belief in the politics of profit?

The whisper from the first serpent has grown into a roar by the newer serpents. More and more become gods each day. The world now postures to gain advantage by commerce rather than conflict. But the coming conflict caused by all the world chasing the same dollar is certain. Worldwide, the classes grow farther and farther apart in wealth and in number. Soon the promises of the leadership will no longer feed the hope of the poor. The widespread use of drugs in the world is indicative of the effect of frustration, not the cause. Crack cocaine is the Prozac of the underclass. Though infinitely more expensive, it is more readily available to the poor. Under the influence of the illusion drugs paint over reality, the army of users will begin to dismantle the mortarless wall of our society. The jury deliberates now on the crime of human greed, the fruits of which have been infinitely too much for infinitely too few, and infinitely too little for infinitely too many.

God where did that all come from? Must have been the double pepperoni on that pizza.

March 20, Vernal Equinox. Bill called, asked me to give him my budget by Friday for completion of the book. He suggested the title remain as it was. Hooo—ray! Moving again.

Kay called from Hawaii. She will be going back to California next Monday. I'll be in Hawaii in May. The city is building a huge tent in the park in Honolulu to house 30 homeless families. They built dividers on the park benches so the poor can't stretch out to sleep.

It will be good to see John Rolloff and Danny Almonte again. I miss their goodness.

March 21. Gave the car back today. I'm walking again. Jay stopped in. He may have located a car for the Starts. I called Ruth; she was thankful. Start seems to be a willing worker and worthy recipient. I hope he never walks to work again.

Kay and I have gotten back together since the book began. If she had not been so strong, I wonder if I ever would have been again. Jay loaned me his car. He's a buddy. Going to Hawaii to check on the homeless. What a place to be homeless. First you bomb it, then you buy it, then you move the native into the street. "Nothing personal pal, it's just business. Have some raw fish."

130

The journal above covers only eleven days, some of the entries have been deleted to protect the innocent (me). Eleven days may as well be eleven years to the crippled ones waiting for relief from their distraction. Frustration is seldom a clear prism. Confused action and inappropriate response is often the product of the clouded prism. Panic and anger is often the feeling of the hungry hand in the empty pocket. This is what I would convey if I were able. The measure of time and its safety or distraction depends entirely on our comfort or pain of the moment. The next chapter will give you the value of understanding between two people who share the same moment of time.

CHAPTER FOURTEEN

Buddies or Friends

Allow me to introduce you to someone accessible, someone who would grant the time and audience for discussion. He perhaps gave me greater insight than any official stance or prepared statement.

A friend of mine named Powell (pronounced "Pall"), heard about the book I was writing. He said he thought it was a needed project but he didn't want me to be disappointed with the results it might bring. We were sitting at Harrigan's Restaurant at the bar, where the good guys gather to get life right. Most of the world's problems are solved there every night. Everyone was adding something to the book project, they all had opinions about the condition and its cause and cure.

Steve Sluder had just placed a plate of something new before me to try. I am the "let Mikey try it" guy. Being hungry on command, I dug into the platter of deep fry and decided to let everyone discharge a little exhaust. Powell said, "While Noah eats, let me tell you boys two stories:"

One time, a long time ago there were two friends. They were on the road. They didn't have jobs, couldn't find any. Oh, they did pick up work here and there, but nothing steady, you know. One night they were cold and hungry, starving, hadn't eaten in three days. They saw this farmhouse down the road with its lights on. One of the men said to his buddy, "I'll tell you what we're going to do. You knock on the door and tell them you're hungry. They'll probably ask you in and give you something to eat. Then you just take a little extra and give it to me later." Now remember, these guys were starving.

So the first man knocked on the door and a farmer answered it. This guy told the farmer he was hungry and could he get a little food. Well, the farmer said they were just sitting down to eat and he told him to come in. In the kitchen was this long table. It had everything on it. There was chicken and roast beef and mashed potatoes and gravy and rolls and corn and green beans and sliced tomatoes and three kinds of pie and coffee. It was a feast. Well, the guy just sat there, he looked at the food but he didn't move. He put his head down and closed his eyes. Well, everybody stopped eating and the farmer asked, "Is anything wrong? I thought you were hungry."

So the guy looked up at the farmer and said, "I am, but I got my buddy outside waiting and he's just as hungry as I am, and I just can't eat thinking about him out there in the cold."

Well, the farmer said, "Get him in here. There's plenty for both of you."

Then Powell looked around, stopped speaking for a minute, and slowly said, "That's what a buddy is. Now here's another story:"

These two friends were talking. One of them just got forty dollars, the second knew that. So he said to his friend, "If I was hungry and you had a lot of food would you give me a meal?" The first guy said, "If I had a lot of food and you were hungry, I'd give you half of the food, we're friends."

The second says, "And if you had three cars would you loan me one?" "Heck, if I had three cars I'd give you one."

The second continues, "And if you had a couple of houses, would you let me live in one?" "Hey we're friends. If I had two houses I'd probably just give you one."

133

"Well that's great," says the second. "I'm broke. Why don't you give me twenty dollars?" "Heck no, you crazy! I got that."

Powell sat there looking at the men at the bar. Everything was suddenly quiet. His stories were quite different from most heard at Harrigan's. Then Powell smiled a perfect piano-ivory smile, and said, "So you see, a lot of people will give you what they don't have, but they won't share what they do have. And there are a lot more friends to the poor than there are buddies. Good luck, Noah. Do some good."

E.E.P., Elvatus Elvatus Powell, born October 2, 1914, in Jefferson County, Mississippi, is a man without a wrinkle inside or out, and my buddy. Love is one of those things that is or isn't.

Three Thousand Years of Warning

The question I hear most often is "How can we help?" The answer lies at the end of each arm, directed by the device that lives and beats beneath the second button on our own shirt. While speaking to various groups, the most frequent suggestion for repair of the homeless problem is that the government must do more. The second most popular suggestion is that the church must do more. I agree. The government could perhaps do more for the homeless and the poor by redirecting funds. But the main thing the government must do is manufacture or create jobs. Some churches are doing a great deal. Some churches could be doing more than they are currently doing. Some are doing nothing. But the action of the church could be to first fill the empty belly and provide a place to sleep.

The issue that we sometimes fail to recognize is that the government and the church are not autonomous creatures. You and I are the cells that make up the body of the government and the church. And while we have our individual duties within those bodies we also have some say as to the direction and actions they take. The government and the church are convenient masks that we individually wear, under which we often hide from ourselves and our own responsibility. It is, therefore, our responsibility individually and totally to lobby for change. Our government was formed by, of, and for the people. The church—whether that church is organized or it consists of only one member, yourself— has a mandate that the government does not. Whether we profess to be Christian, Jew, Moslem, or a follower of another faith, with rare exception, we have been given the mandate to help the poor and the homeless. The directive is explicit. The benefits for compliance and the consequences for not doing so are also clearly detailed. For those who are not Christian, yet still base their belief on the Pentateuch, the mandate is the same. The New Testament, the Torah, the Koran, all mandate certain action toward the poor. Within virtually all religious writings, we find divine instruction to those who can help to reach out to those who need help.

When speaking at various churches and religious gatherings, I am invariably reminded by those in attendance of the words of Jesus as recorded in Matthew 26:11:

> The poor you will always have with you, but you will not always have me.

Many further conclude that since the Bible says we will always have the poor we can do little about it. I don't feel that is the correct interpretation. Jesus, well-versed in the Scriptures, was quoting from Deuteronomy 15:11. In the fifteenth chapter, Moses was detailing the covenants God set forth for canceling debts. But in the fourth verse, we find His statement:

> However, there should be no poor among you, for in the land the LORD your God is giving you to possess as your inheritance, he will richly bless you, if only you fully obey the LORD your God and are careful to follow all these commands I am giving you today.

In Deuteronomy 15:4, there should be no poor among you, because of the Lord's reward for obedience and because of the Sabbath year arrangement. And there would be no poor if we obeyed or followed all His commands. His "year for canceling debts," gave Israelites who had experienced economic reverses a way to be released from indebtedness and so, in a measure, a way to equalize wealth. The provisions of the Year of Jubilee were a more graceful way of forgiving debt than our system of bankruptcy.

In Deuteronomy 15:11 we read that there will always be poor people. Even in the best of societies, under the most enlightened laws, the uncertainties of life and the differences among citizens result in some people becoming poor. In such cases the Lord commands that generosity and kindness be extended to them.

My ledger accepts the fact that there are those who refuse to work. I've known some, met some, employed some. And I am aware of the scriptural admonition against these pitiful souls:

Lazy hands make a man poor. (Prov. 10:4)

Solomon also said:

He who loves pleasure will become poor;
whoever loves wine and oil will never be rich. (Prov. 21:17)

Wine and oil were associated with lavish feasting. Oil was used in expensive perfumes and lotions. So the writer was saying two things: first, that excessive spending could lead to poverty; secondly, the love of secular contentment could result in spiritual poverty.

If a man will not work, he shall not eat. (2 Thess. 3:10)

Paul was making the point that he and his brothers worked and paid for even the food they ate, they did this as an example to the congregations that all must pull their weight. If a man or woman has the opportunity to work at a job which will supply their financial requirements of home, food, clothing, transportation, insurance, etc., and refuses, then they perhaps deserve to be homeless. I am not writing about these. I am writing for the souls that cannot find suitable sustainable work. I am writing for the children in the fields working side by side with their parents eight to ten hours per day for a few dollars. The ones who, for a few dollars per day, are forced to sell their chance at an education and a future.

> Do not take advantage of a hired man who is poor and needy. (Deut. 24:12, paraphrase)

Perhaps we, the purchasing public, should agree to pay an additional nickel per orange so that the parent in the field will not feel forced to lock his child into a transient life-style forever because the family needs the child's income. Perhaps the minimum wage should more reflect the cost of existing. Who could possibly believe the poor have enough?

> You evildoers frustrate the plans of the poor,
> but the LORD is their refuge. (Ps. 14:6)

> He who oppresses the poor shows contempt for their Maker,
> but whoever is kind to the needy honors God. (Prov. 14:31)

> He who mocks the poor shows contempt for
> their Maker. (Prov. 17:5)

I have interviewed many children who have been the target of slurs and jokes by their wealthier peers. In some cases the young people have decided to leave school; the parent, understanding the pressure, reluctantly agrees. For the parent who is well off financially, he or she would be kind to instruct the child in the ways of grace, so as to put no further weight on the poor child. We can be financially well-off and poor in grace.

> Hear this word, you cows of Bashan on Mount Samaria,
> you women who oppress the poor and crush the needy
> and say to your husbands, "Bring us some drinks!"
> The Sovereign LORD has sworn by his holiness: "The time
>   will surely come
> when you will be taken away with hooks,
> the last of you with fishhooks.

You will each go straight out through breaks in the wall,
and you will be cast out toward Harmon," declares the
LORD. (Amos 4:1–3)

Hear this word: The Lord is calling His people to account because of their sins. Cows of Bashan were the upper-class women. He directly addressed them and compared them with the best breed of cattle in ancient Canaan, which were raised and pampered in the pastures of northern Transjordan. Whether the metaphor was intended as an insult or as an irony is uncertain.

Paul's charge to Timothy indicates God's love for all people, rich or poor, for whom he loves he disciplines. And his warning to the rich not to fall prey to their wealth was an attempt to save them.

Command those who are rich in this present world not to be
arrogant nor to put their hope in wealth, which is so uncertain,
but to put their hope in God, who richly provides us with everything for our enjoyment. Command them to do good, to be rich
in good deeds, and to be generous and willing to share. In this
way they will lay up treasure for themselves as a firm foundation for the coming age, so that they may take hold of the life
that is truly life. (1 Tim. 6:17–19)

He has brought down rulers from their thrones
but has lifted up the humble.
He has filled the hungry with good things
but he has sent the rich away empty. (Luke 1:52–53)

When I am speaking to the hungry and the poor, I tell them that Jesus made them a promise, believe it, work at what is available, be gentle, forgive those who hold you from comfort. All things will be evened out, but not by you. To you young ones who have been mocked in school because of your poverty, be proud of your station in life, it holds the greater reward. I tell them to work as hard as they can to get out of the situation so that they can help others. And to you who have risen from poverty, remember how you felt; pay back your blessing by remembering the ones still in need.

Here are a few more words to the poor and the wealthy:

139

Blessed are you who are poor, for yours is the kingdom of God. Blessed are you who hunger now, for you will be satisfied. Blessed are you who weep now, for you will laugh. Blessed are you when men hate you, when they exclude you and insult you and reject your name as evil, because of the Son of Man.

Rejoice in that day and leap for joy, because great is your reward in heaven. For that is how their fathers treated the prophets. But woe to you who are rich, for you have already received your comfort.

Woe to you who are well fed now, for you will go hungry. Woe to you who laugh now, for you will mourn and weep. Woe to you when all men speak well of you, for that is how their fathers treated the false prophets. (Matt. 5:20–26, paraphrase)

A generous man will prosper;
he who refreshes others will himself be refreshed. (Prov.
   11:25)

We are all given the mandate to care for the needy.

Defend the cause of the weak and fatherless;
maintain the rights of the poor and oppressed.
Rescue the weak and the needy;
deliver them from the hand of the wicked. (Ps. 82:3–4)

The poor and homeless need hope, they need possibility and promise, not promises. In Job 5:15 we read,

He saves the needy from the sword in their mouth;
he saves them from the clutches of the powerful.

Hope, promise, commitment, act now, not at some more convenient time. The only convenient time is when it is needed. If we hear a fire alarm in our home we would not wait to leave or investigate when we got around to it. We would not appoint a committee to study the source of the disturbance. We would get the heck out. The alarm is sounding, a large percentage of our neighbors are in distress. They need our help, they need our hope, they need our hands and hearts, they need our love and understanding, they need some of our money and our excess. They need us, you and me.

140

THREE THOUSAND YEARS OF WARNING

The choice is ours individually, we can be like the Cows of Bashan or like the Samaritan:

On one occasion an expert in the law stood up to test Jesus. "Teacher," he asked, "what must I do to inherit eternal life?"

"What is written in the Law?" he replied. "How do you read it?"

He answered: "'Love the LORD your God with all your heart and with all your soul and with all your strength and with all your mind;' and, 'Love your neighbor as yourself.'"

"You have answered correctly," Jesus replied. "Do this and you will live."

But he wanted to justify himself, so he asked Jesus, "And who is my neighbor?"

In reply Jesus said: "A man was going down from Jerusalem to Jericho, when he fell into the hands of robbers. They stripped him of his clothes, beat him and went away, leaving him half dead. A priest happened to be going down the same road, and when he saw the man, he passed by on the other side. So too, a Levite, when he came to the place and saw him, passed by on the other side. But a Samaritan, as he traveled, came where the man was; and when he saw him, he took pity on him. He went to him and bandaged his wounds, pouring on oil and wine. Then he put the man on his own donkey, took him to the inn and took care of him. The next day he took out two silver coins and gave them to the innkeeper. 'Look after him,' he said, 'and when I return, I will reimburse you for any extra expense you may have.' Which of these three do you think was a neighbor to the man who fell into the hands of robbers?"

The expert in the law replied, "The one who had mercy on him."

Jesus told him, "Go and do likewise." (Luke 10:25–37)

The homeless and the poor who want to be helped need commitment—unconditional love and commitment. Love may be easier than the commitment. For it is the commitment to take care of them until they are better. Like the example of the Samaritan, we must bind their wounds, provide their place of rest and safety, and support them until they heal. And each wounded one will require a varied amount of time and expense both financially and psychologically. We must stay with them, teach them to be productive, make use of them but not use them. We must be patient, understanding that many of the homeless are crippled, skeptical of our promises and our purpose. We must be prepared to never hear a thank you except from the one who *commanded* that we take care of the needy.

When I reluctantly journeyed to the street I could not take care of myself. I could not pull myself up by my bootstraps. I was psychologically shoeless. I was emotionally stripped. I felt deceived, betrayed by the one I trusted most. Until my Samaritans materialized I could not truly begin to heal. And until a sufficient amount of time passed, I could not see that I had placed my trust and faith in things and people not worthy of trust.

An example of how unworthy we can allow ourselves to feel is what I term in my life ledger "The Chapter of the Lamp."

When I returned to Oklahoma City, a friend—no, a buddy— invited me to stay in a house he and his wife had just purchased. The house was empty because they were in the process of painting and wallpapering. I stayed in a back bedroom. I had my guitar and my bedroll and a few clothes and some books. (I wish I could use the names of my Samaritans, but my buddy said it would lessen the joy of his helping. However, those who know my story know who this family of Father, Mother, Little Sister, and Brother Samaritan are.)

One night I was reading. They had set up a cot for me, which I used for a chair. I still preferred sleeping on the floor. To read, it was necessary to pull the cot over to the window so that the street light could reach the pages. I heard the front door open, and lady Samaritan appeared in the darkened doorway to my room. She held a lamp and a small lamp stand in her hands. She said, "This is so you can read. I should have thought of this earlier. We know how you like to read." She asked if I needed anything else. I said I couldn't think of anything, and she left.

I sat there looking into the brightness of that little lamp and suddenly broke down. I am not certain how long I cried, but I remember the intensity because I sobbed long after the tears stopped. I knew I wanted a lamp, but I could not ask for one. I still believed I had what I deserved. I still could not do anything for anyone, including myself. I thanked God for the lamp, for that little light to read by. I thanked Him for my Samaritans. I thanked Him for my bedroll and for my cot chair. I thanked Him for the roof over my head and the shower down the hall. I thanked Him for the books I had. I thanked Him for everything, bugs, cracks in the sidewalk, everything. I thanked Him that doors had knobs and wheels were round. I thanked Him for every cell in every body and every atom in every cell. I thanked Him and I thanked Him and I thanked Him . . . then I thanked Him for bringing me to the point in life where I could be aware of the value of a lamp, the brightness of one proud, tiny light standing on its stand.

Suddenly I realized I did not have to be someone's coliseum lights. I do not have to light up the city in anyone's mind. For the cities in some minds outgrow illumination, and they will choose to hide in the dark alleys of their private lives and secrets. All we have to be is one tiny light. To this day, each time I enter a darkened room and flip the switch, I am humbled, and I thank Him.

Somewhere we have separated from the original message of Jesus, a simple message of love, and the command to love one another. We have made the message complicated with interpretation and personal preference. We have traded the mandates on our actions for the gospel of grace alone. We have preferred to hear only that no matter what we do or how we live, we are forever forgiven. We discount the fact that Jesus warned (and quite sternly) that we as individuals had to observe certain tenets to gain life. He would love us, but the door could close on us again as it did on the Ark.

All of us are to blame for the watered-down message from some of our teachers, for the Bible says that in the latter days people will take teachers to tickle their ears. And there is no shortage of those who will speak what we want to hear. But if the Christ were here in the flesh again, He would spend most of His time kicking temple tables and our behinds. The church must lead in giving, according to Paul in 2 Corinthians 8:1–15:

And now, brothers, we want you to know about the grace that God has given the Macedonian churches. Out of the most severe trial, their overflowing joy and their extreme poverty welled up

143

in rich generosity. For I testify that they gave as much as they were able, and even beyond their ability. Entirely on their own, they urgently pleaded with us for the privilege of sharing in this service to the saints. And they did not do as we expected, but they gave themselves first to the Lord and then to us in keeping with God's will. So we urged Titus, since he had earlier made a beginning, to bring also to completion this act of grace on your part. But just as you excel in everything—in faith, in speech, in knowledge, in complete earnestness and in your love for us—see that you also excel in this grace of giving.

I am not commanding you, but I want to test the sincerity of you love by comparing it with the earnestness of others. For you know the grace of our Lord Jesus Christ, that though he was rich, yet for your sakes he became poor, so that you through his poverty might become rich.

And here is my advice about what is best for you in this matter: Last year you were the first not only to give but also to have the desire to do so. Now finish the work, so that your eager willingness to do it may be matched by your completion of it, according to what one has, not according to what he does not have.

Our desire is not that others might be relieved while you are hard pressed, but that there might be equality. At the present time your plenty will supply what they need, so that in turn their plenty will supply what you need. Then there will be equality, as it is written: "He who gathered much did not have too much, and he who gathered little did not have too little."

This passage contains so much. It applauds the church for their generous giving, but also encourages them to finish the work they started. Paul makes plain that the church is not expected to suffer unduly financially, but giving would more fairly equalize those at the top of the pyramid of wealth with those at the base, so there would not be those with too much and those with too little.

Jesus was a street person. He lived with and walked with the poor. He wept with and for the lowly souls who were oppressed. He felt the oppression from the rich and the pain of their looking down on his social position. They said, "You call this pitiful soul the King of the Jews?" How many who today profess to love Him, if they saw him on the street dressed as He once dressed, would invite Him in or give Him a ride? If we ask how all this Scripture applies to us—to you and to me—we might hear this answer from long ago:

> When the Son of Man comes in his glory, and all the angels with him, he will sit on his throne in heavenly glory. All the nations will be gathered before him, and he will separate the people one from another as a shepherd separates the sheep from the goats. He will put the sheep on his right and the goats on his left.
>
> Then the King will say to those on his right, "Come, you who are blessed by my Father; take your inheritance, the kingdom prepared for you since the creation of the world. For I was hungry and you gave me something to eat, I was thirsty and you gave me something to drink, I was a stranger and you invited me in, I needed clothes and you clothed me, I was sick and you looked after me, I was in prison and you came to visit me."
>
> Then the righteous will answer him, "Lord, when did we see you hungry and feed you, or thirsty and give you something to drink? When did we see you a stranger and invite you in, or needing clothes and clothe you? When did we see you sick or in prison and go to visit you?"
>
> The King will reply, "I tell you the truth, whatever you did for one of the least of these brothers of mine, you did for me."
>
> Then he will say to those on his left, "Depart from me, you who are cursed, into the eternal fire prepared for the devil and his angels. For I was hungry and you gave me nothing to eat, I was thirsty and you gave me nothing to drink, I was a stranger and you did not invite me in, I needed clothes and you did not clothe me, I was sick and you did not look after me."
>
> They also will answer, "Lord, when did we see you hungry or thirsty or a stranger or needing clothes or sick or in prison, and did not help you?"
>
> He will reply, "I tell you the truth, whatever you did not do for one of the least of these, you did not do for me."
>
> Then they will go away to eternal punishment, but the righteous to eternal life. (Matt. 25:31–46)

Few of us like to be preached to when it touches a blemish in our personal life. Fewer still like being told what to do, or having others decide what is best for our lives. We know what is best, even though it is not always best. I am like that, I always have

145

been. I am not a preacher. I am a writer. If you would care to hear me preach, invite me to talk to you about the church Christian vs. the Christ Christian.

We sometimes resist what is best for us. If I would have moved to Nashville as once planed, I would not have written this book. And the answer to the prayer of a pantsless derelict appealing to his God for a direction and purpose, may have been overlooked. Thanks, Anita Bryant, for your strength. You were right; I am a writer. Thanks, Charlie Dry. We were all used in our own way.

REACHING
OUT

PART **5**

CHAPTER
SIXTEEN

Legislating Love

"There should be no limits on how high a man or woman can rise in this country. Let's make the rich people richer and the poor people richer." Secretary Kemp said that in a speech at the Petroleum Club in Oklahoma City. I believe we are working on half of that belief. I wonder about the wisdom or value in a simple lateral move in disparity. I think I'll ask Elvatus Powell about that. He'll know what to do. Boogie men seldom stand on this side of the bush where they can readily be seen. Secretary Kemp doesn't mind being seen. I believe he is a genuinely dedicated steward. He just has a huge sewer to sweeten.

I do have one quote that I almost forgot about. I called both Secretary Kemp's and Anna Kondratas's offices and requested an audience. I received a call from a staff member of one of the parties. We talked at great length and the person was honestly interested in the project and the problem. I told the staff person I was frustrated that I could not use the name of anyone I had talked to. I shared the fact that without names, quotes were somewhat suspect. I needed the assurance of some official that the problem of homelessness was a priority. The staff member sympathized with my dilemma, but could do little to assist me. He said something very important to my question of why no official would talk to me. He said, "You have to be there to get there." Before I would be at the stature required to receive an interview I would have to be at the stature. He mailed a great huge pile of pertinent material and it has been helpful.

"You have to be there to get there." That's it. That's what's wrong. That's what's wrong with trying to tell people what being homeless is like too.

I talked with another staff member. He was most helpful, genuine, straightforward, aboveboard, honest. He said, "Here is a quote you may use. My boss, Anna Kondratas, is committed to greatly reducing the homeless population by 1992 and eradicating it by the year 2000." Perhaps I am naive, but I honestly believe they are genuinely committed to their work. On some level I believe they believe they can accomplish that goal. I wish could be as confident.

I wonder, though, what definition of homelessness will be eradicated. I further wonder how they will erase from our nature and culture the underlying reasons for poverty and homelessness. Homelessness is not the problem, it is a symptom. How do we sift the graft, greed, and corruption from the hearts of some of those whose motive is only self-profit? How do we instill the ethic of love, unconditional love, into our daily life? How do we dissolve the disparity in opportunity of education and a future? What do we do about the one in five adults who cannot read or write? What do we do with the worker who has been replaced by a computer chip that has less appetite than a light bulb, or the worker who lost his job to the foreign worker that will work for a two cents a minute? What method of transfusion will remove the pollutant of prejudice from the arteries of our lives? How are we going to control foreign manufacturing output and placement of their products in the world market? How and when are we going to bite the bullet and do something about our addition to the pollutants now strangling the planet? By what method are we going to stop the reason for the rampant use of drugs and protect ourselves from the crime it causes and the crime that causes it? What are we going to do with the dead and the dying cities where the fungus of human poverty is allowed to grow unchecked? How are we going to convince the terminally lazy to raise their cellulite off the public couch and work for a living? When are we going to stop being held hostage by someone in a houndstooth rag hat and put the result of that action to the cure of our weakness?

Why did we not continue with the alternative energy programs started by former President Jimmy Carter? Could it be that a peanut farmer just could not gather or gain the same credibility as an oil man, or was it that he spoke of God while in office? That should certainly discredit any public official, so many would think. It would seem now that he was on the right track, in both resolves.

I wish these idealistic legislators well. I hope and pray that this administration can do what thousands of years of civilization and all the religious restraints have never accomplished. That is what I wanted to talk to the policy makers about. I wanted to understand what was expected of me and how I could help. I just wanted to talk. I needed to understand. I still do. I was only going to ask, "How are you going to do it?" Guess I'll ask Powell.

The following is a portion of the conversation I had with an official representative of an official representative. I had perhaps a dozen conversations similar to this one. I chose this one because the man did not back down. He was certain. He was concise. He was helpful. He supported the one he worked for not out of fear but respect. He had a great working command of facts and figures. His only difficulty was in convincing me that what was being done was enough or encompassing enough to even stop this tragedy from getting worse, let alone cure it. This is a lengthy transcript. Read it or skip it and come back to it. But if you really wish to get involved in the repair you need to know how bad we are leaking. It was even lengthy for my editor; he said cut it down. Everyone wants to know what we can do and how can we do it. Bottom line, base figures, render the fat out of the problem till only the burnt crumbs remain. Forget it. It is not that simple, as perhaps you have already seen.

Most reporters will take the conversation and remold it into glowing cleaver ringlets of curly thoughts. Friends, it just doesn't happen that way. I am personally sick to death of everything quoted sounding like it came from the same mouth. Let me share a secret, mostly it did, but not here. You hear it like I did. This is not some aloof group of uncaring elitists; they are servants trying to make a gallon of soup go a mile, because someone told them it would. You gave them the job to do. Now help them finish it or elect someone who knows the gallon of soup that covers a mile fills no one's belly.

Hello, Noah Snider.

Hi, Noah. This is _____, and I'm returning your call to Anna Kondratas at HUD.

Good. I need a little help, if I can. I don't know if the secretary mentioned anything at all, but I'm writing a book for Thomas Nelson Publishing Company. The book is an autobiography of the homeless. It contains some of my experiences on the street and the way I felt. The publisher is asking me to come up with some type of conclusion and some of the solutions and programs available for those on the street. I do need a fair amount of statistical information. I was able to acquire information from Adopt-a-Family and from the Emergency Food and Shelter National Program, and fact sheets of HUD material. But I am having no success in getting interviews. I'm doing interviews all over the country with various people in the missions and position of helping, and also with those who are being helped. If possible, I would like to talk to Secretary Kemp. If it were just for five minutes, just so that I would have it for the book. My publisher would like to see that also. Basically my question has been, Where are we and what do we need? And I guess that's what I'm asking you, what are we doing and what are we going to do.

Okay. Well, on the first bet, in terms of meeting Kemp, I would guess the likelihood is very minimal.

Okay.

It's just before the elections, and he's a political official, and he's doing a lot of work, shall we say, on the political side of things.

Sure.

And he's out of the office, it seems like over half the time.

Oh, I would imagine.

Meeting up on the Hill and meeting at the White House, and he's all over the place. So I, I would be shocked, I rarely even see him, I'm supposed to be working for him. I would be shocked if you could have an interview with him.

All right, me too.

As for numbers, I certainly have all sorts of numbers in my head, if you would like to be more focused on exactly what you're looking at—

Well, I have a number of estimates of the homeless, of course they vary depending on advocacy or government posture.

Well, I'd just stick to studies that have a foundation, studies that have a method. There are only four.

Okay.

There is the Urban Institute Study, conducted through the Department of Agriculture, and that is, in my opinion, the most sound study, and it's certainly the most carefully done. It was done in 1987 and it came out with a figure that said that between 567,000 to 600,000 persons are homeless on any given day. Now, over the course of the year, the author of that study said it could be as high as 1.2 million, because people, as you know, fall in and out of homelessness.

Sure, absolutely, it's a short fall for some.

The conversation continued for some time. We covered the assumed validity of numbers and reports. While speaking to the gentleman I realized that I had forgotten for a moment that we were talking about people, little children and lost parents, sick souls, that in this conversation had become simply a part of a statistic. I imagined that conversations like this took place while I was on the street, and no one knew me. No one put my face on a number.

So, they were not looking to get a small number and it's interesting that even the advocates' studies base their start with the

HUD number because it is a fairly solid one, at least for the period of 1983 to 1984. And what I can do is send a one or two-pager that sort of, that really nicely summarizes those four studies, and the numbers they come up with.

Okay, great. If you could mail it,—I'm recording this but if you would send it I'd sure appreciate it.

Okay.

What difficulties are you having? Do you find a great deal of infighting and elbowing within the ranks of those in the posture to help, or wishing to help?

You mean between federal agencies?

Uh-huh.

Not at all.

How about outside the federal agencies?

Well, sure there's posturing. That's what advocates are supposed to do. That's why you get such a ridiculous number like three million. That's not based on anything. There's absolutely no foundation for the three million figure. When you call the National Coalition or the National Law Center on Poverty and Homelessness and you ask for the assumptions that were used for that study, you won't find any. Well, you know, though when I think of 600,000, let's take the low figure from '87. That's enough, isn't it?

That's a huge number.

But that's what I'm saying, you don't need to expand it anymore, let's stick with the facts and work on the problem.

We talked further and he mentioned other government agencies that I might contact to gain numerical estimates. I had already contacted them, and he was last on the list. Since the figures all came from the same source, they did correlate.

And that is a report that's about two years old that, just tell them to send both annual reports, because the more recent one, the one done last year, is really good in terms of numbers, when it breaks down the population in terms of the mentally ill.

Excellent, this book is complicated. I could write it in volumes. I'm ready to end this for awhile, my stomach is killing me. But, it's important to me to relate the feelings of one locked inside the

situation accurately. It is difficult now being on this side of it. We
see the massive myriad of problems differently through a full
stomach.

We talked about the budget for the poor and homeless and the
figures that were basically potential. They were the amounts requested but not yet approved.

It was my most up-to-date table on that one. Okay, for 1991,
this is the money that hopefully Congress is going to be giving us,
it is $985,000,000. Now that is targeted money to the homeless.
Okay. However, as far as I know, there is no program for single
men now, or, unaccompanied men, I believe you call it.
Well, programs like Health Care for the Homeless serve mainly
single men, but if you're talking about housing, there are certainly
few programs to do it. Now it looks like Congress is going to give us
just a small portion of that, but nonetheless—
It's a beginning.
—it looks like something is going to come out of it. Another one
or two programs that can be used by single men are transitional
housing program at HUD, and let me just look at the—we had
asked for about $143,000,000 for that program, and that serves
families, it serves singles, it serves anybody who wants to do transitional housing.
Does that program have a name?
Yeah, it's called, you can simply call it transitional housing.
Oh, okay. All right, That's about one hundred and twenty dol-
lars for each of those on the street in the year . . . we don't want to
look at this problem. By the way, Father Hill in Dallas said he
would like to talk to Secretary Kemp. I think the Secretary would
find in him an interesting and honest conversation. Now, your po-
sition there is what?
I am an analyst.
Okay. Well, it looks like you have plenty to keep you busy for
years and years.
Unfortunately.

We talked at length about programs that have been proposed
and goals of ending the homeless problems by the end of the
century.

My boss actually has said that her goal, and she is an Assistant Secretary, her goal is to measurably reduce homelessness by 1992, and to eliminate it by the end of the century.

Okay. I'll put that in. Good. It brings a number of questions to my mind. I wish that, I certainly hope that takes place.

Yeah, I do too.

And I wish I were more optimistic along those lines. The way I feel about it right now, oh well, whatever increase happens, is better than what has happened, you know?

Well, one thing we have to do is make the normal, traditional welfare programs work for people.

Exactly. Exactly right.

I worked for the food stamp program for six years, and it just doesn't work for homeless people.

No, no, I know, I wish I had answers that would be accepted by everyone. God doesn't even have that.

The conversation ended after the following question:

I have heard one very frightening statistic. And, as with all statistics, you know, we—

Yeah, just say it, let me get my reaction.

Okay, I heard we were going to have the figure of 19,000,000 by the year 2000 on the street.

That figure is baseless.

Okay.

I, is this the MI—I'm sure it's from MIT.

I don't know.

It's called the "knife edge of the homeless" figure?

Perhaps: it was on the Downey show.

Where they say, yeah, that's—I don't know how, I mean, anybody can come up with a number, but if you asked them where they got that there's nothing to look at, because I've looked into that number.

You have too?

Yeah. There's nothing to it because no one knows what the rate of increase of homelessness has been.

Well, that seems to be true.

And as a matter of fact, when they say knife edge of homelessness, what they mean is they're not just talking about homeless persons, but low-income persons.

Uh-huh.

Well, there's 33,000,000 people defined as poor in this country.

Yes, some say more, many more, some reports are twice that figure.

So, if you go to the extreme, and many people will, you can say that 33,000,000 people are at risk of becoming homeless, although I think that's a bunch of garbage. And if we start diluting funds that we now have for the homeless to 33,000,000 people, it's not going to do anything.

Uh-huh, not much to go around now I suppose.

That's why welfare programs should be working better.

Uh-huh. Yes, I know. I know. Well, you know, they're all, investigating it, there are other statistics that support the premise that we will have some deeper difficulties down the pike with our manufacturing segments and so on, and our ecological problems that we're all, or some of us, working to correct and worrying about. They may cause loss of jobs and such, and then require retraining, but we begin to wonder, without being labeled a doomsdayer, if we should pack our tent and go out and sit in the woods until the cloud passes. I wonder how will this be taken care of? What provisions are being done for the rapid changes in our whole social and economic structures, you know? It's an amazing study. I mean, it's too much for me and one little book about a guy who just came off the streets who finally has dry socks and a meal—

Uh-huh.

Because of some of the investigative work that I'm doing and some of the studies that I'm reading, I'm wondering. Are we just naive? Are we putting off the inevitable? Are we just telling everyone that this is where we are and what we are doing, knowing we are losing ground? I wonder.

Yeah.

I wonder. It's difficult, you know? It really is. A difficult situation, for everyone, for everyone involved, well, I'm going to give you my address. If there's anything you'd like to send me, I certainly would appreciate it, and if you don't mind, I'd like to quote the things you have said.

Now, you can quote them, but I'd prefer my name not be used, though.
Would you really?
Yeah.

I spent several days speaking to the people at MIT. I was unable to find the "knife edge report" or its author. I did locate a report titled "One-Third of a Nation: A New Look at Housing Affordability in America" by Michael E. Stone, a professor of community planning at the University of Boston. The notice of the report was sent to me by Michael Mayer, who is the editor of the publication *The Alliance*. Mr. Mayer is with The National Alliance to End Homelessness. You will find their address and publication listed in part seven of the book.

The "One-Third" report concludes that 32 percent of Americans are "shelter poor." "Shelter poor" refers to those people who are unable to afford basic necessities after paying their housing costs. (I took into account the above analyst's warning to be careful of reports that have no basis. The "One-Third" study based its findings on a formula that takes into account income and household size and type, as opposed to the traditional formula which simply measures percent of income paid for housing.) The report found that 27 million households, or 78 million Americans, fall under the heading "shelter poor." Many of these people are at risk of becoming homeless.

I talked at great length with Barry Zigas, Executive Secretary of the Low-Income Housing Information Service. Barry sent a wealth of information for my research and to be used in the book. A listing of reports available has been included in part seven. One of the reports, "Out of Reach" makes the following statements:

- The cost of renting a one-bedroom unit is beyond the reach of at least one-third of renter households in every state.

- Half of all renter households need at least a two-bedroom unit. But they cost even more. Three out of five renter households in Massachusetts and Maine cannot afford a two-bedroom unit. More than half the renters in nineteen other states cannot afford to rent such units. Even in Texas, the most "affordable" state, 38 percent of all renters cannot afford a two-bedroom unit.

- Even families with two, full-time wage earners often cannot afford housing. In Alabama, the state with the lowest housing cost, a worker with a full-time job would have to earn $6.15 per hour to afford a one-bedroom apartment. This is one and a half times the minimum wage. In thirty-nine states, paying for a one-bedroom unit requires two to three times the minimum wage. In six states more than three times the minimum wage is required.

- Earnings need to be higher to pay for larger units. In Massachusetts, the most expensive state, a person must earn $13.65 to afford a two-bedroom unit—more than three times the minimum wage. More than three times the minimum wage is required in eighteen states.

I am not optimistic about the situation, however. I am convinced that any lasting and major repair of the travesty of poverty would only be accomplished by people with the optimism and energy of the analyst in the interview above and dedicated people like Barry Zegis who will not climb off of our complacent shoulders.

LEDGER

I live on a small lake in Oklahoma. The dock is about seventy feet from my door and I spend a great deal of time there talking things over with myself. Poets do that I'm told. I was taking a break from the book this morning and, while fishing, I wondered how God ever designed a creature as foolish as a fish. I catch the same fish everyday on the same bait. I know they are the same fish because some of their mouths look like colanders from the many hook holes. As I said, I was wondering why the need for anything as foolish as a fish and then while washing my hands . . . I looked in the mirror. Some of us have mouths like colanders too.

If we are ever to be successful in crossing the chasm caused by the erosion of doubt and fear and prejudice and greed, we must cross on threads of trust. We are all, to some degree, like the fish biting the same bait over and over and over again. Many leaders know we are prone by the hunger of hope to repeat the process. They use that trait to control our lives, slow our reaction, retard our feeding frenzy, appease our distraction. We bite on the same promises that contain the same hooks. The same artificial bait that is purposely created to look like the genuine thing is presented by new fishermen in the same old way. When we are hungry enough, we bite anything. Eventually, being carnivorous, and given the reason or opportunity, we will eat the fisherman.

We are living in the information age so it is somewhat easy to manipulate what we hear and when we hear it. We will embrace the old bait until we discover the hook in our own mouth. The instantaneous advantage of the news media's feeding us the opinion and assumption of the experts, both government and private, is the absolute knowledge and awareness that something is wrong, that someone is wrong. Or worse, someone is baiting the hook.

If the boat is leaking, the captain should tell everyone so that we may all start bailing with purpose and some are not still shopping while some are reaching casually for the pail while some are already up to their air holes. Further, if the ship is sinking, get everyone to the rail.

Yes, I just needed to know, I still do. "Hello, Washington? I would like to talk to someone about how we're going to get out of all this mess. Sure, I'll hold—"

Much is being done to help homeless people. Many states try to legislate the love and action that's missing. In other cases, private groups have pooled their time and talent and available resources to assist the needy. If you would like to add your help and heart to the solution of the growing problem, you might contact one of the sources noted at the end of the book. It is impossible to detail all or even most of the organizations now in place. However, you may contact the mayor's office in your city or the governor's staff in your state for the closest group in need of support. You will need to personally research the legitimacy of the organization. Unfortunately, all reporting helping hands, even in the obvious suffering of so many, are not altruistically inclined. The con man and the bloodsucker prey even on the disabled.

It was reported that of the $467,000 collected by the Metroplex Fraternal Order of Police in Oklahoma City to purchase Christmas food baskets in 1989, only $62,000 was actually spent on food for the poor. That amounted to 13.3 percent: $193,000 was profit to the promoter, $14,000 was paid for security to guard the money, the balance went to miscellaneous expenses, FOP lodge and negotiation expense, and defense and grievance expense. If the fund-raising event is a union activity for union advantage, it should be advertised as such. At 13 percent it is definitely not a legitimate campaign to feed the hungry. Here we have a reputable group representing a very legitimate and worthy cause. Both the public and the hungry will now be better served by some rapid self-policing by the FOP.

This form of collecting for supposed needy causes by private promoters representing legitimate sponsors is common practice across the country, but is it honorable? Is it just and fair to either the giver who thought he was giving to help a needy soul, or to the hungry and poor who have already been the product of great greed? Next time you get a ticket, why not ask the officer what he thinks of the program. The two I talked with were very upset with the information. I believe all of them would be. The campaign was suspended and refunds granted to those who requested them.

Oklahoma Governor Henry Bellmon's task force on the homeless reported that there were 35,000 homeless people full- or part-time. In Oklahoma, Sam Boman, director of a nonprofit organization, estimated Oklahoma City had 25,000 empty, livable dwellings. Vickie White, ranking Democrat from Norman, Oklahoma, authored House Bill 1957, which allows the homeless to live in vacant dwellings. The bill, approved 63–32, allows homeowners to donate their homes for a year, and the agreement may be extended. In return, nonprofit agencies that select the homeless or those in "imminent danger of being homeless," take responsibility for paying utilities and upkeep.

161

Unfortunately a thread of partisan support or opposition runs through all of the reported legislated processes. For privilege of interview or when quoting newspaper and published articles, it is necessary to indicate the political party of the subject. I am neither a Democrat nor a Republican, for I support those actions and statements that are sensible or sensitive to my ledger. To date it has never been political.

A common theme of newspaper articles is the stand of various politicians on the issue of the homeless. In an article in The Daily Oklahoman detailing the House voting, Leonard Sullivan, (R-Oklahoma City), asked what would happen if "some sweet little lady from Nichols Hills gives her half-million- or million-dollar house to this program." He wondered if the bill would facilitate moving "the winos out from under the North Canadian bridge" and also the mentally insane "into the affluent North Side community."

Vickie White responded that the homeless would be carefully screened by their nonprofit sponsors, such as churches or the Neighborhood Services Organization of Oklahoma City.

She said the most important amendment is one providing for case management of the people who would live in the vacant houses. The case management approach would require the homeless tenants to keep up the property. It also would allow the nonprofit agency to require residents to share the cost once they secure employment and are on the road to economic recovery.

One of the state agencies involved in the case management is the Oklahoma Housing Finance Agency. Republican Jim Istook of Warr Acres pointed out that the agency had failed to use millions of dollars for Section 8 housing for low-income people. White said she is watching closely what that agency does. She also noted that public schools report three thousand homeless children in the 1989–90 school year "and that is probably the tip of the iceberg."

Mr. Sullivan's concern may seem to have been a cold response to the need of the homeless, but in reality it wasn't. Every politician is elected to represent the constituency that voted for him or her. He or she should be sensitive to the wishes of that community. Nichols Hills in Oklahoma City is no different from any

162

other upper-class neighborhood in the country, or for that matter no different from any middle- or lower-class neighborhood. No community wishes to be vested with a social problem that may in any way detract from the quiet enjoyment of their lifestyle, regardless of the social status in the community. We have read newspaper reports of middle- and lower-class neighborhoods fighting the placement of treatment centers or halfway houses for the prison work release programs. It is as frightening to them as the dumping of toxic waste products in their back yard.

No one can force social or moral conscience on any of us; it is something that only happens from within if it is ever to move from simple recognition to corrective action. And the socially mobile who have the finances available, simply move from less desirable to more desirable locations. This is what has happened to the inner cities. Those who were and are able, move to the suburbs, leaving the decaying center to the ones who have no choice but stay. This migration crosses all racial lines.

In an Associated Press release of February 1990, we read:

An aluminum village for the homeless is going up across the street from the pricy Watergate complex, but the high and mighty who live there are telling the city, "Not in my front yard." The object of their dismay is a cluster of seven white trailers tucked into a small triangle in view of some of the loftiest apartments in the capital city. The Doles, Senator Bob and Labor Secretary Elizabeth, live in the Watergate. So do authors, high-ranking military people, and big-name journalists. They live in three apartment buildings and a condominium building flanking the Watergate Office Building which gained fame in 1972 when burglars organized by Richard Nixon's reelection committee were caught red-handed inside Democratic Party Headquarters. The residents have filed suit to block the shelter for the homeless who now roam the streets below, sometimes panhandling money from the motorists and tuxedo-clad socialites on their way to the nearby Kennedy Center for the Performing Arts.

The seven trailers, hooked up to sewer and power lines, are behind the Howard Johnson's Motel on Virginia Avenue. The

163

trailers are ready for up to 112 men and women, many of them now living on steam grates, patches of grass, benches, and doorways in the area.

The 680 homeowners don't come straight out and say, "We don't want to house the homeless." Their lawsuit against the District of Columbia is more discreet, based on a claim that the city failed to run the shelter past the Fine Arts Commission, which decides in certain areas whether a structure is appropriate.

Federal Judge Oliver Gasch handed the residents a setback by refusing to block work on the site. He said the Fine Arts Commission argument would not wash because the area is outside the commission's jurisdiction. The residents still can appeal the judge's ruling.

"What I would like to know is exactly what neighborhood they would like to send these folks to," says Lois Williams, an attorney for the homeless.

The taxpaying residents have an answer, through their lawyer, Vernon W. Johnson, III: a softball field four blocks away would be ideal.

I have a special affinity for the homeless, for as I have detailed, I was homeless. Perhaps I still am, for I don't believe I belong here anymore. However, I can understand the feelings of the residents of the Watergate. They chose the site because of the amenities both in and immediately surrounding the complex. It fit their budget and life-style or taste or convenience. And if the homeless project were there when they selected their home, some perhaps would not have located there—probably most would have. But the choice is no longer their own. And if the homeless had a choice, they probably would opt for the Watergate complex over the trailers in front. Strangely enough some of them would probably then complain about the white trailers across the street containing sixteen poor souls each.

Even though I lived on the street and will campaign for the removal of the street as acceptable housing, I never want to go back to it. And as soon as possible I will place as much distance between these flying fingers and the street as possible. I do not need to suffer more because I am aware others suffer. I already suffer for them. I do not need to live in or near the distraction to remember its reality. I only have to close my eyes.

I'll have a small farm if time and providence provides, and without guilt I will return from this campaign at every opportunity to remove the sounds of sirens and traffic from my ears and mind and listen to the birds, if birds remain. And I will replace the stench of greed and the resulting stink of rotting inner city with the sweet smell of the trees and the wind, if trees still have leaves. I will take from my eyes the Dante vision of the growing numbers of poor and lost and replace it with the sight of tomatoes and hot peppers and flowers growing in my garden, if the earth is still able to sustain them.

When I was on the street, I no more would have wanted to be placed with the wealthy to be constantly reminded of their excess and their judgment of me than they would have wanted to view my desperation. Perhaps that softball field would be the better place. It could have gardens and trees and some high green living screen to protect the privacy and perspective of the 112 lives in the seven white trailers.

LEDGER

At birth, we perhaps are the optimum expression of true and complete unconditional love. We begin to lessen and formulate our love with the first rough touch, the first pain, the first time we feel hunger not instantly satisfied, the first time we are the object of anger in our parents' voices.

We progress through levels of love based on receiving parental, peer, and social understanding. We enter each new moment of our lives as the product of all past love received or perceived, or withheld or perceived to have been withheld. This is reflected in the amount of love we feel and give to one another. Our commitments, too, are jaundiced by every commitment made and kept, or made and broken. Our trust is formulated by the trusted and untrustworthy moments in our lives and relationships. And so, no matter what our words say, our actions are our belief. We are all pliable in the hands of our love quotient as long as we have breath. We perhaps live more the motto "Do unto others what they do unto you," rather than the command "Do unto others what you would have them do unto you." My ledger says this is not an unfair assessment, considering the condition of our world, our society, our family strength.

We have all been lied to, cheated, unjustly accused, misunderstood. Most, if not all of us, have lied to, cheated, unjustly accused, and misunderstood someone. We are all a taste of the good and a bite of the bad. We are so much the same. We become hungry and must eat. We become thirsty and must drink. We all wince at pain and cry at distress. We are all subjects of universal law, and none of us escape its enforcement indefinitely.

We are all single cells in the body of mankind, and just as it is not required that every cell be infected to cause death or distress in our own body, so too it is the same in the greater body. The healthy cells must attend to the healing of the weaker infected cells, or the infection will spread. There is no antidote, whether money or status, that will protect the well from the ill. Amputation or isolation is not a possible or plausible solution. By helping and healing others we help and heal ourselves. By protecting others we protect ourselves. Meet some special people in the next chapter that are doing that.

CHAPTER
SEVENTEEN

Jesus House

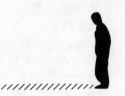

The sleet in hissing waves found its way into my collar and clung to my eyebrows. It drilled into my cheek and my memory. I was not on the street in the winter, but I remember the cold mornings and how the wind blowing through my wet clothes seemed to freeze my weakened body. A person can shiver in the sunshine when he or she is alone and hopeless. As I hurried to the old school building that now houses the Jesus House, I thought of the many street people huddled somewhere in the city trying to escape the molesting sting of nature, further chipping tiny pieces of their remaining faith from their being and dignity, and the humiliation of being the target of even the elements.

While despair may lead us to reality by dissolving the illusion of our own invincibility, hopelessness and helplessness are not positive assumptions of our position in life. They, in fact, imprison the soul in a cell far removed from all possibilities and alternatives.

As I entered the large doors, I revisited the worst period of my life. I shivered with old feelings. The tears that would not come for myself uncontrollably began for those sitting on the cold dirty floor. They sat, knees drawn up to their chest, shoulder to shoulder, the fortunate in chairs once occupied by optimistic children long ago. I wondered if any of these souls sat as children in these chairs in a time full of dreams and promise, only to have returned to the same chair, empty now of childhood illusion and hope.

Santa did not come to them, nor did the prince kiss their sleeping wishes. They found a world void of the Tooth Fairy, the Easter Bunny, and Superman. Instead, they were introduced to the real world of hypocritical professed love. I cried, too, because in this world of real and unreal, of charlatans and shamans, of princes and paupers, angels do exist. For they led each of these helpless souls to the angels of the Jesus House.

I thought, too, about most of us outside the big doors of that Jesus House. We were shopping for luxury; we were working for things. We were lost in the purpose of pleasure. We were living as we wished, knowing that Sunday we would ask for forgiveness and it would be granted. We were dug deeply in the diversions available so that we did not have to think about this place and others like it or the reasons or the causes for its existence. The world outside these doors was running just fast enough to stay ahead of the need to address the needy, to find the lost, to feed the hungry.

We have built many fortresses to protect us from the plight and the sight of the poor, but no man has ever built a wall high enough to hide from the eyes of the God who said,

> But know this, that in the last days critical times hard to deal with will be here. For men will be lovers of themselves, lovers of money, self-assuming, haughty, blasphemers, disobedient to parents, unthankful, disloyal, having no natural affection, not open to any agreement, slanderers, without self-control, fierce, without love of goodness, betrayers, headstrong, puffed up with pride, lovers of pleasures rather than lovers of God, having a form of godly devotion but proving false to its power, and from these turn away. (2 Tim. 3:1–5, paraphrase)

As I was led down the hall, stepping around and over the lost, or perhaps found, I saw little pride, little self-love. There were no haughty ones. Many were reading the Bible or helping each other. The children were standing or quietly sitting by their parent or parents. The feeling of the hall was orderly, warm, welcome. My ledger understood how and why God loved these souls so much, and why he commanded us to take care of them.

A sign on the smoke covered wall read:

NO ALCOHOL,
SPRAY PAINTS,
WEAPONS, OR
X-RATED BOOKS
JESUS IS LORD

I read the sign and thought of the signs in some restaurants that read, no shirt, no shoes, no service. I was led into an office off of the main hall and asked to wait until Sister Ruth could see me. I met Emily Richards who had been with the Jesus House since 1982. Emily's office reminded me of an old attorney's office I once visited to try to buy a piece of property he owned called Pilliod's Island. It was located in the middle of the Maumee River in Maumee, Ohio. The office was full of old books, some shelved, some stacked. An old chair peeked out from under forgotten retired things. On the floor in front of the chair slept a dog who had long since grown accustomed to strangers and the sounds of the gospel being preached and sung in the hall. Above was a loft with more old wooden school chairs piled and piled upon with stacks of yellow wool blankets and frames once used for something now forgotten. Through the sounds of the singing and the ringing of phones and the constant parade of people coming in and out with no real destination in mind, I heard Emily say she had left the Jesus House for a while but had returned because she had found no other place doing what was being done here.

Emily said the Jesus House was doing what the churches should be doing, taking care of the poor and homeless. She reminded me that Jesus was a street person, poor and humble. I thought of the magnificent multimillion-dollar churches I have seen in every city I had visited. The huge edifices seating thousands of Christians giving freely or otherwise, to pay the huge mortgage on the temple. I wondered what the total dollars of interest on the bricks and mortar would be, and how many people that huge sum would feed and house each day. I wondered how Jesus would view our choice of where and how we spend the funds given to God. My ledger seems to remember he said to the rich young ruler, "Sell all the things you have and distribute to the poor people, and you will have treasure in the heavens; and come to be my follower." I wondered how many people could have been fed from the $4,000 spent on the heated doghouse purchased by one of the popular television stewards of souls.

A young man ended my waiting: "Sister Ruth can see you now." I turned off my tape recorder with Emily's words and followed him down more halls filled with the standing and sitting and pacing poor. I thought how they were all locked in the waiting rooms of their mind awaiting deliverance from the pit of poverty. I remembered the sense of urgency that accompanied my own walking and pacing. I felt wherever it was I was going, I had a limited time in which to get there, wherever "there" was. I couldn't have recognized the "there" I was looking for if I found it, for it was never a place. It was a hug, a word of encouragement. It was a voice saying you are important to me. It was someone saying I need you. It was being productive, earning my way, having a purpose to be. I heard that voice. It said, "Noah, I'm Ruth. This is Betty."

Both Sister Ruth Wynne and Sister Betty Adams were dressed in bib overalls, they wore flannel shirts and blue bandannas tied like a hat on their heads. We talked for a few minutes, I told them what I was doing and what I hoped to accomplish with the book. Sister Ruth said they started the Jesus House concept in 1973. They had been working with a few artists at Shepherd Mall in Oklahoma City. Some friends of Ruth and Betty's opened a home called God's Crash House. It was originally opened to assist the flower children who were traveling around the country in the early 1970s. The house was closed by neighborhood complaint. A few of the kids who were involved opened another home with the promise of assistance from two ministers. In a short time the ministers had a disagreement with each other and left the young people to fend for themselves. Ruth and Betty went to see if they could help and as fate and fortune would have it, moved in. I asked Ruth if that was how she and Betty started the Jesus House. She quickly corrected me: "God started it, He just uses us."

She said a number of things began in 1973. The Jesus Movement began to replace the drug problem of some of the young people. Many of our military veterans came back to find themselves searching for the home they left. Some are still searching.

Some of the kids at the home went downtown to see if there might be someone they could help. Sister Ruth said, "They brought home our first alcoholic. He cooked and watched the house." Ruth and Betty and the young people worked to support the growing effort for a year or two until, as Ruth says, "It got out of hand and they could not do both things."

She said it was a faith ministry, they have never solicited funds, they just used what they had each day, but it's worked out. They moved five or six times in a short period because, as Ruth says, "It was not a popular thing to do at the time, until 1983, when the economy in Oklahoma hit bottom and it became the 'in' thing to help the homeless." She said very few people bothered or wanted to be bothered with the poor prior to '83, and that they had very little support.

In 1979, on the coldest day of the year while in a warehouse on 8th Street, the Jesus House was visited by the fire department, the police, the health department, and a television crew. The warehouse home was closed, and the 150 men were put out into the cold. Ruth said years later they learned that the owners of the warehouse had lost it in a poker game and the whole closing was contrived. She said they had a difficult time but were able to grow and, in 1983, began getting help because "people were becoming aware that this was not a handful of derelicts downtown, but more and more people becoming homeless all over the country."

I asked Ruth and Betty my most common question: How many homeless are there? The answer is usually the same. "No one really knows. Even the census will not reflect an accurate count." Betty said there were an estimated five thousand street people in Oklahoma City. The Jesus House feeds between four hundred and a thousand people a day. They have 12,165 people receiving food baskets twice a month. That is a long way from a small family of helpful souls with an alcoholic dishwasher, a group that once worked the dumpsters to find food enough for the hungry. God must have been very angry on that cold night in 1979. But He must giggle when He looks down on these two ladies in their bib overalls. He probably dresses just like that, clothed in love.

Ruth and Betty live with the souls they help. They draw no salary. They eat what everyone eats. They dress from the same clothes bag. Ruth said if anything happened to the Jesus House, she would probably be a bag lady on the street.

I asked if they had noticed an increase in the homeless. I was told the Jesus House had experienced a 35 percent increase per year for the last four years. A particularly disheartening statistic was the increase in homeless families. Dan Mercer, who oversees an annex of the program, said he had a family who came to get food in their Mercedes. They lived in the car. It was all they had left after losing everything. He said they see people from every economic background.

Christine Byrd, who has been with the Jesus House for several years, (recently appointed as homeless coordinator for Oklahoma City) told me she had been on the street with her children for about a year. She said she was certain she could not repeat the experience. She said people do not realize they are just a step away from being without a home. She remembers having to bathe at the bus station. She no longer takes for granted a bar of soap, a clean towel, a toothbrush or her own bathroom. She said, "We who had homes just automatically thought they would always be there." Christine was a victim of abuse at the hands of her husband. She had numerous beatings and resulting cuts and stitches, which can never repair or close the deeper underlying social problems causing the abuse. After having her throat cut, she left—against the advice of her friends. "Stay with him, he'll change. What are you going to do on the street?"

She said she was particularly in touch with the feelings of the children now. How glorious it was to have a clean pair of socks or new underwear. She said her heart broke for the children, who were already emotionally scarred.

I had realized as a child that children are cruel when they emulate the cruelty of their parents. I remember the laughter at my baggy pants, the shoes three sizes too big, the home haircuts, the being trapped in an unfair shell judged by tiny minds of superficial people. Those people who wore their quality on the outside, screaming, "Look at my importance, see the label on my clothes, look at my silver trinkets, my golden barometers of greatness, my position granted by birth, for even if you should somehow acquire the wealth required for elevated status, you can never earn the value of social birth!"

The poor child is shunned like the plague. He is condemned for life for nothing more than the offense of being poor. Is it the child's fault? Some new philosophy postulates that the child wishes to be where he or she is. It even goes so far as to suppose that everyone, regardless of condition, is exactly where he or she most wants to be. This may be true in the case of those who can afford to be where they wish, but I cannot buy the concept totally. Especially the concept that the small child starving in its mother's arms somehow has the power to change its surroundings and condition. However, the acceptance of the concept relieves the believer from the duty to help. For, in effect, everyone then is the physician that can heal himself. It was simpler and safer in this life before so many became gods.

Christine said it's like a war zone, the homeless and the poor coming in greater numbers every day. The growing numbers of young joining the ranks of the swelling army of homeless . . . the drugs, AIDS. She said, "It's a war and we're not ready for it. We're losing it. I really think we're losing it. Man, we are losing the war. We think we know our enemy but we don't have any idea. The enemy is coming from every angle. Even the ones who could help sometimes become the enemy. I really don't think we are going to win this one. I believe as a Christian I'll be all right, because He says I have the victory if I live in His Word. But I'm really worried about what's happening. Everyone's so materialistic. There's a church on every corner, but it doesn't mean a thing. A poor homeless soul has to find his way down here. If he knocks on the church's door, there's nobody home."

Sister Ruth echoed this thought. "The problem can start and end with the church. If the churches would adopt homeless poor families and stay with them until some change happened within the family unit, then some could be helped on their way. This would make way for the abuser and the mentally ill to be cared for. They have absolutely no business on the street. These people need long-term treatment and training. Some will never be rehabilitated."

Sister Ruth told me of the development of a school for the homeless. She asked if I had seen the TV account of the new school. I told her I had, but it seemed a bit far off. She said they did not wait for committees and such, if you have a good idea just jump in and get it done. I believe that is exactly what will happen.

She said when you get locked into committees and bureaucracy, nothing gets accomplished. When a person is hungry, he is hungry today. When she is cold, she is cold now. Ruth believes the private sector will have to help the homeless, that we cannot and perhaps should not depend on the government to solve the problem. The government moves too slowly by plan and bipartisan interest.

Somehow we have come to believe that the government, the Red Cross, and the United Way will take care of everything. We say that charity begins at home, but until our eyes are open and people realize that giving the responsibility to a large bureaucratic organization has obviously not solved the growing problem, until more people are willing to take a hands-on position with the poor and homeless, very little will be done. These people are literally bleeding to death; they need sutures, not Band-Aids.

"We hear so often from the churches that ours is a social gospel; they are into winning souls. If we are as we are told—spirit, soul, and body—we can not separate one from the other. If we do not provide the necessities for basic survival, what are we saving the soul from or for? If people are worried about where they will spend the night or what or where to eat, it does little good to say, 'Jesus loves you,' and then send them out. The poor person thinks, *If Jesus loves me, show me. Show me how He loves me. Otherwise I'm not going to be able to listen.* We can start by living the Scripture 'I was hungry and you fed Me' then the parable of the Good Samaritan and how he helped the needy one and said he would come back. He followed up. If every church just helped one poor or homeless person or family, we could clean up a great deal of this.

"We need to stick with the needy ones until they can take care of themselves, then move on to the next needy souls. It is not an impossibility; it can be done. It is a matter of catching the vision of what Jesus said to do and the benefit and the feeling of doing it. We cannot possibly comprehend that miracle—the spreading, growing goodness from one tiny act of kindness."

Sister Ruth said, "Tell them, Noah. Tell them they can do it. They can help; they can make a difference. They cannot always do it with the reasoning mind. We had a board member who always said, 'That isn't logical; that isn't reasonable.' I finally told him if I were reasonable and logical I wouldn't be here. We were past reason and logic. We've moved into faith, and that's when things get done. Logic bogs down the effort. We begin to be only what we think. This one is getting too much; that one is getting more. Logic moves to judgment, and judgment is not love. So if one fellow over here gets more than he should and doesn't share it, that's his problem between him and the Lord."

"Some people just cannot be down here at the mission in this problem, and that's all right, I understand that. This is not a pleasant place with the depression, the despair, the hopelessness, the hunger, the dirt, the disease. And for some it would be impossible to maintain their denial of all this if they had to come down here every week. But if they cannot add their hands and their hearts to the effort, they can help foot the bill. We cannot depend on government grants. Grants are not that easy to obtain, and you must have a person on staff to write and pursue the funding. You could spend *all* your time on funding and not be about our Father's business.

"We need to provide housing, but not the huge expensive projects that house people like rats. We have thousands of old homes that require repair. The Jesus House has about thirty old homes that we've renovated, but that is costly for us when we first try to feed hungry people. We must first feed and take care of the immediate needs of the poor and homeless, then teach

175

them to take care of themselves. You cannot just put them in a house with no job and no money and expect them to survive. Society will have to manufacture jobs—we need jobs. We also need transportation. We want to get a small garage somewhere and hire a mechanic who is unemployed and have him repair donated cars. This would provide transportation for some who could not go to work otherwise."

Ruth believes that if more of us became more spiritually involved, more accepting of the love message of the Christ, we would reduce the number of the homeless by half. This would then expose the alcohol and substance abusers and the mentally impaired to the needed long-term treatment they need. She said the street and the despair cause a portion of the mental and abuse problems, for some become mentally unbalanced simply in the course of the daily panic to survive. And some turn to alcohol and drugs to escape their plight. Survival takes all the time and energy of the poor, and soon it just seems easier to find a way out through chemical release because the distressed soul has come to believe there is no way out. Some of these people, given the opportunity to straighten out, will change. The Jesus House and many other efforts have success stories to support that belief. The Lord never says anyone is hopeless, but the individual must regain hope before he changes.

The Jesus Houses of the country would be good stewards of your financial assistance.

CHAPTER
EIGHTEEN

A Jubilee for Aaron

I swore when I began this project I would refrain from any and all conclusions until the book was completed. I did not do that. My attempted objectivity was tempered by my experience, pain, and anger. So it happens with all of us. Our experiences shape and reshape who we are and what we see. If they didn't, we would never grow, never risk, never fall in love, never learn, never really live. And although I have made and changed my conclusions a dozen times, one conclusion emerged as a constant: We cannot fix everything; or perhaps I should say we *will* not fix everything. Resolving our problems is sometimes a matter of ability; either it's possible for us to do it or not. Most of the time, however, ability is not the issue—desire is. "I can't take out the garbage now" means "I don't want to do it now because _____." Jesus was right; the poor and homeless will be with us always. But why? Because we can't address their needs, or because we won't? And if we won't why not?

We must have a plan. Otherwise, all the great compassion born at the first moment of our wanting to help can turn to frustrated, frenzied activity, not action. I know many compassionate and sensitive people would do more if they could be assured that the effort and money expended would go directly to the ones who need it. We have all seen the man or woman standing on the corner with a sign: "I will work for food." Some, I believe, mean it, but we have all read the accounts of some of these users who make as much as $175 a day. We have heard reports of our tax dollars being misdirected from the intended purpose, and in so doing, monies are stolen both from the taxpayer and the needy.

Recently one hundred million dollars was granted to a number of well-known hospitals in various cities around the country, for the purpose of establishing care for the mentally ill who are homeless and poor. The money, as reported by CNN, was diverted to the improvement of facilities for the benefit of those who are able to pay. CNN reported the building of swimming pools (at the cost of seven hundred thousand dollars) and other luxuries that will never be seen by the needy. In one case, the money was received but nothing ever done. The government never asked the hospitals to return the funds.

Caution needs no justification. But sometimes it is understandably mistaken for lack of concern. I recognized this after my first talk on the subject of homelessness at the Chapel Hill United Methodist Church in Oklahoma City. I truly do not remember what I said to the small study group. I do remember it was quite animated. Later that night after the meeting, I received a call from Jay Davis saying everyone was excited. Several people had heard about the talk and had stopped over at Jay and Ann's house to meet me. The church wanted to do something about the adopt-a-family idea that I had shared with them. They wanted me to set up a day for them to visit the Jesus House so they might find a needy family. They wanted to help, and they wanted to help now. They wanted me to write a manual now. It does seem to me as if we are living more and more in the want of others. I was only at the expanded outline point of the book. And this dyslexic writer can burn up the keyboard and pound it out at the unbelievable rate of about a page an hour. But I did not see how I could write a how-to manual. Yet if they were going to do this, they needed a guide or it would be mass confusion.

I had this vision of a basketball team running around bumping into each other, everybody on the team going through the motion of shooting, while everyone in the stands could see that the other team had the ball. Soon all the spectators were rolling in the aisles laughing. I was the ill-equipped coach without a clue. There was a good guide; I simply had not found it yet.

I tried to stall and told Jay that I was at an important point in the book and I would meet with him as soon as I could. He quickly reminded me that it was I who told them we need to do something now, not later, that people are hungry every day, not just when the cook feels like cooking. He said, "I know you have to finish the book, but use us to test the idea. If we are successful, use us as a model. If we're not, you can say so; but we are ready, willing, and excited." And they were. So I agreed to help.

It was raining on Saturday when Jay Davis, Larry Clements, and Jim Svetgoff met me at the Jesus House. The grassless yard in front of the old school building provided abundant mud for the footprints we left in the hall. The tracks seemed to exaggerate the embarrassment of the need for this place and others like it, and they followed us down the halls like reminders of the disrespectful stepping on the downtrodden. I noticed the embarrassment of my three guests for the mud they had tracked in and the sensitivity with which they regarded the feelings of those who had to and those who chose to be there. The muddy tracks soon became counterpoint in purpose and lost their contempt.

I had advised Sister Ruth of our intentions and she arranged a tour of the facility. We were met by Wesley, a young man who had come to the Jesus House with a drug problem and had stayed to be a part of the solution. He led us through the facility with frequent and appropriate Scripture. Pointing to the second floor he led us to where the women sleep or wait for whatever it is the lost wait for. In patience or submission the women sat on the row of cots and beds, surrounded and protected by the invisible walls of the mind, oblivious to our presence, or so it seemed. Each cot resembled a nest, containing a small pile of belongings, like eggs fiercely guarded the pile of things peeked from under pillows or rested on their laps. The scene was like some surrealistic painting void of color, as if even the companionship of color is withheld from the ones who most need it.

How many times have we heard or said, "There but for the grace of God go I?" The grace of God has nothing to do with it. In my ledger it is the greed and the selfishness of man, not the grace of God, that requires the building of warehouses for bent people and broken lives. God would have no one go here. But our sayings somehow elevate our position in the eyes of our self-made and controllable gods, and give some perverted permission for allowing this condition of homelessness to exist without effort to change it—as if God has some figure in mind, some percentage of mankind that must live a life of hopelessness, and chooses who will live out his or her life condemned. I cannot believe it is God who rewards the ones who steal the money targeted to help the poor. Where did He ever say if you follow Me I will give you country club memberships, new cars and huge homes? But my ledger believes that the crime of stealing from the poor will be punished. We have just begun to see the backlash to that action.

Wesley led us through the old school and over to the annex where a hundred or more people hid from the rain. In the annex is a stage where local bands and performers come to donate their talent to the ones who could not buy a radio even if it were only a buck and a half. Some people were sitting in the uneven rows of old wooden folding chairs, some standing or shuffling around waiting for the band to set up. This was a far cry from the gala event put on ten miles to the north for the debutantes that year. People were piled and stacked everywhere, and again the remarkable lack of color was vividly apparent. Brown and gray and faded blue is the color of the rainbow here. Though the rain freshened the air outside, it did not have the same effect inside. Dogs slept through it all, uncaring of the size of the bank account behind the hands feeding and stroking them. Here at the Jesus House even hungry homeless dogs are welcome. We then went back to the main building to meet with Sister Ruth and Sister Betty, who were busy feeding and stroking strays of another kind.

We met Aaron in the hallway outside the cafeteria, where we were to talk to Ruth and Betty. It was not the accidental meeting it appeared to be, for Ruth had decided the Starts were the family the church should assist. Aaron Start was twelve, the oldest of eight children. He was in special education classes at the fifth grade center and attended three days per week. The class is for children who have been unruly or have not attended school for the required amount of time to qualify for their normal grade-to-age placement. Ruth estimates the Starts had moved ten times in the last three years. It is difficult for a child to fight the battles necessary to establish acceptance or territory one time, let alone ten times. For all our assumed civilized evolution, we still, like the animal that will not leave the human in us, urinate on our private boundaries, and woe to the one who stumbles into our territory uninvited, either psychologically or physically.

Mr. Start worked at a computer company as a custodian. Aaron said his father used to walk the four miles to work, but now he had a bicycle. Ruth told us she had a special feeling for the Starts, as Mr. Start worked very hard to keep the family together and would work or do anything he could to ensure the family remained intact. We learned that Mr. Start could not read. An estimated one in five American adults cannot read. The term *illiterate* has always had a chilling effect, as if the person who wore the title somehow had a social disease. The fact is, illiteracy is a social disease—one of the most serious.

Ruth and Betty had arranged to have the Starts move into a house that had been donated to the Jesus House. Mr. Start was working and his job requirement was filled for the moment, but there were matters of transportation, furniture, phone service, and a few other items that would make the operation of the household smoother, like a washer and dryer, a refrigerator, and a heater or furnace. The church committee decided they would consider the Starts for their adopted family and would bring up the proposal at the next Sunday meeting.

The committee decided they wanted to meet the Starts. They had gotten a tip on a pickup truck that might be available from an attorney they knew. Further, some of the members of the church, who were accredited to teach remedial reading, wanted to teach Mr. Start to read. One of the committee members, Larry, said he would teach Mr. Start to run a press as soon as he

could read, which would enable him to get a job almost anywhere in the country. He could work at his new trade while he
learned. Another member of the Sunday school class wanted to
help the Starts with their tax return to ensure they were getting every benefit possible. Another who knew about nutrition
volunteered to help. Jim was concerned with Mrs. Start's not
having any free time away from the children, which spoke loudly
of his respect for his own wife and her needs. He was trying to
enlist help from some of the women to baby-sit or take Mrs.
Start out of the house for diversion. Another member knew of a
clothes dryer, and someone else wanted to plant grass in the
front yard of the Starts' house. Others in the group wanted to
tutor the children. Another was trying to get a swing set. We
arranged a meeting with the Starts.

The meeting was tentatively set for Wednesday night at 6:30.
We wanted to meet Mr. Start and assumed he would be home
from work by then. The Starts have no phone (which is a problem with many poor and homeless), so we were unable to con-
firm the meeting. Since we heard nothing from them, we did not
go. I called Betty the next morning to schedule a new time. She
told me the Starts had been expecting us, so we chose Saturday
at 1:00 as the time for our visit.

Only Jay and I went, which was probably best. We drove
down the street. Many empty, boarded-up houses lined each
side. Piles of trash and junk rested against the curbs and slept in
the yards. I thought of the offer to seed the yard; seed was not
the problem. We parked and walked up to the tired old porch
that was losing its grip on the house. There was an old, brown,
stand-up space heater leaning on the doorjamb, some boxes and
papers scattered around the porch, and a little black dog about
the size of a squirrel with anorexia, defending his food dish with
a bark that sounded like somebody stepping on one of those tiny,
yellow, squishy duck toys. Some windows were covered with old
sheets, some with newspaper, but there could not have been any
light getting in.

Mrs. Start answered the door and I thought we had awakened
her from a nap, then I realized her eyes were adjusting to the
sun. Maybe by staying in the dark we are never forced to see
where we are. Maybe for some the sun doesn't make things

brighter. Personally, I can't stand dark rooms with windows that won't open. It reminds me of an older person's home, where they now only look inward and live in the past. Mrs. Start stepped barefoot onto the porch and closed the door quickly behind her. We introduced ourselves and told her we came to see if we could help. Two of the children squeezed out the door and ran around the porch a few times. One checked the dog and gave it a look as if to say, "It's never going to be a real dog," then squeezed back into the darkness of the living room. Why do so many poor children seem to have liquid dirt running out of their noses? Somehow this was not what I expected.

I am not sure what I expected but this wasn't it. I wanted to holler, "Get the soap!" I wanted to move the junk off the porch. I wanted to paint the front of the house. I wanted to see the children shiny clean, all lined up by size, saying, "I'm going to be a doctor; I'm going to be a lawyer; I'm going to run my own business; I'm going to be a scientist." I guess I wanted to see some change—change in attitude, change in hygiene . . . change.

Jay asked if they needed any furniture. Betty said they needed beds. They had only one bed in the house. One bed for ten people. That's one that ten will not go into. She said they needed dressers for their clothing. I remembered they had been homeless, they probably needed everything—curtains, towels, sheets, everything.

Bill Start had an opportunity to work overtime, and so was unable to meet us. I asked Betty if Bill was able to read. She said he used to, but had been injured in a fall from a collapsing building in 1971, and that part of his memory was damaged. Three other men died in the accident. He had spent some time in the hospital as a result of the accident, but he was all right now, except for his memory.

We all seem to be products of our environment to some degree, and as such, our assumption of how things should be tends to color our acceptance of how they are. Jay and I left. He took me home, as I still had no car. The ride home was unusually quiet. When we went in to talk over what we had found, we were both quite disturbed. I told Jay this was bigger than I had realized. I had seen much of this on the street, but I had only seen it with my eyes, not with my heart. What could really be done to change the scars that years of poverty make? Even with a house and a car and a job, there are some living skills and social graces that, when lacking, will keep people from the mainstream of our society and, further, may keep some from receiving help because they will be judged to be beyond help. The tap root of poverty is centuries deep and will not be completely pulled out or destroyed by one act of kindness or one attempt to right a social wrong, it will take time and patience and understanding. The tap root of the condition of some poor, however, is growing in their own laziness.

All of the homeless did not grow up in poverty. Many are broke, not poor; when helped, these will respond to society's values more rapidly. We must be appalled at the level of life of some of our brothers, but we must love them enough to overlook their lack of social graces. We must also teach them in a compassionate way, if they are willing.

I remember a friend telling us of the time he volunteered to assist a group that was replacing screens on some shack houses in the South. He said they worked all day screening in porches so the flies would not be in the houses. He and the group were exhausted when they finished and returned to their vans for the night, but they all felt a great sense of accomplishment. The next day, when they returned to work on the remaining porches, they found the previous day's work destroyed. The screens on most of the homes were already torn out in at least one place. It seems the people were used to throwing their dirty water and garbage out the door and off the porch. The screens hampered their habit, so they just kicked them out. The group left without finishing the job and did not return. Some of them quit the volunteer group and are bitter to this day.

We cannot help everyone. Nor can we expect those we help to act as if they lived in Beverly Hills before their misfortune. But we still have the obligation to help all to the extent they can be helped, without judging or imposing our standards on them. Some will choose flies over screens; flies are free, effort and screens are not.

We must also remember that the gift of our help is to be given freely. That means we may never get a thank you or see the response we expect. The gift should be used as the recipient chooses. We must also remember, I must remember, that helping people is a requirement of my belief—the gift is for my benefit. The steward of that gift is the receiver, and it is up to him to use it wisely. However, I have found that giving is sometimes best by contract so that both sides will know what to expect. The contract may contain conditions or be void of them.

We finally met Bill Start two weeks later when the committee delivered four beds, a dresser, and a large television set. Someone once said, "Where you stand is where you sit." How true that is, for while we sat in the car on the way to the Starts', it was apparent where we stood. We still had a disabling doubt that the help we were trying to give was doing any good at all. It seemed to be less than a Band-Aid on an amputation. It was as if emotion had visited a month ago, and she was now disappearing over the horizon. The feeling she inspired was disappearing with her. Honesty in a person is always refreshing or frightening, and being with Jay, Larry, and Jim was like sitting in a sea breeze, yet feeling a storm was about to blow the beach and the beauty and the comfort and safety away. The job of any cheerleader is to keep the fans in the stands cheering even when their team is down by fifty points. It appeared we were down. Jim said he was discouraged and wondered whether we had selected the right family to help. His commitment was not waning, he only wanted to help someone who could and would be bettered by the effort.

I shared some of my personal battle with the problem and how I justified what we were doing, and Jay repeated some of our earlier discussions as to what our responsibility was and the need to drop the judgment. None of us wanted to judge, but we all, without exception, wanted to optimize our effort. We simply wanted to see some evidence that we were actually making life a little easier for someone. So many are willing to help when they can see results.

When we pulled up to the house, several of the children were playing in the yard. One hollered, "Mom, some people are here!" Another small boy with his pants unbuttoned at the waist ran around the back to get his father. Bill was a slight man with a kind face and a swollen and bleeding thumb. He told us he was building rabbit pens and had just delivered a misdirected hammer shot to the thumb instead of the nail.

We untied the ropes holding the mattresses and suddenly had eighteen extra hands helping. We were all taken with the children. They were enthusiastic, animated, smiling, outgoing, and totally full of joy. They were also amazingly well behaved. This was a family that, while lacking what most of us determine as the better things in life, seemed to possess the most valuable of all commodities: love and respect. They worked with the precision of an ant colony, even the smallest of the children helped carry the beds into the front room without complaint, then rode back to the trailer on the arms of Larry, Jim, and Jay. The trailer was emptied in a flash, and Aaron rolled up the ropes and handed them to me.

Bill showed us the two rabbits that would soon do what rabbits do best, and thereby subsidize the Starts' protein requirement. We asked Bill if he needed anything else. He said they needed a heater; the floor furnace had been removed. We noticed they had been using a tiny, unventilated space heater to heat the whole house. There were no complaints, no whining, no tears, no sadness, just overwhelming gratitude and smiles.

Emotion had returned from the horizon and was leaning on the car smiling as we crawled in to leave. I am sure now that she had been watching the whole event. Hearts were melted and refined there that afternoon, and perspective surfaced to be skimmed off and made into tiny mental medallions that we would wear the rest of our lives. That Saturday the genuine wish of three special people, that they find someone who could and would be helped, was filled. And eight beautiful little children would sleep that night on a bed, instead of a pile of clothing on the floor. A Band-Aid? Perhaps in the whole scheme of things, but a heart transplant to this writer.

The Starts will not be abandoned without cause by the church committee, Jay, Jim, and Larry. I have a feeling those helping hands hold much more for the Starts, and I am just as sure that the proud man with the swollen finger will continue to do all he can to raise his family in love and dedication. And perhaps, just perhaps, there will be a Jubilee for Aaron and for all the Starts.

In Washington D.C., at Calworth Parkside, a program to purchase apartments by the poor has been established. The most interesting program they have initiated is an orientation class, which is mandatory for prospective owners. The class covers home ownership, maintenance of the unit, and the social practices that ensure the value of the property through keeping the project clean and in good repair.

The above was an excerpt from an article in a Washington, D.C., newspaper. I purchased and read newspapers from all parts of the country to determine what was being said and done about the homeless. I missed the importance of the above article. It was the notice that an orientation class was mandatory for prospective buyers. People must know what is expected of them. Further they must know how to meet that expectation. That contract of understanding between the Starts and their helping hands would have been more than helpful in this effort.

I thought the story of Aaron and his family would end with the wish for a Jubilee for Aaron. It appeared that that was going to happen. But life just doesn't seem to be that simple. Just before the finish of this book, Jay gave me a letter he had received from a member of the committee. It appeared the grip on the Starts was loosening and they were slipping away.

I had not intended to print this letter, but my ledger says that not to report everything as it is, is to report nothing as it is. So here is the letter:

Jay,

How are things in the Motor City? Do you live next door to the Supremes or Lee Iacocca? Things are going well for us but we are busy. Friends from Malaysia stayed with us over the weekend and we had a great time. I'm teaching the next two weeks in Sunday school. The subject is abortion. It ought to be an interesting experience. I have no idea about the type of reception I will get. Pray for me that it goes well.

We've been back to the Start family several times since you left. Bill lost his job. One of the boys got hit in the head with a brick and needed stitches. Aaron and several of the other boys now have Mohawk hair cuts.

The Bible school class gathered clothes and food as a

187

project. About two-thirds of the clothes (most were very nice) were given to the Starts. The kids were glad to have the clothes, especially the girls. The Sunday after we gave the kids the clothes, they all attended Sunday school. Maybe the nice clothes made a difference. Reba John was in charge of the Bible school program and it was she who decided to give them the clothing. She also went with us to deliver it. Mrs. Start was happy to see a female face for a change. Anyway, Reba deserves a lot of credit.

Wiley Walker donated a refrigerator to the family. Larry and I will deliver it to them tonight. Will Harms is going to give eye tests to the whole family Saturday morning. We're making some progress with the Starts, but I hope to see them make some basic changes in their lives also, especially cleanliness. When I was there last night I got into the kitchen. It was the foulest room I have ever seen. The class took up a collection to buy cleaning supplies two weeks ago. Carol and I went to "Sam's" last night and bought $145 worth of cleaning supplies. We'll deliver them tonight.

I'll keep you posted on how we are doing in OKC. Let us know how life in Detroit is treating you. . . .

P.S. Either Brandy or Anita Start drew this picture for you. Your name is on the back.

You asked for a list of contributors to the Starts; it's enclosed. If you still want to write "thank you" notes let me know, I'll send half of them.

It is imperative to understand what motivates people to donate their money, resources, and time to help other people. It is also imperative to understand what circumstances and conditions cause some to stop that assistance. Both the giver and the receiver have a special duty to the gift.

A gift of a meal to a hungry person may not inspire a show of appreciation on the part of the one fed. The giver, however, in that same act, may feel his gift to be too modest and therefore apologize for its value. A gift of a meal most often requires only the eating. A gift of commitment to the healing and helping of an individual or family requires more. It requires commitment and effort on the part of the one or ones being helped. It requires that the ones being helped work at least as hard to get out and stay out of their problem as the ones who are helping them. As the number of poor and homeless grow, so will the competition between the needy ones for the assistance, for it will undoubtedly be given to the ones who are willing to work the hardest.

To ask parents to wash themselves and their children is not unreasonable. Showing respect for the gifts of food and clothing by taking the best care possible and using them to the fullest without waste is little payment on the part of the receiver.

This conclusion I made and changed and changed again. The gift of unconditional love has nothing to do with conditional giving. One can love unconditionally and still give conditionally. A giver has the right to say she will give no more to someone who wastes the gift that she has worked hard to afford to give. That condition should be mutually understood early in the giving process.

My ledger says: I can give food; a person can eat it. I can give space; a person can require it. I can give love; a person can do what he or she will with it. I gave it; I have more. However, I cannot give change; a person must make it.

I met one last time with the committee helping the Starts. We met at my apartment and I recorded the conversation. The committee was confused and struggling with the definition of duty—duty to themselves and their own families and duty to others in need. They were frustrated, saddened, and tired, but they didn't want to quit. The very best way to say what was said is how it was said. Please refrain from any judgment until the end; then, if you must, toss a stone.

CHAPTER
NINETEEN

The Meeting

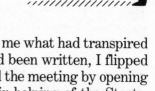

Jay, Jim, and Larry were anxious to tell me what had transpired with the Starts. Although the story had been written, I flipped on the recorder. I'm glad I did. I started the meeting by opening where I had left the committee in their helping of the Starts. The last I had heard was that the Starts had no car again.

Jim explained that it was a truck. "Bill needed a way to transport all the family at once so he traded his truck for a van. The truck was running; the van wasn't. The van had not been licensed since 1985. The man totaled the truck before they transferred the titles, so now legally, Start owns a totalled out truck and the man owns a van that Mr. Start still owes some money on. The van is in the front yard, and the Starts have no transportation."

Jay mentioned the Pinto that had been in the front yard. Larry said the car never had run, and it had been repossessed. He could not understand who would have financed it. The following is a common problem in the transportation requirements of the poor.

Jim: Who would even want to repossess it?
Noah: It was probably one of those half down lots where you pay half down and a hundred a month on a twelve dollar car. How are the children doing?

We talked more about the difficulties of getting and paying for insurance and repairs on cars that are ready to be pressed into steel cakes. I asked about Aaron. The three were quiet for a moment. Then Jim asked, "Who wants to tell him?"

Jay: Well, Aaron's been in some trouble.
Noah: What flavor of trouble?
Jay: Running around the wrong crowd at night. Getting in trouble in school. When we were over there the other day, he had been expelled from school.

We began the discussion about Aaron's problems and Larry mentioned that Betty had left the house and the family. I was interested to know whether Aaron's attitude was a result of his mother's leaving.

Jim: No, I don't believe that had much to do with it. I talked to his teachers yesterday. They said he had a file an inch thick, from different schools, on the trouble he had caused.
Noah: How does the trouble manifest itself, did the teacher share that with you?
Jim: No. We all think . . . oh, they did say he cusses the teachers out to their faces for one thing. He seems to be an agitator, "disruptive in class" were her words. He has cafeteria duty basically every day because he acts up in the cafeteria. Then the cafeteria duty makes him late for his next class which is a P.E. class. He told me last night it's no big deal. He . . .
Jay: How did he do last night?
Jim: Good, perfect, like always. Pleasant, well-mannered.
Noah: Seems to be a huge difference between what he shows us and the report we get from school.

191

Jim: What he is around us, that's exactly right. The boy knows right from wrong, and he has values and manners. He can act as nice as he wants to.

The following part of the conversation will indicate how involved the committee had been with Aaron and his school. This effort to help had become complete in its coverage.

Jay: Do you think he just knows how to get what he wants?
Larry: I think that is a large part of it. He knows what we want to hear. He knows how to treat us when we go around there. He seems innocent and I want to believe him. I really want to believe in him, that he's trying hard but I think the boy can lie to you just as easily as he can tell you the truth. Do you agree?

Jim and Jay both agreed and I asked if they had ever caught Aaron in a lie. Jim thought that either Aaron was lying or his teacher was and he trusted the teacher. I noted the "no big deal" comment indicated that Aaron placed little value on the school experience. I wondered if the other children in his class were in the same social place Aaron was.

Jim: I don't think so. He's going to _____ Middle School. Aaron said there were about seven white students in the school. I believe there are more than that. I believe the school has regular classes, and then they have the emotionally disturbed program which has different class schedules. He is scheduled to go to school half a day, three days a week, because he's too disruptive to go any longer than that. I guess his attention span has something to do with that. Going to _____, however, disallows him to have that schedule because they have no transportation in the middle of the day. So, he goes to school two full days a week.
Jay: What does he do the other three days?
Jim: He goofs off!
Jay: He's not in school the other three days?
Jim: No . . . no . . . nothing, when I talked to his teacher yesterday , I told her he needs more school, not less. She said he can't be here, he's too disruptive. He's too much of a troublemaker. A

half day, three days a week might be too much, she seemed to think. He's just evidently a problem she or the school is not prepared to deal with.

I agreed that he obviously had a problem. He did not fit. I had noticed he dialogued far better with adults than he did with children. He did not fit within the "normal" school format. We cannot blame the teacher, she did what her ability, grace and job description allowed. And when Aaron came to her with a folder an inch thick, the folder, to some degree, set her opinion of possibility. And further, when he took a bite out of her authority by cussing her in public, she had to make some example so as to not lose complete control of the class.

I told them I thought what they were experiencing was the frustration of a system built for the norm, whatever that is. The system is ill-equipped to handle problems with efficiency and total fairness. What Aaron was experiencing in school he was also experiencing in his family life of homelessness.

I reminded the committee that Aaron and his family had moved ten times in eight years. If we thought for one minute that the teacher is frustrated, how about Aaron? Does a twelve year old have the right to feel frustrated with a system that would make him totally responsible to change his square shape to fit the roundness of society's. Aaron has been the new kid with no territory. It seemed reasonable to me that he would have a problem with discipline. What wasn't reasonable is that he has not had more severe problems. I postulated that if something was not changed in Aaron's life, we may one day read about the boy with the beautiful name who climbed a bell tower to spray the regular people with his frustration.

Our educational system is too rigid. Children are silently encouraged by the inaudible whisper of their difference to be different, yet they are allowed little room in the box of our educational sameness to grow to the shape of their difference. Any system that cannot or will not teach to the interest of the individual becomes a system that rejects or is intolerant to the true individual. At least until and if that individual attains sufficient stature either financially or socially and becomes elevated to the posture of the eccentric. Aaron, too small in both deed and size for the eccentric label, is just another problem that society will either change or dispose of. Maybe we live in an educational climate that makes no provision for the Aarons in our population, and simply finds it easier to one day inventory them on the welfare or homeless rolls.

We discussed the various rolls of the committee, Aaron, his parents, the school and the other children. The frustration was building in the room. As I mentioned I had not been involved with the Starts for at least two months. So much had happened to and for the Starts and with the helping hands. Counter pressures grew and pressed reason and patience out of shape. This happened not only with those helping but with the Starts.

Jim thought the number one problem was that Aaron would have a huge impact on his brothers and sisters. Jay agreed, and said if Aaron were to get into trouble, how he treated it or how he was treated would have some great impact on the other children.

I saw an additional problem. If Aaron caused too much difficulty for the school's tolerance, or if he got into extracurricular difficulty, the DHS might investigate and separate the family. If the teacher reported an additional behavior problem and attributed it to the mother's leaving, the DHS might not have a choice.

We can understand how the authorities would view a family of eight children whose mother chose leaving over cleaning up, and a father who could not leave the family to work. The DHS could make the Starts wards of the court. I imagined what that would do to Bill Start.

Jim: That's why he's fighting so hard to maintain the family right now. That's his sole purpose in life right now, to keep his family together.

Jim: Aaron's teachers told me he was a smart boy.

Jay: He just isn't being challenged in school.

Jim: Yes, but after talking to him last night, I think he feels he is in a situation where the number one goal is to survive. He goes to that school and those kids beat him up constantly. He may be wetting all over the floor, but it's just to hold them off a little bit. There's no territory there for Aaron Start. I asked if he was afraid to go to the rest room because he was afraid he would be beaten up.

194

He said no, they beat him up in front of the principal's office. They put a sign on his locker saying, "If you open this locker, we're going to lock you in it."

Noah: Are the teachers or his counselors aware of this?

Jim: I don't know, there isn't much they can do anyway. They can't be everywhere, and Aaron is afraid to tell on the ones torturing him.

Larry: He can't fight it.

Jim: He's just in a real bad environment and it's not going to get better at that school.

Jay: He isn't equipped to fight it.

Jim: He's doing what he can to survive at school, and an education isn't even a consideration right now.

Larry: He's just interested in his basic needs.

Jay: That boils down to what we started off with. It's time to provide that basic secure home life.

I wondered if that were possible. I wondered if we could provide anyone with a basic secure anything. First, what is the definition of *basic?* It is basically different. We could not provide for the Starts the same start any of us had in life. The basic secure home life is vastly different between the poor and those who are basically secure. That is a part of the great frustration in helping. The distance between life-styles of the poor and those who are more comfortable must be measured in more than the miles separating them.

Jim: Even a secure home life would dissipate once he got to school.

Jay: Yes, but if he had a secure home life, he wouldn't have to go to there.

Jim: Shirley checked into changing schools. He can't.

Larry: Why is that?

Jim: I don't know if it's because of the special ed class or where he lives. There must be a middle school closer.

Jay: Would Aaron be interested in going voluntarily into a foster home?

Jim: I doubt if he would.

Jay: Why?

Jim: Why? Because he probably thinks he needs to stay home and help his dad.

Larry: His dad needs all the help he can get right now.

Jim: He's doing it. I mean he's helping. He's staying right in there and helping. He told me last night he doesn't like to. He wishes his mother would come back so he could run around with his friends.

Jim: Except she doesn't do anything for him when she's home.

Noah: Well, if she did nothing more than be there to unlock the door so the kids could come in, it would be better than having no mother at home.

Larry: My wife called the Methodist Boys' Home, thinking that might be an alternative to the situation. They said he fits all of the qualifications to go to a place like that. All that would have to be done is the paperwork. But it's a long way from here, and at this point I don't think Bill would agree to the idea. Three weeks ago when Aaron ran off, Bill told me he was ready to put him somewhere. He was just worn down. He couldn't stand the thought of going out one night looking for Aaron and finding him in one of the vacant houses, dead or with the crack users. He thought there was the chance of getting shot or stabbed himself. He could not leave the other children to look for Aaron, and at that point wanted to put him anywhere he would be safe. But right now, with the mother being gone, I don't feel he thinks he can let him go.

Jay: Thank God we have so many people involved now. These guys could not do it alone anymore.

I did not know what had precipitated Betty's leaving the family. Everything seemed all right when I last saw them. I asked how that had happened. I raised the question earlier "What is the definition of basic secure home life?" For most of us it begins with a clean environment. Jim opened his hands palms up, as if he were delivering a plateful of story. And he did. It was a smorgasbord of different tastes and diets in life-style that provide some of the distance between our understanding of each other.

Jim: Well, we got a hundred-dollar donation from another Sunday school class, and I went up to thank them. I gave them a little background on the Starts and told them the condition of the Starts' house. One of the gentlemen volunteered to come out and exterminate the place. Anyway, he came out a week ago yesterday to tell them what to do so he could exterminate. He told them to remove the dishes and take the food out of the cupboards and off the shelves. He told them if the house was not maintained in a better fashion, his work would not help. Well, that made Betty mad because he insulted her housekeeping. Bill agreed with the exterminator and told Betty she would have to start cleaning the house. So here they both were ganging up on Betty to clean. Bill had been after Betty for a long time because if Welfare came and saw the house in that condition again, the kids would be gone. Well, that was Tuesday and she left Wednesday.

Noah: Where did she go, and how did she get there?

Jim: She was from out-of-state, but she had some relative here and we assume she went there.

Noah: She hasn't tried to see the children or talk to Bill?

Jim: No. Aaron told me he went over to the house where they think she's staying. The lady wouldn't let him upstairs.

Noah: Did he ride his bike all the way down there?

Larry: He doesn't have the bike anymore, he walked.

Noah: But that's miles from the house.

Jim: Yes, but I think they pawned the bike.

Larry: Noah, so much has been going on here since you were here last it's hard to believe this keeps happening. Jim and I found out they needed a refrigerator.

It hadn't been that long or it did not seem that long. But that is a point I have tried to make. It wasn't that long ago in my life. It was a lifetime in the Starts' life. It seemed only moments before we had taken pictures of the Starts with their new bedding, shortly after that I heard one of the children stepped on a nail. Then I heard Bill lost his job, and that's why we were meeting to bring me up to speed. They were about to get to a distasteful part of the updating. Time gets loose from all of us no matter how we grip it, the sequence of things and events become tangled in frustration's knot. The events relayed below are at times out of sync, but then we all are at times.

Jim: We are a little out of sequence here. The refrigerator was before the Bible school stuff with the exterminator.

Larry: It doesn't matter much what was first, but the Sunday school class gathered a bunch of things and took it over there, Reba, Jim, and myself, and they were all pretty excited about it. Then came the eye exams. Will, a member of the Sunday school class is an ophthalmologist and he volunteered to give the Starts free eye exams. It took Will all Saturday morning to do that. He examined everyone from Bill on down to the smallest one. I took the Starts over to Midwest City for the exams. Then Will arranged to get the Starts the glasses they needed. Aaron needed glasses, but he did not want them. So we got glasses for Bill and Betty and Paul and Anita.

Jay: Neither Bill or Paul were wearing glasses the other day when I was over there.

Larry: Paul wears his most of the time but Bill doesn't too often. I think he is afraid of breaking them.

Jay: I thought Paul was the four year old.

Noah: Paul's the one who doesn't like to zip his pants.

Jim: No, that's Randall.

Larry: So, anyway after the eye exam we asked them if there was anything they absolutely needed. They said they needed a refrigerator. They thought that would help. So, Wiley Walker at our church had this great big side-by-side really nice refrigerator. It had the water dispenser in the door, it was in excellent shape. We took it over. That was the first time we really realized how much the house needed cleaning.

Now we were getting to what separates men from boys and men from mice and mice from man. Mice are not always careful what drops in their nest; some men are, some are not.

Jim: I went in to measure the space so we would be sure to have enough room. I was appalled. I told Larry about it but I didn't think he believed me.

Larry: I'll tell you what. I believed him, but I wasn't ready. My mother was a caseworker in Missouri when I was a kid. I thought I was in some dirty houses but I've never seen anything like this. I was not prepared for this at all. I went in to double-check the space we had since we had to dismantle the thing to get it through the door. We had to take the front doors off to get it in. So, we took the doors off on the front porch. Sitting on the front porch the smell of the urine was bad from the kids using the front porch for a toilet.

Jim: I didn't think it could get any worse, but it went down hill from there.

Larry: We got back in the kitchen, and we realized we were going to have to go buy a wrench because we did not bring enough tools. I told Betty to go back and clean the floor for a spot to put the refrigerator in. When we got back she was sitting in the same chair; she hadn't moved. I asked her if she had taken care of it. She said she had sent one of the girls in to do it. When I went back to look, I could not tell anything had been cleaned.

Jim: Here we are with a thousand dollar refrigerator and she would not even clean a place to put it. I'm getting mad just thinking about it.

Larry: So, we got the doors off and we had to go back in the kitchen to move the other refrigerator out of the way. About a hundred roaches took off, just going nuts trying to get away. Then I asked one of the girls for a broom to sweep the spot out. There was quite an accumulation of food on the floor that had been thrown or swept there.

Jim: We're talking smashed tomatoes that had turned black.

Larry: So we shoved the refrigerator out of the way. It wouldn't sweep. Some of it would, most of it would not. We had to scrape the stuff off the floor.

Jim: The kids were smashing cockroaches with their bare feet. They were walking in all this stuff.

Larry: Then I got ready to put the doors back on, and I offered to let Jim do it. I told him to lie on the floor to put the screws back in the bottom of the door. He didn't like the idea, but I told him I just couldn't get down on this floor. He couldn't either, so I got this tarp from the back of the truck to lie on. The only time Betty got up was when I had a paper tag on the back window of the truck and a bug got caught between the tag and the window. The kids noticed it and Betty went to see it.

Jim: She got out of her chair to look at that dead bug in his rear window. She would not move to help get a thousand-dollar refrigerator into the kitchen.

Larry: So what should have been a thirty-minute visit became a two-hour marathon.

Jim: We left after ten o'clock.

Larry: But that was when we first found out what the living conditions really were for the kids.

Jim: It was the week before all that when Reba went with us and suggested we put an advertisement in the church paper for a refrigerator. It got in the paper, Wiley saw it and donated this refrigerator. So, I'm telling you, Noah, we had some people who wanted to do something. It was a positive feeling.

Larry: The ad did run asking for donations of one type or another. The Trinity class donated one hundred dollars to go to whatever we wanted it to go to. Whether it was shoes for the kids or paint for the house it did not matter. We were starting to get some people involved. Up until then it was just the four of us.

I have noticed that people who really help, those in the trenches of the homeless problem, are slow to take credit and quick to give it. Helping is one of the best forms of virus we ever catch, and it is very contagious.

Jim: I think it is important to mention that Reba organized a clothing drive and a food drive for another cause but wound up giving two-thirds to the Starts. It came at the most opportune time because Betty had run out of food stamps and was not to receive more until the next week. We pulled up with boxes of food, and that was one of the times Betty seemed grateful to me. Also the clothing was really nice. The ladies checked the sizes the Sunday before and took it over there. I don't think it was an accident that, after they got some nice clothes, the next Sunday they went to church.

This was the first time I had heard anyone mention that the Starts had been to church together. I asked if everyone that had been helping had the opportunity to meet the Starts. The answer was interesting in that there were even more hands helping the Starts. Jim told me that the Starts did not go to their church. They went to Del City Baptist. Del City had a bus and the children continued to go there. The church sent the bus every week. Jim thought that was truly fine that the Baptist church would come to get the children every week. He said he was going to call and tell them so.

Jay: How did the Baptist church hear about the Starts?

Jim: Either Ruth or Betty at the Jesus house set them up with some people from there. Buddy, when you run a bus that far for people you know can't put a penny in the pot, you know their heart's in the right place.

Noah: You're not telling me there's some move to merge the Baptist and the Methodist Church are you?

Jim: No, but they must be fine people, and we're thankful for them.

Perhaps only in the effort to assist the needy would the churches grow closer together. Perhaps if enough needy were assisted, the churches would become one again. Perhaps not.

Larry: Okay, let's see where we are. After the refrigerator . . .

Jim: Wait a minute. I want to make some comments. Larry and I were not going to go back after that night with the dirt. We were washing our hands of the whole thing. But, we had been set up to go to Will's for the eye exams that Saturday morning. So we were going to make that final commitment and never see them again. That was my feeling. I was sick and tired of all that.

Noah: I can appreciate that.

Jim: But Saturday morning Larry and I pulled up. Will was sitting in his van. And, it was like . . . it seemed that they were plotting against us. All these little kids pop out—they just had a bath, their hair was washed. They were wearing the clothes we had given them. And even Betty and Bill were all spiffed up. The kids were just loving on us, and hugging on us and talking to us all at once. The difference was this time they were all clean and like our own. We just melted and things were A-okay again.

Larry: The first special collection our class took was one hundred and forty-five bucks. It was a spur of the moment deal.

Jim: Carol and I bought cleaning supplies. I'm talking indus-trial size and strength stuff. We took it down with the fridge. And that Saturday when we arrived, there were garbage bags of stuff at the curb. We felt better about doing it. We understand from the kids that Bill threw a bunch of trash away. Let's see, what was the next thing that happened? Oh yes, Larry, you and Shirley and Be-verly went down there. Shirley is a reading specialist and teaches at Casady. She was interested in trying to get the kids up to speed in school.

Larry: Yes, it was hard to tell her that it may not be possible in the few short weeks before school started. They needed a lot of work. The first week we got crossed up on our time. She was wait-ing one place and I was at another. The next week I picked her up and we went to the Starts'. She took a pile of test papers and books to get some idea where the various children were in their education, alphabet identification, numerical knowledge, etc. Randall, what grade should he be in?

Jim: He's not that old. I think he would be in the second grade.

Larry: I think he's eight. He tested in the first grade special ed group. I don't think he could go past E in the alphabet and could not count to ten. She tested the other kids. The girls seemed to be fairly good, they were behind, but with hard work they could catch up. Aaron was farther behind than he should be and Paul was behind. So she realized they all needed a lot of work. She decided she would find a few volunteers to come every other weekend to tutor the children. She was surprised by how far behind they were. She expected a better response. We spent three or four hours down there that morning. I made a mistake and wore white pants that morning. We did what we could in the time frame. The chil-dren were tested on the front porch, you couldn't really spend any time in the house, you know. It was much more pleasant on the porch. She came back and talked to the class about what she needed, and got a few more people involved.

Jim: That was on a Saturday and school was still out. Then on Monday, Shirley, Carol, and Lisa went down there.

Jay: Sounds like everyone was getting involved.

Larry: You bet.

Larry: Anyhow, they wanted to establish a rapport with the chil-dren and read to them and spent some time down there. A day or so later David Schuller and I—he's our youth director—went down there. Shirley had been down there and saw what terrible condition the house was in. The youth group from church had just gotten back from Arizona and New Mexico where they were cleaning up and painting up the houses for the poor. Shirley's daughter had been with the group so she suggested that the youth group paint the Start's house. Her daughter, I believe, went down there and helped with the reading and the baby-sitting. So, we went down there and talked to them about painting the house. Of course, the Jesus House owns the place. At the same time, Dave and I mentioned that we would like to have the family come up to the church Sunday afternoon for a tutoring lesson. A couple of days later I went back to see if we could take the kids to the zoo just to get them out of there while the house was being painted. Bill said okay.

Noah: Was Betty gone at this time?

Larry: No, she was still home. So Bill said all right. He thought I was going to be on the trip, but I did not make it. We got some other people to do it. At that time we had two new people enter into the show, Rick and Jenny. Up until this time they were not involved but when we asked for help in class, they were the only ones who volunteered for zoo duty. I think it was Jenny's idea, but we met them down there. That was all it took to hook Rick; He's been extremely active ever since. He's concerned and he's been down there many times. Well, they only got part of the house painted.

Noah: Inside or out?

Larry: Outside, these were the teenagers in the youth group. Is that the time I went down there with the stuff?

Larry: Evidently, before you went back, Carol and Lisa went down and talked to Betty to answer specific questions she might have and to talk to her about home hygiene and health needs. They promised the children new shoes if they would bathe for school. Also, they found out from Betty that the washer would not fill with water anymore. The sink in the kitchen had no hot water and the lavatory in the bathroom would not drain properly. We had been going down there for two months and did not know any of that.

Jay: They had never mentioned any of that.

Larry: No, it was like pulling teeth to get anything out of them as far as what they needed. They seemed to need everything.

Jim: You had to ask specific questions.

Larry: If you asked, "What do you need?" they would say, "Whatever you want to do or bring." So we found out the drains and the plumbing were not working right. So we decided to take some Drano down there and open the drains. The drain in the bathroom was stopped up. The drain in the kitchen and the one in the tub were not clear. The washing machine drain was clogged. So I told Bill what I had and he took me back to the bathroom first. I opened it up and Bill said, "Don't pour it down there, it doesn't drain right." I said I knew that, that's why we were going to open the drain. He said, "No you don't understand. It's not hooked up right." So he showed me where the drain pipe was not soldered into the hole in the wall where it should have been, so the water just ran on the floor. I asked about the toilet, he said it was fine. So I poured some into the bath tub then we went to the kitchen. He said the sink drain was all right but go ahead and pour some anyway, so I poured the rest of the bottle down there. I opened the next bottle and told Bill I was going to pour it down the washing machine drain. He said it drains, but it drains under the house. It was not hooked into the sewer lines. He showed me the hot water side just barely trickles. It had some water pressure but it was just plugged up. So the next day at Sunday school we talked about it. Jenny said she had a plumber that owed her some money and she would send him out. It took him a couple of days to get there, but his report said all the plumbing needed to be replaced under the house and it would cost two thousand dollars. The sewer line was all right. The bathtub was draining under the house and the washing machine was draining under the house. The lines had been patched so many times, they were not worth patching anymore.

Jim: He said it would cost two thousand dollars, but he did not want to do the job.

Noah: What did you feel you needed to do at this time?

Jim: Well, we didn't know if we would need a quarter of a million or what for this project. You know, we are not a big money group. So we started having meetings at the church, there were five or six of us.

The three were sitting back now and I wondered if we were settled in for the night. I wanted to get back to my writing but I could not believe all the effort and time these people were devoting to the Start family. And the numbers of those that were helping was a pleasant surprise. This was sounding much like an audible Rube Goldburg cartoon. I could not ask them to leave or hurry up. I had a feeling that this was leading up to bad news. I was wrong. It was leading to bad news then worse news.

Larry: There were so many things going on. It was like a bad soap opera. There is so much to do, it's so big and the needs so many, and it never quits.

Jay: Just take a bite at a time.

Jim: We're going to give you some bites. It sure is good to have you back from Detroit.

Noah: The Father must be very happy with you guys. He must giggle at your frustration and smile at your effort.

Jim: Larry and Carol and Cindy picked the kids up and took them down to get new shoes and socks.

Larry: All but Aaron, we could not find him. That was the weekend he took off. Bill was just beside himself. He took off Saturday afternoon and was gone all night. I was there about 3:00 on Sunday and he wasn't home yet. Bill was pretty sure he knew where Aaron was, but every time he went to this house, they told him they did not know where he was. He felt he was there or at the flea market on Northeast 23rd and Choctaw or something.

Jay: Man, how does that little kid get around like that?

Jim: I don't know, but he does get around. He doesn't mind asking you for a ride.

Larry: It was quite an experience taking all those kids to Payless for shoes. The weekend before school started, the place was already busy. Here we came with seven little Start kids. Carol brought her little girl and Cindy had her boy. We had lots of kids. They divided up the kids. They said Okay, Larry, you take three kids. The two of them took the other three apiece or whatever. I was assigned three boys—they're easier to buy for than girls. But I got Crystal too. She got some little red shoes. That was a real experience. The one I thought would not care what his shoes looked like was Randall, but he was the pickiest one. He changed his shoes three or four times until he got it just right.

Jim: It was interesting that Betty made them take the shoes off when they got home. They had to put them up and could not wear them except to school. We thought that was great. The kids did not complain. Some of the children said that these were the first new shoes they had. They were real proud of those shoes.

Jay: When we were down there Monday, the house was almost empty.

Noah: You mean the clothes on the floor and things?

Jay: No, the furniture and beds and such.

Larry: Well, that gets into another story.

Jim: We're not quite ready for that part yet. You want to hear it or should we try to stay in some order? Okay, the same day they got the shoes was the first day for their tutoring lesson. That's when we had another person come up and help out. Kathy came up. To my knowledge she was there this past Sunday too. Anyway, Shirley and Jenny volunteered to do that and Lynn was up there. They got the class going and they had some of the teenagers helping too. I want to say that Bill and Betty were there too. I believe they were that time.

Larry: I think we have this out of order. I think the shoes came later because when Lynn took the kids home from the class one of the nursery workers asked Lynn where the kids shoes were. One of the kids said they didn't have any. That's how the shoe thing happened. Shirley saw Lynn getting into her wallet and thought she was going to pay the nursery workers. What it was, was the nursery workers were donating to buy the kids shoes. One of them gave twenty dollars and another gave twenty-five.

Jim: I didn't know that.

Larry: Yeah, that needs to be known. It was a spur of the moment deal. But so much was happening and so many were coming in to help that we get mixed up a bit as to what happened when. That just shows the heart of these people.

Noah: This started, remember, with the three of you. Look how your seed of help grew. This is good.

Larry: Okay, we talked about the shoe store right?

Jim: Right. I'm not sure how all this fits together exactly, but the longer we do this the better we get to know these people and their life-style. We are not guessing so much anymore. We are gaining more knowledge about their personal life.

Noah: What are you learning about your own life?

Jim: Ah . . . depends on the day.

Noah: That may be a profound answer. How about the rest of you, what are you learning about yourselves?

Larry: That's hard to say, I haven't thought about myself in this.

Jay: Nor I.

Noah: Think about it. I'll ask again some day.

Jim: I mean, it amazes me. We have maybe a couple dozen people here now and none of us, none of us, have ever done this before, anything like this. I mean we don't know these people. They are so different from us. We have absolutely nothing in common. Ah . . . what are we doing?

Jay: Answer your own question, what are we doing?

Jim: Um . . . there's no doubt in my mind.

Larry: You talked to the class, remember?

Jim: Yes, there's another story or two before we get into last Saturday.

We took a small break as they warned me I would not want to miss the next part of the Start episode. Jim had me check the tape on the recorder and I knew we were getting close to the make or break moment. I only hoped they were not going to ask me what to do.

Jim: When we get to Saturday you may want to get on all eight channels. You don't want to miss it.

Noah: Don't want to miss anything.

Jim: Anyway, where did we end up a minute ago? Oh yes, the tutoring session at Chapel Hill. Everybody drove from far northwest Oklahoma City, picked them up, took them up to the church then took them home afterward. An hour-and-a-half drive time at least, plus the time at the church. Anyway, the next thing I have down here is, that was the same week Bill was so upset cause Aaron ran off. Well, I could not do a thing about it. I left for Wyoming Monday morning, didn't get back until Thursday. Of course,

Larry's over at El Reno at the college, so I got back Friday and went over there on my lunch hour. Larry was really concerned about Bill because he was really upset about Aaron.

Larry: He was just upset period! He thought he was going to be the one to take off. He just told me . . . he didn't think he could handle this anymore.

Jim: He said he just wanted to leave.

Jim: He sounded pretty sincere about it. So, I was afraid that was what he might do.

Noah: It's interesting that he shared that with you. His feeling seemed to have been driven so deeply inside. He's been rather closed-mouthed about most things. He is stoic about all that is happening to him. It seems you have established a bond with the man. To think that he was comfortable and safe enough to share is very telling.

Jim: I got back and went down Friday and asked permission to talk to Aaron. I asked if it would be all right if I came down Saturday and picked Aaron up. I wanted to ask him why he ran off, why he was treating his dad like this, how about school etc. We decided I would pick him up at 1:00 Saturday afternoon. I told Aaron, Betty and Bill, everyone that was there. So I go back Saturday at one o'clock . . . no Aaron. Betty said he was with his dad over cashing a check or something, they should be here any minute. Well, I was getting frustrated because he was not there as agreed. I talked to Betty for awhile and she kept saying they'll be here. An hour later I got up to leave and they came home. So, I took Aaron and we left. We talked and I asked him why he ran off. He denied it.

Jay: Denied what?

Jim: That he ran off! And that he had cussed his mother out, and he was running around with bad friends. He didn't miss a beat. I don't think Bill's lying. When I confronted Aaron his response was very cool, smooth and slick and he said he was only gone about eight hours. He said he was just helping a friend throw newspapers. I don't know if he meant handbills or what. He said he had asked another friend to tell Bill and Betty that he was going to be doing that. That was his story. I hadn't talked to Bill, so I didn't know if it was true or not. Anyway, we drove around a bit and tried to get to know more about each other. This was the first time Aaron and I had a chance to just talk. That was a week ago this past Saturday. Then Tuesday I called Chuck from the Trinity class. He volunteered to exterminate the house. We talked about it, he went over and told them they had to clean the place up or nothing would keep the bugs away. She got mad and Wednesday she left. We did not know about that until Friday. By chance, Don drove past and went up to the house.

Jay: Had Don been there before?

Larry: He had been there several times. One time he took some plaster to Bill to fix the walls where the plaster had been knocked off. We were all concerned about Bill and interested to see if Aaron was still at home. He was just stopping to check on Bill and Aaron. The dates are all confused, but I think that's how it happened. Not to get off of this, but wasn't it a week or two prior to this that Paul and Brandy broke some windows in an empty house and got caught. So they're in trouble somewhat. Jim probably knows that story a lot better than I do.

Jim: It is just another burden for Bill. The kids were breaking windows and the neighbors caught them and called the police. They have to go to some type of educational skill class. I believe the DHS conducts it. It is located at 6th and Hudson. They have to go two hours a night, two nights a week for three weeks.

Jay: How are they going to get there? Bill doesn't have transportation.

Jim: That's what we would like to know. I called the lady, Bill can't read and he handed me a piece of paper last Saturday morning and asked me what it meant. I told him I don't know but I'll call and find out. Monday I called the lady who sent the letter and she said it was an alternative to some type of juvenile delinquency proceeding. I asked if they could furnish a ride for these kids to attend as they have no way to get there. She said no. They had hundreds of people in the same position and they could not furnish rides. I asked about baby-sitting services for the other kids when Bill walks down there with the children. No, they don't have any baby-sitting services. So Bill doesn't have a baby-sitter, doesn't have a car, and he's thinking he has to take the entire family on a ten-mile walk and wait outside while the two kids serve their time, wait until 8:30 at night then walk back two hours back home in the dark in this neighborhood at 10:00 P.M. . . . and he may have to do that! I found out that information Monday morning, and drove over with Larry to tell Bill, and told him there's a chance we could get it postponed. So I called back that afternoon and talked to the lady. We postponed it for two weeks to try to find some way to work it out.

Noah: What would happen if it were disregarded?

Larry: There's no alternative! They do it or go to juvenile court.

Jay: Of course, then they will be turned over to DHS and the family is gone. When they send a caseworker out here they won't do what we are doing.

Jim: It's the easy way out, if they can get there. Anyway we got that postponed for two weeks. That was just something else . . . just another thing to worry about. Aaron's expelled.

Jay: That was just one day wasn't it?

Jim: No, he's still out. He's OUT, O-U-T, Aaron's expelled Monday, they are supposed to have their meetings downtown on Tuesday. Oh man, he's up against it. We were down there Monday. Tuesday I called Aaron's teachers to find out what was going on. Shirley had called one of them also on Monday. She got back with me and I wanted to verify it. So I called his two teachers. One said he was expelled indefinitely or until Bill and Aaron can meet with the principal. They must decide what Aaron's attitude will be and if he really wants to go back to school. They want to set up some program where he'll cooperate.

Noah: Aaron is still terrified of the situation. So, it is a moot point what Bill and the teachers and the principal decide is a reasonable program. Or, for that matter what society reasons is best for Aaron, may not have Aaron's sanction. He may agree to something he cannot live up to.

Larry: He has this chance and one more, then he goes into some school where he is locked in. A hard core location and he will have no choice.

Jay: Maybe that isn't such a bad thing.

Larry: I don't know about that. But he does have an alternative before that. The Methodist Boy's Home will take him. That must be better than a children's prison. It's very structured too.

Jay: Where is it located? Is it the one up here by Edmond? That's not too far.

Larry: No, it's the one up by Gore, in northeast Oklahoma. It's a long way from here but maybe that would be best.

Jay: It would be too far for him to sneak out and come home.

Noah: A few miles or many miles . . . there is no difference to someone as independent as Aaron. Only his feet are that of a boy, not the motor that drives them. If he can routinely get twenty or thirty miles around town on his ingenuity, a few more miles is no hill for a stepper.

The knots that tie the poor to their situation are like those in a wet rope. The longer they are there the more they set. Approximately fifty people were or had been involved with the repair of the Starts at this point. I have no guess at the number from the Baptist church. The repair of the home and the homelife is a difficult one when we attempt to patch up the old breaks. The "new wine in old skins" statement takes on new meaning. The helpers not only took on the task of cleaning the dirt from the life of the Starts. But they now found that there was no door on the Starts' life-style to keep dirt out.

Larry: We need to go back in the story to where Don went by to check on Aaron and Bill.

Jim: Okay, so Don went there to check on Bill and he found Bill and the three smallest kids huddled up in the van. The place had just been exterminated and of course, they could not go right back in there. Well, Don talked to them and found out that Betty had left two days before. He found they were out of food and had not eaten for two days. Betty took care of the paperwork and cashed the checks. Bill could not read so that was what she did for the family. Bill gave her the check, she cashed it and paid the bills. Don went immediately across the street and bought some peanut butter and milk to eat. The phone lines were busy so he could not contact us.

Larry: The gas was also shut off. Bill said Betty had been taking the money lately and not paying the bills. So, they didn't have any hot water to bathe in. If they did bathe it was in cold. They didn't have any gas to heat anything out of cans. They had no way to cook.

Jim: We're talking dire straights here. Bill doesn't know anything about food stamps I'm sure. He can't read to fill out forms, he's got these kids to watch, Betty left. All he could say was, "I'm going crazy." The next morning the Saints showed up. Don and Carol and John, another first timer, got down on his hands and knees and scraped that filth off of the floor. He went out in the yard and tried to rake the glass shards up so the kids would not cut their feet.

Jay: You mean Carol? I thought she didn't want much to do with this.

Jim: Well, we thought so too. But, she came down here once and she's been leading the charge.

Jay: Yeah, remember, we said if she would get involved she would be dynamite.

Larry: You know, a lot of people started that way. My wife was somewhat like that. She said she could not go down there. She said if she went she would not be able to stop. She was right, she can't.

Jim: Anyway, let me finish this Saturday story. So everyone's down there and they're working on the house. Well, I guess Don found out Friday that the school nurse found head lice on one or more of the kids.

Larry: I think it was the exterminator. He found lice in the bed, that's when he told Betty she would have to keep the place cleaner.

Jim: Okay, so they found out about the lice. What did Bill do? What can he do? He shaved their heads. The boys . . . the boys have this short, short burr and Bill tried to shampoo them. I'm telling you he's trying to do what he can. No wonder he ganged up on Betty. This living condition was not healthy for the kids or anyone else.

Larry and I were down there too, on Saturday and we were going to divide up the responsibilities with the others and, OH . . . Oh! . . . the clothing, the clothing we had given was in plastic bags and the bags were infested with roaches and lice eggs. Literally they were crawling all over the clothes, they could not use them or wear them. This was the clothing we had just given. So, the clothing had to be cleaned. Don and Carol picked up the clothing and took it to the laundromat and they were completely grossed out.

212

The bugs and the cockroaches were swimming . . . for . . . their . . . lives as they lower the clothes into the washing machine. And this money is out of their pocket, I mean, no collection to help defray the cost. They are cleaning and paying. They finally paid somebody thirty-five dollars to do the work. Then they went back to clean the filthy refrigerator.

Noah: Is that the one you just gave?

Jim: Yes, they were down on their hands and knees and cleaning all this stuff. And you tell Noah what you guys were doing.

Larry: Well, tell a little more about what they were doing first.

The meeting was to attempt to allow me to understand what had transpired with the Starts and the church, so that I would be supportive of whatever the decision of the committee would be. I had always been supportive and tried to stay out of the guidance of the direction of the help. The church members had already gone a great deal farther than many would have. An author has the desire to lead the story to his or her conclusion. I fought that, and I fight the conclusion.

Jim: Oh, I went down there to try to encourage Bill first thing Saturday morning. I walked in before they all got there, and there sat this poor pathetic guy that didn't know anybody's coming down. He had no idea, yet he was back there and he'd been up all night long, he had everything out of the kitchen cabinets. He's on a step ladder painting the inside, trying to clean the place up because he's terrified that the DHS is going to come out to take his kids away from him.

Larry: We got there a little behind Don and Carol and John, because we were trying to get a key to the McKee Center to take the kids down to scrub them. That was the cleanest I had ever seen the house. Bill had swept the floors as best he could. The roaches had been sprayed a few days before and there were a lot of dead roaches.

Jim: And many live ones too.

Larry: Yes, there were. The roaches were quite active. They were running for their lives. He was up there painting away and he had placed anything that was salvageable in plastic bags. As far as food goes he had rice and things like that. As Jim said, the rest of

213

the dishes were out in the middle of the kitchen floor. So we sat down to talk it over and divide the duty. We ended up just putting dishes and stuff in a truck. And Lynn and I took the kids in the back of the truck and this other lady who was one of Betty's friends, who lives in Mulligan Flats. Bill asked us to take her with us. We had special shampoo for the lice. Bill said he had already taken care of the lice, but we thought we better do it again, since the eggs were still in the clothes and everything. One of the things we wanted to do was find some clean clothes for the kids. The McGee Center has clothes. The smallest kids did not have any clothes at all. They had on dirty underwear. The rest of the clothes were in the bags full of bugs on the way to the wash. We put the clothes in back of a trailer and a second forty-pound box of soap and took it down there. I don't know were the first one went but it disappeared. When we brought all that cleaning stuff to the house before, we had another forty-pound box. When I picked the clothes up from the laundry that forty-pound box was gone too.

We loaded the kids up, I think Bill wanted this woman to go with us to make sure nothing happened to them. We were just going to take them down to put some clothes on them and wash the dishes. We had loaded every dish they had in the house on the back of my pickup. Same way with the laundry. We took every piece of clothing in the house. We went through every drawer, I mean everything. All the drawers were infested with cockroaches. Even after the spraying, the roaches were hiding in the clothing and under things. There were thousands of them. We knew that it would not do much good unless we took everything out of the house and exterminated again.

We put the children in the back of the truck and took them to the McGee Center. She took the kids to one end of the Center and bathed them with the special soap. That is the small ones, the older children took care of their own showers. But she used a special shampoo on all the children to be sure the lice were destroyed.

Crystal, if you noticed, always has a running nose. The lady down there also said she was sure she had impetigo. She gave Bill some medicine to clear it up. Patrick or William also had a large sore on his leg, and we were sure he was infected. The children are always covered with scabs and bug bites. You wonder how a mother could let this happen. If she had just kept them clean. As she was washing them, I decided to wash the dishes. They had a sink at the other end of the center and the lady was kind enough to allow us to use it.

So, I started to carry a box of dishes in to wash, and I noticed there were cockroaches running on the dishes in the box. I thought the center probably had some roaches, but I did not want it to be worse because of us, so I pulled the truck out into the middle of the parking lot. I set the boxes in the middle of the drive and started to shake everything off. I carried the things inside. The kids who were finished with their baths, and some other people, helped carry the dishes in, so all the bugs did not stay in the drive.

I could only wash about a dozen things at a time and then I had to empty the water from the sink. There were so many dead and dying roaches floating and swimming around. I would pick up a dish and it would look all right and there would be some bugs on the other side of it. They were crawling all over me, or it felt like it.

Jim: We're talking serious, serious roaches here folks.

While they were talking to me, they had their arms folded across their chests and they hugged their shoulders as if to hug the goose bumps out of their memory. Larry shuddered as he continued the story.

Larry: No matter how the dishes looked, roaches seemed to be hiding behind them, and those that were supposed to be clean still had spots all over them. I don't know how she could have fed the children on those dishes. The dishes had these little spots all over them. I don't know what that stuff was, but I think I do. I hope it wasn't what I think it was but I'm sure it was. Anyway I washed every dish they had. It took two or two-and-a-half hours to do it. Like I said he had a lot of electric skillets, there were four or five of them. Every one of them had old food and stuff sticking to it. The frying pans had leftover food in them. I asked Aaron if he had any idea why they had so many bugs. He had absolutely no idea. I told him it was because of things like this. The dishes would have to be rinsed off after meals, and the pots and pans would have to be cleaned or you would never get rid of the roaches. So I think it was an eye opening experience to him. He had just never been taught that we cannot live that way and be healthy.

After an hour or so, the other kids were just going nuts hammering on the piano and things. They had an electric organ in there that Paul figured out how to turn on. They flipped every switch and pulled every knob on that thing. I worried that it would not work the next day when they came in for church services. But we finally loaded the dishes and the children in the truck. We looked for a place to get them something to eat as it was about 1:30 or 2:00.

They had some Crispy Treats candy that the youth group had brought earlier. Lynn took them and bought twenty-six hamburgers for the seven kids. The woman had one and Lynn had one and the children devoured the rest of them. Then she bought six more hamburgers and kept three to give to Aaron and his dad. When they got back one of the kids tore one in half and gave it to me. I wasn't sure I had the stomach for it. I did not have an appetite after washing the dishes. I choked it down so the kids would know I appreciated it. Aaron ate only one hamburger and kept two for his dad. We promised we would buy his dad some more burgers before we got back to the house, so Aaron ate the other two.

When we went back to their house they were clean, full and dressed. All the children got clean underwear but because school had just started, the center had a shortage of children's clothes.

Jim: Yes, the lady at the center said they had just clothed six hundred children.

Larry: So, when we went back to the house, Carol and Don and John were still there working. Carol mentioned she had picked up a clock on the mantle and a dozen or so cockroaches ran out. By this time when we walked through the house, the house looked clean except for the hundreds of cockroaches running around. All the cleaning had them stirred up. They were on the walls and ceiling and the floors. They were behind and under everything.

Jim: This was after a professional exterminator had treated the house!

Larry: It was as if you had a whole box of roaches and you shook it and let them out all at once to watch them run.

Jim: They really were. Everything was in motion, across the

216

floor up the walls, across the ceiling, absolutely everywhere. When I went in there Saturday morning to talk to Bill, we went in the bedroom to get away from the children for a private talk. The roaches were falling off the ceiling on our heads. I think the exterminating just stirred them up. There were thousands of them dead but that many more alive.

Larry: I will say that last night was the first night since that weekend that I did not wake up thinking bugs were crawling over the bed and the room. That first night after the lice thing with the children and the roaches, I remember picking up my pillow and going into the bathroom to look at it in the light to see if I had something crawling around on it.

Well anyway, when we got back they were still cleaning. Carol . . . you have to know Carol to know how special she is. She mentioned the roaches and the house and she said they started cleaning the floor and they were walking around this stuff. It was kind of dark, sort of dark. And, they kept walking around this stuff. Lynn and Carol were both wearing rubber gloves up to here you know. They were walking around this stuff and Carol said there was something on the floor that would have to be cleaned up. So she looked at it. She did not want to say what it was. She said she was trying to think of a way to get it up and thought, oh, what the heck, and just reached down and scooped it up and threw it away. Crystal and Paul, or Patrick, it's Patrick he's four, and Crystal's three now, they wet their pants and defecate wherever they are.

Jim: I don't know if Crystal has any diapers. I don't remember seeing any. The children should be over that by now, I think.

Jay: The four year old sure ought to be over that.

Larry: When we took the kids to Will for their eye exam, the four year old wet all over one of Will's good chairs. We didn't go around and check but he was wet and he was sitting in several chairs.

Jim: Like Noah said, he was just marking his territory. That's Patrick's spot.

This was the last time we all laughed that night. These three men all with families of their own had given hours and days and weeks and months to the healing of one needy family. They had enlisted perhaps one hundred additional hands to help. They slowed now that they were nearing the end of their report. All three were sitting on the edge of their chairs with their hands folded in front of them. It appeared to be choreographed as the six thumbs would all stand up at the same time and their shoulders would shrug in unison.

Larry: He's wet all the time. Anyway, they had used a whole gallon of insecticide and we went to the hardware store to get another gallon. We went past the laundromat to pick up the clothes and then we went to get Bill's hamburgers. Aaron kept reminding us about his dad's burgers.

Jim: This is about 4:00 or later in the afternoon. Some of the people had been down there seven hours or so.

Larry: We left and they said they might still be there when we got back with the burgers and the bug killer. When we got back some of the people were gone. Aaron was with me all that day. He was a perfect gentleman. He stayed right by my side and helped with the dishes. He stayed and pitched right in even though he was as hungry as the rest of the children. He also said he really appreciated doing that because that was his job and he would have to do it all by himself if I had not helped. So he dried the dishes while I washed them.

After we left to run the errands, we stopped to get the clothing and the lady said she was not completely finished. So, I told her I would come back the next day and get the rest. We were not gone very long, but while we were away, the store across the street was robbed. It was an armed robbery. Someone had gone in with a gun in broad daylight and taken the money. As we pulled up, I saw this nicely dressed girl talking to Bill. I wondered what was going on. She was not one of our Sunday school class people. I wondered if it was someone from the DHS or something. I thought it was more trouble.

When we pulled up, Bill shouted, "They just got robbed." This girl was running back and forth. She did not know what to do. She said she was walking to the store and a black guy told her not to walk around the corner. Bill was waiting for us on the front porch when these two guys ran out of the store and jumped in a car in front of him and tore off. She asked if he had seen a couple of black guys. He said yes, that they were right in front of him, he saw the whole thing. Of course that's all it took. Now there was a witness, Bill!

Now, Bill was on the porch talking to Lynn. He told her he just could not get involved in this. He was trying to stay away from the police since he felt the men might come back and harm the children. He was so afraid he could not remember anything anyway. He thought the car was a Chrysler and someone else thought it was a Mercury. Since he couldn't read, he told them he didn't get the license number, the other witness was a small child but he didn't remember anything either. But, he may have been a more reliable witness than Bill. We told Bill it was time to leave and we left.

Noah: That was last week?

Larry: Last Saturday. The next morning at church, Carol spent an hour telling the class what we had found down there and what was done. She told what shape the family was in, that the gas was shut off and final notices for the water and electricity were in. They did not have any food. We took up another offering. How much did we raise?

Larry: I think it was a little over four hundred dollars. Lynn called and sent checks to all of the utilities and arranged to have the gas turned back on. I don't know everything she did. Bill had all these envelopes and he no idea of what was inside. Betty had told Bill they had a letter from a collection agency. Do you know what that was about? Was it on the car?

Larry: No, he showed me all these bills and this one from a collection agency for $3,700. They wanted the Starts to pay for back charges. Bill did not know why. I called Monday and found it was for medical bills. They would take the kids down to the emergency room rather than going to a doctor. Since it was a non-life-threatening situation, they would have to pay. Plus, I found that to qualify for the DHS or state assistance for medical charges, they would have to have a case worker come to the house to check the condition of the house and the children. That is called an in-house interview. Someone said that Betty knew what was needed, but she knew that the house would have to be cleaned up so they never went through the simple process of filling out the paperwork for government assistance for medical care. She must have known if the case worker came the kids were gone because the house was such a pit.

Jay: The house is okay now. The DHS would not take the kids; now, because of the house, would they?

Again like the history in the beginning of the book, we seem so often to get no farther then where we began. This is almost where we met the Starts, by bringing the bedding they needed.

Jim: I don't know, but the other thing is, with all the lice and roaches, the exterminator told them to throw all the mattresses out. So, now they are sleeping on the floor again.

Larry: I guess the bugs laid eggs in them and they had to go.

Jim: I believe the house was so bad you needed to burn about everything inside and put a bag over the whole house and fog it. Anyway the exterminator is going back again this Saturday to give it another blast. He told me eventually he could control it, if they would keep it clean.

Larry: There are a few broken windows now too. When we went back to take that other gallon of bug killer, we also took a candle that was supposed to kill roaches. It emits a poison. Of course, they can't be in there when it's used. We did not try to use it because the windows were broken and it would not work anyway. We also thought the candle might fall over and burn the house down. That would get rid of the bugs, but we did not leave the candle.

We also went back Sunday for the tutoring session. Shirley made arrangements to use Epworth Methodist Church as a location for the session. We got there about 4:15. Even Bill wanted to go. When we finally got in they worked with him on his reading.

Jim: We had a mix up on the time. The church people thought we should have been there at 2:30, not 4:30.

Larry: The doors were locked and I did not notice the bell for a while. When some of the people inside came out, we told them what we were doing and they gave us a key and told us to lock up and turn off the lights when we were through. So, when I left it was Jenny, Lynn, Shirley, and Kathy who stayed with Bill, Aaron, Brandy, Anita, Randall, and Paul. I took the other three kids . . .

yeah, let's see, three kids. There was Crystal, Patrick, William and my son. My daughter stayed down there with Lynn. Rick was with me so we went to get the rest of the laundry. I don't know if we got the right laundry or not. The lady was not the same one as the night before. But, she said it was the right stuff. The forty pound box of soap wasn't there and none of the bags were marked. There were eight or nine bags of clothing all together. So, we just loaded them in the truck and left.

We then went to the grocery store and bought about fifty dollars worth of food. I've never seen a child get as excited as little Crystal when she saw a little horse that cost a quarter to ride. Her eyes lit up and she got excited and there was no way I could walk past without putting a quarter in and allowing her to ride. So, I had every one of them ride the horse.

The three sat there for a minute or two. They looked at each other as if to silently ask what this had all been about. No one added anything more so Jim concluded with what probably would have been sufficient in the first place. Except one paragraph can not convey the frustration of the attempt to help, or the extent or depth of help necessary. These three men and all those that were involved with the Start family had touched the worst symptom of a sick global society. The symptom of homelessness and poverty is rooted deep within the marrow of our system. It is not cured by a topical dressing; it needs major surgery and extended periods of therapy to heal the system.

Jim: So that's about where we are. The Starts have glasses. They are being tutored. The house is as clean as it ever has been, and Bill's keeping it that way. The exterminator is going back until the bug problem is solved. We are trying to find new beds and everyone is still behind the project. We have found work for Bill as soon as he is able to get there. But, Betty is still gone and Aaron's still in trouble in school.

So perhaps it is back to the fear that tomorrow may bring to the Starts. Back to the same old same old, just like the history in the beginning. Back to the lice and the roaches and the sleeping on the hard floor for a while. Back to the fear of going to school and the sure failure for not doing so. Back to the concern of the ones helping and the frustrations that lives with and in that process. Back to realizing that basic life tools are imperative for a successful living experience in this society and the realization that many do not possess the skills and knowledge needed.

Since the meeting I heard that Betty is back. The class members no longer go into the house as that condition is back where it was. Aaron was sent to the boys' home in Gore, Oklahoma. He was asked to leave after a week. He started classes at a special learning center but has since run away from home. No one has seen or heard from him for several weeks. The men on the committee still drive around looking for him, for the little boy with the burr haircut has become a part of their lives and family and they feel a deep loss.

Maybe Aaron still has a shot at his jubilee from the poverty wheel. Jay told me Aaron was talking about going to college someday. He wanted to become someone. He wanted the things he saw in the various homes of his classmates. He wanted the cleanliness he had enjoyed for such a short time. He had tasted more and he wanted it. He wasn't happy at home anymore.

If the class had the information in *Adopt-a-Family*, written by Jan Johnson of the Community Enrichment Center of Fort Worth, and followed the suggested contract between giver and receiver, the Starts may not have received help. They would not have qualified because of the mother's refusal to maintain a healthful level of hygiene practices. She would have had to change, or the children and Aaron would not have received the assistance they did: no clothes, no shoes, no beds, no glasses, no tutoring, no glimpse at more.

The Adopt-a-Family program written by Jan Johnson is a carefully designed program. It was created to assist just such a group as the church committee involved with the Starts. The participating family must sign an agreement and participate in follow-up counseling. If you have a group that would like to sponsor a family, you may want to contact Jan Johnson for her outline.

The committee has decided it will no longer invest in beds and bedding that must be replaced every so often like spoiled milk on the shelf. What has expired is the tolerance of the giver to the waste of the receiver. The action of the parent is visited on the children.

The class has gone to class in the effort to help the Starts. We have gone to school on them. They are very special people, and still are assisting the Start family. Again, my ledger says there is a difference between conditional love and conditional giving.

My ledger says I must go on now and leave the Starts, for we are all bound to different illusions. However, I can not release the hope and the prayer that the Start children and Aaron and his family will be together.[1]

LEDGER

Special thoughts are special gifts. My ledger reminds me of a special gift given to me by my buddy, Chad Ransdell. It was a book by Don Marquis titled, "Archy and Mehitabel." The remembering was prompted by all the talk of roaches. Archy was a cockroach who lived in a newspaper office with a cat named Mehitabel. Archy was a poet in another life, and Mehitabel was Cleopatra. Archy was my kind of writer. He was not strong enough to make capital letters, so he used all lower case and no punctuation. I wished Archy had lived at the Starts', for they and everyone involved would have found his typewritten note: "believe that everything is for you until you discover that you are for it."[2]

GETTING STARTED

PART **6**

CHAPTER TWENTY

The Eyes
of the Heart

The view is much the same for all of us regardless of the size of the window, for we all see outwardly only through our private glass, be it tempered and refined or raw and cloudy. It is a product of our own experience and willingness to extend our vision.

We must remember that majorities vote only on information received, then accept or reject according to individual persuasion, based to some degree on the confidence in the one presenting the information. Confidence lost is chaos born. So leaders need to provide clean windows through which the issues can be seen.

We have a right to disagree with the direction of those in the lead. And we have a personal mandate to object when that direction opposes our belief or our good. We must, however, expect to experience censure and increased control.

Something happened to me on my journey to despair and back. I am strong enough now to cry. I am able to cry over anything I wish and in front of anyone present. However, I have become weak enough to fight. I will gladly lash out now at any tormenter. I have never understood some people's anger before. However, I have never before so thoroughly understood the need to control that anger. There is a part of all of us that would break windows and throw what is behind them into the street. There is a part of all of us that will finally strike out at our perceived persecutor. I cannot yet erase the judgmental stares and snubs of those who readily judged and assessed me to be of less value because of my appearance. It is most difficult to be patient with petty, selfish harassment.

We are all to some degree living within the shape forged by the parent and the past, but we exist in our present form only by our continued acceptance of it. There are times when we must break away and suffer the wrath of those who cannot accept having less than complete control. Otherwise, without some dissent, complacency will allow some windows to get dirty.

Yes, the view is the same, whether through the tiny window of a few who believe they are superior and would judge a man undesirable because he dares to challenge the status quo, or the view through the huge window of those who control our society and can raise the volume of confusion and red tape to any level necessary to drown the cry of the dissenter. That is why windows are broken, why children with stones face soldiers with guns, why anger replaces reason, why change occurs.

Now the point of this whole piece is that if a gentle, articulate, generous, peaceable, contented, pretty wonderful person like myself could be pushed to want to punch some guy's lights out, how much frustration must the poor and homeless feel when someone mislabels him as an undesirable, lazy, unworthy drunk or druggie? I know what it is to be judged undesirable by people who possess only money and things, not character or class. I never have to accept that again. And to you with the tiniest windows, who would judge me undesirable because I will not participate in, nor pay for your foolishness, you will have spanked a scorpion.

We are all paying for a silting problem that should have been stopped a long time ago. The opposite is true: It is worsening. Those who are judged to be silt have grown tired of the confinement. Plant the seeds or be the seeds that grow to end the erosion. Plant truth and weed out the lies. Stop judging who is worthy of a comfortable life. Listen to the growing protest of the ones you would judge. Do not attribute your own weakness to them; they might call you to the street over it. Clean your windows before you have to board them up.

CHAPTER
TWENTY-ONE

What You and
I Can Do

I have ridden an emotional merry-go-round on this project. I began with an intense inner anger, angry with everything having to do with the poor and homeless condition. Perhaps anger is conceived in ignorance, but it grows best in confusion, watered by frustration. I have gone through periods when I wanted to quit and just go back to the street and other times I swore the street was not an option. There were times when time was the enemy, and other moments when it was my strongest ally.

I have learned much about myself and my sameness with all others, no matter what their opinion or stand on this subject. I have been the crusader and believed my purpose, the peacemaker proposing that the poor be patient, the revolutionary telling the poor to rise up and take what is theirs. I have been abused by panhandlers to satisfy their addictions and have been angered to the point of wanting to sweep them from this life. Yet I have told people to drop a buck in the pot. I have scolded and

screamed at people to have more compassion in their understanding of the importance of time, to do something now, not at
their convenience. A day to people in control of their lives may
seem like a month to someone in distress. Yet knowing this and
having lived with that frustration, I have been guilty of making
some wait. They waited because of my personal priority or frustration. And in so doing, I have become more understanding of
those who seem to be somewhat cool or unconcerned.

Perhaps we are all locked into our social priorities as my
friend Brian Clark suggests, judging ourselves and our success
by our very limited illusions. I believe now that our view of life
will forever remain limited when we subscribe to the belief that
we are more important than anyone else.

I turned fifty before this book was completed, and in these
fifty years I have searched for the truth, for the meaning of the
word and concept, for the location where only truth lives and all
other distraction waits outside. I have searched many doctrines
and beliefs hoping to find the ready-made, acceptable schematic
for living. But still I find myself continuing to customize all I
experience and hear into my changing ledger. I have cut the
parts of my life into a collage of shapes my experience and understanding have allowed, and I paste them on the pages of my
ledger. I continue to use the glue of my faith and reasoning,
which has proven in the past to be soluble through the changing
condition of my todays. Yet I still do not know exactly what I
believe to be pure truth.

I have used the disclaimer *perhaps* many times in this book,
much to the frustration of many, at least many who critiqued the
manuscript along the way. But my ledger says I am not an expert in the subject of the self, only in *my*self. I find me in the
best of those I respect and also in the worst of those I revile. I
have come to believe that I am best able to empathize with a
condition while I am experiencing it. *Perhaps* allows the cutting
and pasting of my ledger to continue, for I am not near completion. I no longer live in and with so many absolutes because possibilities and probabilities have melted them.

It appears the world will not yet sing its song in harmony;
there are too many individual songs being sung in too many
keys. I still can hear Elton John singing "Skyline Pigeon Fly"

and how his voice and words connected everyone watching or attending Ryan White's funeral. It was a bonding of those of us not able to understand, to the struggle of one small boy who was forced to. I cannot help but believe one day the whole world remaining will be invited to sing in unison, and the world's harmonic discord will no longer be heard in our inner ear or in our actions.

My ledger concludes that universal law is not a respecter of persons or conditions outside it's parameters and, whatever the actions or pleadings of the individual or group, the universe will not be bribed to change or slow or bend or break. We must change our shape to fit the requirements of the universal law of love. Until we do there is no harmony.

We live in a world of contradictions. Our own lives from hour to hour may contradict what we say and what we believe. Our interest and understanding of the word *hunger* can change with a full stomach. It is somewhat easy for us to project how we would react to a certain event or situation that *might* happen. A number of people I have met truly believe that they could not be homeless, that they could not be without a job—and a good job at that. They believe that here in America, anyone can have anything they want. Others I met truly believe they may never have anything and only death will remove them from an uncaring and callous world controlled by those with money. Perhaps there is some truth in both extremes of belief.

Those families who have risen to social prominence and power based on the fortunes made by their ancestors by stealing this country from its original owners, seem to have done and are doing precious little to remove the despair and poverty existing in and on the reservations now void of resources. These reservations now house the nation of people bilked of their future and deprived of their culture. These people now exist somewhere between their tradition and today in a cultural homelessness. This travesty is the subject of potential volumes of work and I have no new bright lights of change to report.

We most readily acknowledge distress when it is our own distress. It is almost always easier to relate to a condition or an experience that we ourselves have or are going through. Most of us have never been homeless or tragically poor. There is an infinite difference between "poor" and "broke." Many of us have been broke. Most of us cannot imagine what it would be like to live in this world today without the ability to read, yet one out of five American adults do.

But there are conditions existing that are so visibly tragic, experience is not a prerequisite to empathy. Homelessness is one such condition. What can you and I do about the growing national calamity? What can we really do? We have shared together some of the efforts of groups and individuals who have taken the initiative to do something. But the problem continues to worsen and is far outstripping the effort to heal. The role of the individual—you and me—is not always clearly defined. However, the rapidly growing number of concerned souls indicate our concern and our contempt for the plight of those who have lost their lifeline.

Contradiction's shadow, confusion, grows in direct proportion to dialog and debate. Some groups press to legislate mandatory assistance for the mentally ill by requiring the cities to pick up, house, and care for the street patient. Another group says that action is an infringement upon our civil rights and fights to ensure that each citizen occupy the territory he or she chooses. And so the mentally ill soul now urinates and defecates in front of any shop window he or she chooses as an expression of personal civil rights. The issue of civil rights verses civil responsibility continues to evade resolution.

Our leaders speak in contradictions. In one ear we hear the shout that all will get better; in the other we hear the whisper that the number of homeless will be even higher by the year 2000. We have heard the report that one out of four jobs now existing will soon fall victim to technology and world competition; yet we hear that more jobs will be available because of trade agreements with Mexico.

Contradiction grows with our disgust of abuses in the welfare system, both by those receiving assistance and those who divert money to the wealthy. Contradiction builds in our realizing we must do something to help the needy family that will be helped, but not the one who will not help themselves. Those contradictions grow in our inability to judge which is which; it is not always blatantly apparent.

The biggest contradiction of all is that the problem of the poor and homeless now and always has been a moral problem that will not be solved with only moral support. The role of the church will only grow if compassion gains direction, if people help people in a real way, not just in well wishes. That effort is expanding in many faiths and the variant names of belief. However, the effort must increase. There are many churches and organizations that have not yet added their resources and effort to the problem.

While the church and the individual have the responsibility to help the needy, the elected arm of the individual has a responsibility to create jobs, if not in the economic sector, then in the repair of our infrastructure which is in extremely ill health. We could use an army of workers to rebuild our bridges, rail systems, roads, airports, sewer systems, water treatment facilities, to help clean up the soil, the lakes and streams, the environment. We need an army of workers to tear down the rotting inner cites and replace them with new buildings and landscape the scars. We have need of more watersheds and lakes for fresh drinking water and irrigation.

We have all of these needy, wanting, and willing hands that are being treated like the fallow acreage of the land bank. People are not crops. We can not control their numbers by reducing them to the poverty of subsidization. In fact the contrary is true. There is so much to be done and we have so many able hands, it seems we could find the way or incentive to marry the needs.

One incentive might be the knowledge that it has always been easier to defend a fort than a tent village. We have concentrated our efforts for the security of our country on the building of walls that fly, or walls that explode. We have neglected the morale of many of the inhabitants of this fortress America. It does little good to have strong walls when many inside are waiting to pick off their own sentries. The most secure fortress is a combination of well-constructed walls and defenders with common purpose.

Another contradiction is that we live in an age where technology and scientific revelation can provide enough for all. Yet, armed with greed and love of the self, we seem intent on never realizing that potential. The sun shines and the wind blows on all of us, and can provide most of the power to operate this country.

234

They are nonpolluting and free, after the cost of building the harness to hold them. They are resources we need never import. They never cross boundaries that can be closed by dispute or disagreement. The jobless can supply the muscle and the dedication needed to build the systems. That dedication comes with work and purpose.

If we ever arrive at the decision to match the volume of wasted human resources with the problem of the volume of wasted resources we could reduce two overwhelming problems.

One study estimates that the government spends three dollars for every dollar it gives to the poor and homeless. This is somewhat misleading when we consider the number of people provided with jobs helping those without jobs. These programs seem to lack effectiveness partially because more and more people fall through the proverbial crack. In actuality the crack may have become a huge and growing sinkhole, caused by the washing away of the subterranean social and economic substructure made obsolete by progress through technological revelation. That hole will continue to grow until we fill it in with a new base.

A total revamping of our society is imperative, both in purpose and direction. The great experiment of man for the most part has been a violent and fierce history of controlling and being controlled. The human species is the first and only living organism that has the ability to control its destination and environment. As long as this small globe called earth exists, we could live comfortably and in harmony. But we do not. The potential for total world revolution is greater now than ever before, recent changes in many of the world's political systems notwithstanding. The changes have not drawn us closer in brotherhood.

There seems to be a sense of frustration and distraction and fear sweeping the world like a solar wind. In this world family of five and a half billion souls, eight hundred million believe we are approaching the holy war, *jihad*. Their duty is to defend against and destroy the infidel. This belief disallows the possibility of true peace and harmony with the rest of the worlds of belief, because all others are identified as the unbeliever. We have perhaps a billion more who are trying to identify the Antichrist and are preparing to fight against it or them or him.

We are divided by every difference that man has been able to imagine. We are divided by color, social class, education, religious preference, language, culture, climate and resources, time and space. Some live in a world that no longer exists, some in a world not yet born. We are divided by distrust and judgment. We are divided by fear, by need, and by greed.

We all, however, have the will to survive, and that survival instinct is the most powerful of forces in the human makeup. If the human family is to survive, it must not clench its composite fist in defense, but must lower its hand and drop its weapons. We seem not yet ready or willing to do that because in the history of man against man we know that laying down the weapon will not ensure peace. So we remain armed with weapon and suspicion, with fear and division.

I am not at all convinced that the problem will be cured. In fact the opposite is true. The plight of some of the homeless will not be solved by the addition of a roof to their lives. It is not just a problem of a dwelling. The state of homelessness is more than sleeping on a cardboard bed in the bushes or on a mat in a mission. It is going to sleep wishing this to be the last night of wishing and finally going to sleep not wishing.

As Robert Bly said, "We got here one at a time, and we will only get better the same way." The best we may be able to expect is to retract one soul, one family at a time, from the couches of the curb. We may only choose to sanitize the slime of skid row by demolishing the structures hiding the occupants from our eyes. But as the army of pitiful souls flees the falling rubble and scurries to the next dark ruins, they will indelibly tatoo a number on the wrist of a world intent and content with a newer holocaust of lives.

It is an abhorrent travesty charged to the family of humankind that we have millions of souls whose optimum possibility in life is a fast and painless death. Or as the song says, "The best you can hope for is to die in your sleep."

As a sailor, I learned that shifting the weight on my boat would keep it from listing. I realized that slight carelessness to that duty, combined with a sudden huge gust of wind, would put me over. I knew that during a storm I had to lower the sails and retain just enough sail to keep me "bow to the wind." Perhaps we need to lower and trim and come about, instead of foolishly sailing between the waves.

For those families who are still on deck of this ship America, and are listing under the luggage of two jobs and debt to the limit, remember: A sudden wave washing one of your jobs from your ability to meet monthly installments can send you to the hold too. And suddenly you may be introduced to mutinous thoughts that you may discount now.

There are many wealthy people dedicated to helping the poor and homeless. Most perhaps by choice are not recognized for their effort or concern. Prominent families like the Kennedys have always spoken out in defense of the poor. The theme of their service has not been to their profit, for it has cost that family greatly.

Former President Carter and his wife, Rosalyn, work tirelessly at bettering this life for all people. They are among the most active public servants working to eliminate suffering. They are acutely aware of the almost insurmountable mountain of problems standing between the way things are and the way we would have them be. Yet they continue to do what can be done within the time left to accomplish it. The work of the Carter Center is an international effort addressing the world agenda of problems from ecology to homelessness.

Few business people have been as verbal or visible as H. Ross Perot in campaigning for change. He uses his resource of wealth and will and risks peer and public opinion to try to shake us from our apathy. More high profile personalities could stand to add their lives and voice to changing inequitable conditions. That stance requires first commitment, then courage.

Humans are truly strange cousins to the ostrich, and we have become very skilled at hiding our heads in the confusion of others. When speaking about the homeless to various groups, I find most of those who listen to be very compassionate. However, I occasionally sense resentment. It is as if we all know at some level that things are not right, not fair, not just, not acceptable, but we do not want to be reminded of it. I find that most sincerely want to help repair the condition, yet upon seeing the complexity of the problem and its origins, we tend to bury our

237

composite head. It is as if we want to enter the cave and pull the sky in with us. We just can't do that. The sky's too big and it belongs to everyone, and the cave's too small and belongs only to us.

During the "question and answer" portion of my talk I usually encounter a small but intense pocket of interest. This group of people, while in the beginning opposed to the message, gives birth to the ones who have become the most active advocates. I find the anger, which usually is the catalyst for their comments, is not anger at the messenger or the message, but total disgust and frustration with the problem. Before a repairman can fix anything broken, he ought to know how it works and what its purpose is. We need people dedicated to repair. This is not a Maytag world.

Now that the Gulf War is over and the patriotic euphoria of victory begins to ebb, our domestic problems will be heard, for they have not slept voluntarily or quietly. The condition of our poor and struggling population did not become brighter with the discharging of billions of dollars in smart bombs. Poverty will once again be the subject of media attention. The thin film covering the tragedy of the poor and the disenfranchised will dissipate, and the economic realities of a world grown smaller yet apart will again be the visible scars that have not healed but keloided. It will reveal a more severe problem ahead for our working population and those who cannot find work. The cost of war is always deducted from funds earmarked or proposed for the poor and needy. That is precisely the message of this book. If you become unemployed in this crazy volatile global economic climate, you will experience great stress. And your voice will not be heard from down there in your need. Use your voice now while it will be heard. The only difference between you and many in the soup line is that they have already lost their job and their voice.

We know once again we can pull together when we feel threatened. We have all met together in discussion over breakfast, lunch, and dinner, courtesy of CNN. If it were possible to gather 90 percent of our population to support the war effort, and gather an army of several million who volunteered to die for it, is it not then possible to gather a majority who will support the repair of our society and an army of several million who would work for it? We are threatened. We are all threatened, every man woman and child, rich or poor, black or white or brown, yellow or red. We are all threatened.

In Part Seven you will find a listing of agencies, both governmental and private, that assist the homeless. They need your help. Get involved by donating your time or money. If you have a special talent or skill that can help the needy, give an hour a month to the cause. Build a house, pound a nail, paint a wall, make a sandwich, bake a cake, give your shirt, dry a tear, shake a hand, write or call your congressman and ask what he can do for the mentally ill, talk to your governor's staff and ask them what you can do to help.

If you own or run a restaurant, what do you do with the extra food at night? Get together and visit a mission; make this a mission. If you are an employer, would the bottom line be bent too severely if you hired one additional worker? Is your church now actively working to lessen the burden of the homeless? If not, perhaps you might be the catalyst that makes that a reality. Start with one family or person in need. Doctor, do you have room in your schedule for one free family? Dentist, can you pull a bad tooth for free? Family, if you have a relative on the street or nearing it, can you make a place for him or her? Can you teach someone to read? Leaders, can you trust us with the truth of our condition so that we can help you help us? Ministers of all faiths, can't you take off your robes, join hands, teach to our sameness, and lay away the differences that keep us separate?

Whether or not we will or can do anything about the total issue is not important. The important thing is, if you can do something for one soul, you have done something of great value.

Do something! Do something! Do something!

There is just a sliver of moon outside the window tonight. It smiles at me through the clouds drifting in. A part of me smiles back. A thunderstorm is beginning to boil just west of here. I believe that last flash of lightning was right over the lake house where Katy is sleeping tonight. A part of me is clouding up, too, thinking of how much we have to do. The city has grown quiet. Not much happening in here with me now; it's all happening out there somewhere. Some are escaping from the growing distress; some are not able to. Tomorrow will be much like today: somebody died, someone born, somebody killed somebody, someone helped someone. Somebody is trying to sleep above the crying of an empty stomach. Someone is trying to sleep after eating and drinking too much at a late dinner.

The book is done, finished, over. I'm through with it. It's yours now; you bought it. It's part of your ledger now, and you'll do what you will or won't. That's just the way it was in this illusion today.

I just realized you know me now about as well as most people do and I do not know you. Write to me at:

NOAH
6957 N.W. Exp. Suite 278
Oklahoma City, OK 73132

If you are on the edge of despair, write. Perhaps we can help. If you want to help, write. We need you. If you take issue with my statements, write. Perhaps we will talk. At any rate, write. I do want to hear from you.

The rain is flashing now in the silhouette of the street light. I could not help but come out here to feel it on my cheek. I love the rain's touch. It's clean; it smells good. It's an old friend.

That reminds me of a time in New Orleans in the parking lot of a shopping center. I was pasted like a poster to the dryness of the doorway and I saw these two shadows moving across the parking lot . . .

And then something happened.

MORE HELP WANTED

PART **7**

CHAPTER
TWENTY-TWO

Reference Material

The following are advocacy groups and governmental agencies
and their publications available to the public. You may wish to
join or subscribe to their literature. I relied greatly on the information available from the first two groups on this list. I highly
recommend them.

National Low-Income Housing Coalition

Low-Income Housing Information Service
Barry Zigas
1012 14th Street, NW, Suite 1500
Washington, DC 20005

Low-Income Housing in America: An Introduction by Larry
Yates
order #P101

A Place to Call Home: The Crisis in Housing for the Poor by Paul Leonard, Cushing N. Dolbear, and Edward Lazere. order #R201

Out of Reach: Why Everyday People Can't Find Affordable Housing by Cushing N. Dolbear. order #R202

The Housing and Community Development Act: HR 1180 by Barry Zigas. order #T501

At a Snail's Pace by Cushing N. Dolbear. order #R203

Low-Income Housing Needs by Cushing N. Dolbear. order #R204

Low-Income Housing and Homeless: Facts And Myths by Barry Zigas and Cushing N. Dolbear. order #SM302

Unlocking the Door: Women and Housing, NLIHC. order #P102

A Program to End the Low-Income Housing Crisis by Barry Zigas. order #P103

National Alliance to End Homelessness
Nan Roman, Director
Michael Mayer, Assistant Director
1518 K Street, NW, Suite 206
Washington, D.C. 20005

This group publishes *The Alliance,* an excellent, informative monthly update of information relating to the homeless problem. The publication details upcoming conferences and govermental policies that affect the homeless.

The following publications are by HUD, U.S. Department of Housing and Urban Development, Office of Policy and Research.

Non-McKinney Federal Programs

Interagency Council on the Homeless
451 Seventh Street, SW, Suite 10158
Washington, D.C. 20410–0000

Fact Sheet

National Survey of Shelters For the Homeless

GAO Report to Congressional Requesters

Homelessness: Changes in the Interagency Council on the Homeless Make it More Effective

Homelessness: Issues and Legislation in the 101st Congress, CRS Issue Brief, Library of Congress
Order #IB88070

Emergency Food and Shelter National Board Program
601 North Fairfax Street, Suite 225
Alexandria, Virginia 22314

Federal Dollars, Local Concerns.

CHAPTER
TWENTY-THREE

List of State Agencies

The following is a list of agencies or organizations that are in place to assist the homeless and those that wish to help. This is but a partial list of groups that are prepared to act as clearing houses for information or assistance.

ALABAMA

Alabama Department of Economic
   and Community Affairs
Community Services Division
Joe McNees/Andre Epps
3465 Norman Bridge Road
Montgomery, AL 36105
Phone: 205-284-8955
Fax: 205-284-8670

Alabama Low-Income Housing
   Coalition
Cleo Askew
P.O. Box 95
Epes, AL 35460
Phone: 205-652-9676

Travelers Aid Society of
   Birmingham
Molly Hester
3600 Eighth Avenue South, Suite
   110-West
Birmingham, AL 36106
Phone: 205-322-5426

Family Guidance Center
Christopher Dumas
Walter White, Executive Director
925 Forrest Avenue
Montgomery, AL 36106
Phone: 205-265-0568

ALASKA

Alaska Coalition for the Homeless
Paul Day
C/o Department of Community and
  Regional Affairs
949 East 36th Street, Suite 402
Anchorage, AK 99508
Phone: 907-563-1073

Department of Community and
  Regional Affairs
State of Alaska
David G. Hoffman
P.O. Box B
Juneau, AK 99801
Phone: 907-465-4700

ARIZONA

Arizona Department of Economic
  Security
Community Services
  Administration
Karen Novache/Terry R. Cook
P.O. Box 6123–0867
Phoenix, AZ 85005
Phone: 602-229-2736

Homeless Task Force/Arizona
  Human Services Coalition
Mark Clark
C/o Traveler's Aid
40 West Veterans Boulevard
Tucson, AZ 85713
Phone: 602-622-8900

ARKANSAS

Alliance of Shelter Providers
Joe Flaherty
C/o Our House
P.O. Box 34155
Little Rock, AR 72203
Phone: 501-375-2416

Office of Community Services
Thomas Green
P.O. Box 1437/Slot 1330
Little Rock, AR 72203
Phone: 501-682-8715

CALIFORNIA

California Coalition for Rural
  Housing (CCRH)
Collie Hutchison
2000 "O" Street, Suite 230
Sacramento, CA 95814
Phone: 916-443-5128

California Homeless Coalition
Kay Knepprath
926 "J" Street, Suite 906
Sacramento, CA 95814
Phone: 916-447-0390

California Homeless Coalition
Toni Reinis
1010 South Flower, Suite 500
Los Angeles, CA 90015
Phone: 213-746-7690

California Right to Housing
  Campaign
Marc Brown
2000 "O" Street, Suite 230
Sacramento, CA 95814
Phone: 916-443-5128

California Right to Housing
  Campaign
Tim Carpenter
3400 Irvine Avenue, Suite 216
Newport Beach, CA 92660
Phone: 714-852-0523

Health and Welfare Agency/Office
  of the Secretary
Margaret Debow
1600 Ninth Street, Suite 450
Sacramento, CA 95814
Phone: 916-445-0196

Travelers Aid of Alameda County,
Inc.
William Groth
1761 Broadway
Oakland, CA 94612
Phone: 415-444-6834

Travelers Aid Society of Long
Beach, Inc.
Norma Mueller
947 East Fourth Street
Long Beach, CA 90802
Phone: 213-432-3485

Travelers Aid Society of Los
Angeles
Wayne Hinrichs
453 South Spring Street, Suite 901
Los Angeles, CA 90013
Phone: 213-625-2501

Travelers Aid of San Diego
Mary Colacicco
1122 Fourth Avenue, Suite 201
San Diego, CA 92101–4816
Phone: 619-232-7991

COLORADO
Colorado Affordable Housing
Partnership
Mary Booker
1981 Blake Street
Denver, CO 80202
Phone: 303-297-2548

Colorado Coalition for the Homeless
John Parvensky/Mary Wilham
2100 Broadway
Denver, CO 80205
Phone: 303-293-2217

Colorado Division of Housing
John Maldonado
1313 Sherman, Suite 623
Denver, CO 80203
Phone: 303-866-2033

Governor's Task Force on the
Homeless
Swanee Hunt
1981 Blake Street
Denver, CO 80202
Phone: 303-297-7355

Human Services, Inc.
Noreen Keleshian
899 Logan, Suite 500
Denver, CO 80203
Phone: 303-830-2714

Travelers Aid Services
Steven Rees
1245 East Colfax Avenue, Suite 408
Denver, CO 80218
Phone: 303-832-8194

CONNECTICUT
Connecticut Coalition for the
Homeless
Jane McNichol
30 Jordan Lane
Wethersfield, CT 06109
Phone: 203-721-7876

Department of Human Resources
Elliot Ginsberg/Alan Carbenneau
1049 Asylum Avenue
Hartford, CT 06105
Phone: 203-566-3318

Travelers Aid of Hartford
Jane P. Stanke/John R. Morrison
Catholic Charities
896 Asylum Avenue
Hartford, CT 06105
Phone: 203-522-2247 or 203-522-8241

Family Counseling of Greater New
Haven
Bill Mecca
1 State Street
New Haven, CT 06511
Phone: 203-865-6765

DELAWARE

Delaware Coalition for the
   Homeless
Delaware Housing Now
Ken Shuman
P.O. Box 25291
Wilmington, DE 19899
Phone: 302-656-1667 or 302-762-2779

Delaware Housing Coalition
Delores Solberg
317 Treadway Tower
9 East Lockerman Street
Dover, DE 19901
Phone: 302-678-2286

Division of Community Services
Department of Community Affairs
Dennis Savage
820 North French Street, 4th floor
Wilmington, DE 19801
Phone: 302-571-3491

Family Service Delaware, Inc.
Alvin Snyder/Marvis Hollowell
809 Washington Street
Wilmington, DE 19801
Phone: 302-658-9885

DISTRICT OF COLUMBIA

Churches Conference on Shelter
   and Housing
Keary Kincannon
1711 14th Street, NW
Washington, DC 20009
Phone: 202-232-6748

Commission on Social Services
Jan Woodward
609 "H" Street, NE, Suite 512
Washington, DC 20002
Phone: 202-727-5930

Community for Creative
   Nonviolence/Housing Now
Carol Fennelly
425 Second Street, NW
Washington, DC 20001
Phone: 202-393-1909 or 202-393-4409

DC Commission on Homelessness
Annie Goodson
801 North Capitol Street, NE,
   Suite 700
Washington, DC 20002
Phone: 202-727-0518

Low-Income Housing Information
   Service
Barry Zigas
1012 14th Street, NW, Suite 1006
Washington, DC 20005
Phone: 202-662-1530

Mayor's Homeless Coordinating
   Council
Ken Long
609 "H" Street, NE, 5th floor
Washington, DC 20002
Phone: 202-727-5930

National Alliance to End
   Homelessness
Nan Roman/Michael Mayer
1518 "K" Street, NW, Suite 206
Washington, DC 20005
Phone: 202-638-4664

Travelers Aid of Washington, DC,
   Inc.
Pauline L. Dunn
512 "C" Street, NE
Washington, DC 20005
Phone: 202-546-3120

Women's Shelter Providers
Tracy Newell
C/o New Endeavors for Women
611 "N" Street, NW
Washington, DC 20001
Phone: 202-662-5825

249

FLORIDA

Community Service Council of
    Broward County
Arthur Ellick
1300 South Andrews Avenue
Fort Lauderdale, FL 33315
Phone: 305-524-4877

Florida Coalition for the Homeless
Fred Karnas, Jr.
P.O. Box 76301
Tampa, FL 33675
Phone: 407-425-5307

Florida Department of HRS
Office of Program Policy and
    Development
Bill Hanson
1317 Winewood Boulevard
Tallahassee, FL 32399
Phone: 904-488-2761

Florida Low-Income Housing
    Coalition
Claudia Frese
P.O. Box 932
Tallahassee, FL 32302
Phone: 904-878-4219

Florida Non-Profit Housing
Carol Noel
P.O. Box 1987
Sebring, FL 33871
Phone: 813-385-2519

Governor's Task Force on
    Homelessness
Florida Departmert of HRS
Jill Sandler
1317 Winewood Boulevard
Building No. 1, Room 216
Tallahassee, FL 32399
Phone: 904-488-2761

First Call for Help
Marie Robinson
16 Southeast 13th Street
Fort Lauderdale, FL 33316
305-467-6333

Travelers Aid of Daytona Beach
L. Strait Hollis
330 Magnolia Avenue
Daytona Beach, FL 32014
Phone: 904-252-4752

The Center for Family Services
Tom Cimock
2218 South Dixie Highway
West Palm Beach, FL 33401
Phone: 407-655-4483

Travelers Aid of Tampa
Donna Todd
920 West Kennedy Boulevard
Tampa, FL 33606
Phone: 813-253-5936

GEORGIA

Georgia Homeless Resource
    Network
Bill Holland
363 Georgia Avenue, SE
Atlanta, GA 30312
Phone: 404-589-9495

Georgia Housing Coalition
Verlee Fowler
250 Georgia Avenue, Suite 363
Atlanta, GA 30312
Phone: 404-523-0896

Habitat for Humanity
    International, Inc.
121 Habitat Street
Americus, GA 31709–9987
Phone: 912-924-6935

Office of Community and
  Intergovernmental Resources
Georgia Department of Human
  Resources
Don Mathis
47 Trinity Avenue, Suite 541-H
Atlanta, GA 30334
Phone: 404-656-3479

Special Housing Projects
Georgia Residential Finance
  Authority
Terry E. Ball
60 Executive Parkway South, Suite
  250
Atlanta, GA 30329
Phone: 404-320-4840

Travelers Aid of Atlanta
Dr. Eleanor Hynes
40 Pryor Street, SW, Suite 400
Atlanta, GA 30303
Phone: 404-527-7400

Travelers Aid of Savannah
Helen Ludlow
P.O. Box 23975
Savannah, GA 31403–3975
Phone: 912-233-2801

HAWAII
Affordable Housing Alliance
Betty Lou Larsen
1164 Bishop Street, Suite 1605
Honolulu, HI 96813
Phone: 808-536-9758

Hawaii Housing Authority
Aric Arakaki
P.O. Box 17907
Honolulu, HI 96817
Phone: 808-848-3228

Homeless Aloha, Inc.
Clarence Liu
333 Queen Street, Suite 408
Honolulu, HI 96813
Phone: 808-537-1399

IDAHO
Division of Community
  Rehabilitation
Department of Health and Welfare
Joseph Brunson
450 West State Street
Boise, ID 83702
Phone: 208-334-5531

Idaho Rural Housing Coalition
Tim Lopez
P.O. Box 490
Caldwell, ID 83606
Phone: 208-454-1652

ILLINOIS
Illinois Coalition for the Homeless
Michael Marubio
522 East Monroe Street, Suite 304
Springfield, IL 62705
Phone: 217-788-8060

Illinois Coalition for the Homeless
Michael Marubio
P.O. Box 2751
Chicago, IL 60690
Phone: 312-435-4548

Illinois Department of Public Aid
Kathleen Kustra
Harris Building, 100 South Grand
Springfield, IL 62762
Phone: 217-782-1200

Information and Referral Service of
  the Quad Cities
Genevieve Rafferty
2002 Third Avenue
Rock Island, IL 61201
Phone: 309-786-5424

Office of the Governor/Human
  Services
Ginger Ostro
100 West Randolph Street, 16th
  floor
Chicago, IL 60601
Phone: 312-814-6725

Statewide Housing Action Coalition
  (SHAC)
Fran Tobin
202 South State Street, Suite 1414
Chicago, IL 60604
Phone: 312-939-6074

Travelers and Immigrants Aid of
  Chicago
Sid Mohn
327 South LaSalle Street, Room
  1500
Chicago, IL 60604
Phone: 312-435-4500

INDIANA

Indiana Coalition for the Homeless
Barbara Anderson
C/o Hoosier Valley Economic
  Opportunity Corporation
P.O. Box 843
Jeffersonville, IN 47130
Phone: 812-288-6451

Indiana Housing Network
Jim Taylor
C/o Indiana Interreligious
  Commission on Human Equality
1100 West 42nd Street, Suite 320
Indianapolis, IN 46208
Phone: 317-924-4226 or 317-924-4245

Office of the Governor
John Delap
Statehouse, Suite 206
Indianapolis, IN 46207
Phone: 317-232-1079

IOWA

Department of Economic
  Development
Lane Palmer
200 East Grand Avenue
Des Moines, IA 50309
Phone: 515-281-7240

Iowa Coalition for the Homeless
Ben Zachrich
1111 Ninth Street, Suite 370
Des Moines, IA 50314
Phone: 515-244-9748

KANSAS

Kansas Department of Commerce/
  Office of Housing
Phil Dubach
400 West Eighth Street, 5th Floor
Topeka, KS 66603
Phone: 913-296-4100

Kansas Homeless and Hunger
  Action Coalition
Jim Olson
C/o CRC, 121 East Sixth Street,
  Suite 4
Topeka, KS 66603
Phone: 913-233-1365

Topeka Housing Information Center
Karen Hiller
1195 SW Buchanan, Suite 508
Topeka, KS 66604
Phone: 913-234-0217

KENTUCKY

Advisory Council for the Homeless
Kentucky Office of the Governor
Joan Taylor
State Capitol
Frankfort, KY 40601
Phone: 502-564-2611

Cabinet for Human Resources/
  Office of the Secretary
Ronnie Dunn
275 East Main Street
Frankfort, KY 40621
Phone: 502-564-7130

Family and Children's Agency
Daniel Fox/Jane E. Panther
1115 Garvin Place
Louisville, KY 40201-3784
Phone: 502-583-1741

Federation of Appalachian Housing
  Enterprises
David Lollis
P.O. Drawer B
Berea, KY 40621
Phone: 606-986-2321

Kentucky Coalition for the
  Homeless
Mary Beth Gregg
C/o Welcome House
141 Pike Street
Covington, KY 41011
Phone: 606-431-8717

LOUISIANA
Division of Community Services
Marilyn N. Hayes
P.O. Box 44367
Baton Rouge, LA 70804
Phone: 504-342-2297

Travelers Aid of Greater New
  Orleans
Crystal Pope
846 Baronne Street
New Orleans, LA 70113
Phone: 504-525-8726

MAINE
Department of Economic and
  Community Development
Margaret R. Marshall
State House Station, Suite 130
Augusta, ME 04333
Phone: 207-289-6800

Governor's Interdepartmental
  Council on the Homeless
Marta Wenger
State House Station, Suite 146
Augusta, ME 04333
Phone: 207-289-3862

Maine Coalition for the Homeless
C/o York County Shelter, Inc.
Donald Gean
P.O. Box 20
Alfred, ME 04002
Phone: 207-324-1137

MARYLAND
Action for the Homeless
Norma Pinette
2539 St. Paul Street
Baltimore, MD 21218
Phone: 301-467-3800

Governor's Advisory Board on
  Homelessness
Kathleen Riley
C/o Department of Human
  Resources
311 West Saratoga Street, Suite
  229
Baltimore, MD 21201
Phone: 301-333-0276

Homeless Services Program
Harriet Goldman
311 West Saratoga Street, Suite
  229
Baltimore, MD 21201
Phone: 301-333-0147

253

Maryland Low-Income Housing
  Coalition
Ron Halbright
28 East Ostend
Baltimore, MD 21230
Phone: 301-727-4200

PATH: People Aiding Travelers and
  the Homeless
Nancy Friedman/Dawn Thomsen
204 North Liberty Street, Suite
  200
Baltimore, MD 21201
Phone: 301-685-3569
Emergency Number: 301-685-5874

Break-the-Cycle Employment
  Program
Nancy Friedman
4 West 26th Street
Baltimore, MD 21218
Phone: 301-243-0420

MASSACHUSSETTS
Executive Office of Human
  Services
Division of Homelessness and
  Housing
Social Policy Unit
Irene Lee
1 Ashburton Place, Suite 1109
Boston, MA 02108
Phone: 617-727-8036

Massachusetts Affordable Housing
  Alliance
Lou Finfer
25 West Street, 3rd floor
Boston, MA 02111
Phone: 617-728-9100

Massachusetts Coalition for the
  Homeless
Sue Marsh
33 Farnsworth Street
Boston, MA 02210
Phone: 617-451-0707

Massachusetts Housing Now
Jim Stewart
C/o First Church Shelter
11 Garden Street
Cambridge, MA 02138
Phone: 617-661-1873

Massachusetts Shelter Providers
  Association
Mark Baker
444 Harrison Avenue
Boston, MA 02118
Phone: 617-482-4944

Travelers Aid of Boston
Richard Soricelli
711 Atlantic Avenue at 17 East
  Street
Boston, MA 02111
Phone: 617-542-7286

MICHIGAN
Michigan Housing Coalition
Kris Wisniewski/Therese Porn
P.O. Box 14038
Lansing, MI 48901
Phone: 517-377-0509

Michigan Housing Coordinating
  Council
Ted S. Rozeboom
309 North Washington Square,
  Suite 203
P.O. Box 30249
Lansing, MI 48909
Phone: 517-335-0923

Travelers Aid of Detroit
Earnestine Coates
211 West Congress, 3rd Floor
Detroit, MI 48226
Phone: 313-962-6740

MINNESOTA

Interagency Task Force on
Homelessness
Minnesota Housing Finance
Agency
James Solem
400 Sibley Street, Suite 300
St. Paul, MN 55101
Phone: 612-296-5738

Minnesota Coalition for the
Homeless
Val Baertlein/Sue Phillips
666 Broadway Street, NE
Minneapolis, MN 55413
Phone: 612-379-2779 or 612-379-8920

Minnesota Housing Partnership
Chip Helbach
520 20th Avenue South
Minneapolis, MN 55454
Phone: 612-339-5255

Minnesota Department of Jobs and
Training
Patrick Leary
150 East Kellogg Boulevard, Suite
670
St. Paul, MN 55418
Phone: 612-297-3409

United Way First Call for Help
Rita Hayden
404 South Eighth Street
Minneapolis, MN 55404
Phone: 612-335-5000

MISSISSIPPI

Governor's Office of Federal/State
Programs
Community Services Branch
Larry Christian
421 West Pascagoula Street
Jackson, MS 39203
Phone: 601-949-2041, ext. 4266

Mississippi Housing Coalition
Linda McMurtrey
P.O. Box 373
Jackson, MS 39205
Phone: 601-545-4595

Mississippi Task Force on
Homelessness
Division of Budget and Policy
Royal Walker
421 West Pascagoula Street
Jackson, MS 39203
Phone: 601-960-4280

Salvation Army/ Travelers Aid
Tom Hitt
426 West Pascagoula Street
Jackson, MS 39203
Phone: 601-968-3972

MISSOURI

Division of General Services
Department of Social Services
Al Gage
P.O. Box 1643
Jefferson City, MO 65102
Phone: 314-751-3870

Low-Income Housing Task Force
Missouri Association for Social
Welfare
Peter DeSimone
515 East High Street
Jefferson City, MO 65101
Phone: 314-634-2901

Missouri Coalition for the Homeless
Larry Rice
C/o New Life Evangelistic Center
P.O. Box 473
St. Louis, MO 63166
Phone: 314-421-3020 or 314-896-9109

Mullanphy Travelers Aid
Vivien Hopper
Greyhound Bus Station
809 North Broadway
Street Louis, MO 63102
Phone: 314-241-5820

MONTANA
Intergovernmental Human Services
  Bureau
Family Services Division
Department of Social and
  Rehabilitation Services
Jim Nolan
P.O. Box 4210
Helena, MT 59604
Phone: 406-444-4540

Montana Low-Income Coalition
Marcia Schreder
P.O. Box 1029
Helena, MT 59624
Phone: 406-449-8801

NEBRASKA
Governor's Policy Research Office
Gary L. Rex
State Capitol, Suite 1319
Lincoln, NE 66509
Phone: 402-471-2414

Nebraska Coalition for the
  Homeless
John Mata
3915 "N" Street
Omaha, NE 68107
Phone: 402-559-7115

NEVADA
Nevada Homeless Coalition
Nancy Paolini
C/o Department of Social Work
University of Nevada/Reno, Mail
  Stop 90
Reno, NV 89557
Phone: 702-784-6542

Nevada State Welfare Division
Linda A. Ryan/Anthoula Sullivan
2527 North Carson Street
Carson City, NV 89710
Phone: 702-687-4715

NEW HAMPSHIRE
New Hampshire Coalition for the
  Homeless
Henrietta Charest
P.O. Box 46
Manchester, NH 03105
Phone: 603-623-4888

New Hampshire Commission on
  Homelessness
Msgr. John Quinn
C/o New Hampshire Catholic
  Charities
P.O. Box 686
Manchester, NH 03105
Phone: 603-669-3030

Office of the Governor
Nancy Baybutt
State Capitol
Concord, NH 03301
Phone: 603-271-2121

NEW JERSEY
Governor's Office of Management
  and Planning
Christina Klotz
State House, CN-001
Trenton, NJ 08625
Phone: 609-777-1265

New Jersey Department of
  Community Affairs
Anthony Cancro
101 South Broad, Suite CN-800
Trenton, NJ 08625
Phone: 609-292-2705

Right to Housing Coalition of New
  Jersey
Peggy Earisman
217 Howe Avenue
Passaic, NJ 07055
Phone: 201-932-6812

NEW MEXICO
Human Services Department
Community Assistance Section/
  Income Support Division
Dorian Dodson
P.O. Box 2348
Santa Fe, NM 87504
Phone: 505-827-7264

New Mexico Housing Coalition
Michael A. Varela
P.O. Box CC
Santa Fe, NM 87502
Phone: 505-988-2859

NEW YORK
Child and Family Services
Ivy K. Diggs
Ellicott Square Building
295 Main Street, Room 828
Buffalo, NY 14203
Phone: 716-854-8661

Family Services of Greater Utica
Eleanor Wertimer
401 Colombia Street
Utica, NY 13502
Phone: 315-735-2236

Housing Now: New York City/State
Larry Wood
C/o Cathedral of St. John the Divine
1047 Amsterdam Avenue
New York City, NY 10025
Phone: 212-316-7544

Metropolitan Assistance
  Corporation
Lucy Friedman/Helene Lauffer
2 Lafayette Street, 3rd floor
New York, NY 10007
Phone: 212-577-7700

New York State Coalition for the
  Homeless
Fred Griesbach
90 State Street, Suite 1505
Albany, NY 12207
Phone: 518-436-5612

New York State Rural Housing
  Coalition
Tim Palmer
350 Northern Boulevard, Suites
  101–102
Albany, NY 12210
Phone: 518-434-1314

Office of Shelter and Supportive
  Housing Programs
Department of Social Services
Peter R. Brest
40 North Pearl Street, Floor 10-A
Albany, NY 12243
Phone: 518-474-9059 or 212-804-1295

NORTH CAROLINA
Division of Community Assistance
Bob Chandler
P.O. Box 27687
Raleigh, NC 27611
Phone: 919-733-2850

Family Services
Sid Bradsher
P.O. Box 944
Wilmington, NC 28402
Phone: 919-392-7051

Family Services of Winston-Salem
Sarah Y. Austin
610 Coliseum Drive
Winston-Salem, NC 27106–5393
Phone: 919-722-8173

North Carolina Low-Income
    Housing Coalition
Linda Shaw
P.O. Box 27863
Raleigh, NC 27611
Phone: 919-833-6201

Travelers Aid of Wake County
George O'Neal/Willie Reddick
1100 Wake Forrest Road
Raleigh, NC 27604–1354
Phone: 919-821-0790

TAS of Charlotte, Inc.
Martha Brown
500 Spratt Street
Charlotte, NC 28206
Phone: 704-334-7288

NORTH DAKOTA

North Dakota Coalition for
    Homeless People
Barbara Stanton
C/o YWCA
1616 12th Avenue North
Fargo, ND 58102
Phone: 701-232-2547

Office of Intergovernmental
    Assistance
Shirley Dykshoorn
State Capitol Building, 14th floor
Bismarck, ND 58505
Phone: 701-224-2094

OHIO

Family Service Association
Robert Nelson/Keith Daugherty
184 Salem, Room 790
Dayton, OH 45406
Phone: 513-222-9481

International Institute
Dr. Ernest Barbeau
632 Vine Street, Suite 505
Cinncinnati, OH 45202
Phone: 513-721-7660

Office of the Governor/Human
    Services and Policy
Dan Pollack
77 South High Street, 30th floor
Columbus, OH 43266
Phone: 614-466-7781

Ohio Coalition for the Homeless
Bill Faith
1066 North High Street
Columbus, OH 43201
Phone: 614-291-1984 or 614-944-4114

Ohio Department of Development/
    Community Development
Roberta "Bobbie" Garber
P.O. Box 1001
Columbus, OH 43266
Phone: 614-466-5863

Ohio Department of Mental Health
Interagency Homeless Cluster
Grace Lewis
30 East Broad Street
Columbus, OH 43215
Phone: 614-466-7460

Ohio Housing Coalition
Julie A. Keil
1066 North High Street
Columbus, OH 43201
Phone: 614-299-0544

Ohio Rural Housing Coalition
Roger McCauley
P.O. Box 787
Athens, OH 45701
Phone: 614-594-8499

Travelers Aid
Penelope Talley
Joseph Bruening Red Cross Center
3747 Euclid
Cleveland, OH 44115
Phone: 216-431-3010

OKLAHOMA

Governor's Task Force on
  Homelessness
Office of the Governor
State Capitol, Suite 210
Oklahoma City, OK 73105
Phone: 405-523-4254

Oklahoma Housing Finance
  Agency/Homeless Programs
Shirley Williams
P.O. Box 26720
Oklahoma City, OK 73126
Phone: 405-848-1144

Jesus House
Sister Ruth Wynne
1335 West Sheridan
Oklahoma City, OK 73106
Phone: 405-232-7164

Homeless Coordinator of Oklahoma
  City
Christine Byrd
1335 West Sheridan 73106
Oklahoma City, OK
Phone: 405-232-7164

Traveler's Aid Society of Oklahoma
  City
Marrie Hollenbeck
412 Northwest Fifth Street
Oklahoma City, OK 73102
Phone: 405-232-5507

OREGON

Oregon Housing Now Coalition
Diane Hess
C/o MCA; 812 SW Washington
  Street, Suite 300
Portland, OR 97205
Phone: 503-295-6790

Oregon Rural Housing Coalition
Darlee Rex
525 Glen Creek Road, NW, Suite
  210
Salem, OR 97304
Phone: 503-585-6193

Oregon Shelter Network
Robert B. More
363 South Second Street
Coos Bay, OR 97420
Phone: 503-756-3176

State Community Services
Victor Vasquez/Alan Kramer
207 Public Service Building
Salem, OR 97310
Phone: 503-378-4729

PENNSYLVANIA

Coalition on Homelessness in
  Pennsylvania
Phyllis Ryan
802 North Broad Street
Philadelphia, PA 19130
Phone: 215-232-2300

Commission on Economic
  Opportunity
Eugene M. Brady/David Ritter
211–213 South Main Street
Wilkes-Barre, PA 18701
Phone: 717-826-0510

Governor's Policy Office
Annette Mayer
Finance Building, Suite 506
Harrisburg, PA 17120
Phone: 717-787-1954

259

Pennsylvania Low-Income Housing
  Coalition
Mary Ann Holloway
4 South Easton Road
Glenside, PA 19038
Phone: 215-576-7044

Travelers Aid of Pittsburgh
Robert Lindner
Greyhound Bus Terminal
11th and Liberty Avenue
Pittsburgh, PA 15222
Phone: 412-281-5466

Travelers Aid of Philadelphia
Ernest Eskin
311 South Juniper Street, Suite
  500–05
Philadelphia, PA 19107
Phone: 215-546-0571

RHODE ISLAND

Division of Economic and Social
  Services
Department of Human Services
Thomas A. McDonough
600 New London Avenue
Cranston, RI 02920
Phone: 401-464-2371

Rhode Island Coalition for the
  Homeless
David McCreadie, Jr.
P.O. Box 23505
Providence, RI 02903
Phone: 401-521-2255

Rhode Island Right to Housing
  Coalition
Jim Tull
C/o Amos House
P.O. Box 2873
Providence, RI 02907
Phone: 401-272-0220

Travelers Aid of Rhode Island
Marion Avarista
177 Union Street
Providence, RI 02903
Phone: 401-421-7410

SOUTH CAROLINA

Economic Development
William Gunn
1205 Pendleton Street, Suite 357
Columbia, SC 29201
Phone: 803-734-0662

South Carolina Coalition for the
  Homeless
Marie Toner
C/o South Carolina Department of
  Social Services
P.O. Box 1520
Columbia, SC 29202
Phone: 803-734-6183

South Carolina Low-Income
  Housing Coalition
Marvin Lare
P.O. Box 1520
Columbia, SC 29202
Phone: 803-734-6122

SOUTH DAKOTA

Office of the Governor
Ruth Hultgren Henneman
State Capitol Building
Pierre, SD 57501
Phone: 605-773-3212

TENNESSEE

Knoxville Travelers Aid
Keith Richardson
107 South Gay Street
Knoxville, TN 37902
Phone: 615-533-8718

Nashville Union Mission
Rev. Carl Resener
129 Seventh Avenue South
Nashville, TN 37203
Phone: 615-255-2475

Tennessee Coalition for the
  Homeless
Ed J. Wallin
C/o Veterans Center
1 North Third Street
Memphis, TN 38103
Phone: 901-544-3506

Tennessee Department of Human
  Services
Steven Meinbresse
400 Deaderick Street, 14th floor
Nashville, TN 37219
Phone: 615-741-3335

Travelers Aid Society
Joyce Wesley
46 North Third Street, Suite 708
Memphis, TN 38103
Phone: 901-525-5466

TEXAS
Adopt-a-Family Network
Jan Johnson
6250 NE Loop 820
Fort Worth, TX 76180
Phone: 817-281-1164

Austin Street Mission
Father Jerry Hill
723 South Austin Street
Dallas, TX 75202
Phone: 214-742-7282

Texas Alliance for Human Needs
Jude Filler
2520 Longview, Suite 311
Austin, TX 78705
Phone: 512-474-5019

Texas Department of Community
  Affairs
General Willie L. Scott
P.O. Box 13166
Austin, TX 78711
Phone: 512-834-6022

Texas Homeless Network
Kent C. Miller
C/o Benedictine Health Service
400 East Anderson Lane, Suite 306
Austin, TX 78752
Phone: 512-339-9724

Travelers of Houston
Joan Chellberg
2630 Westridge
Houston,TX 77054
Phone: 713-668-0911

UTAH
State Homeless Coordinating
  Committee
Department of Community and
  Economic Development
Alice Shearer
324 South State Street, 3rd floor
Salt Lake City, UT 84111
Phone: 801-538-8722

Utah Housing Coalition
Mark Smith
C/o Independent Living Center
764 South 200 West
Salt Lake City, UT 84101
Phone: 801-359-2444

Travelers Aid of Salt Lake City
Patrick Poulin
210 Rio Grande
Salt Lake City, UT 84101
Phone: 801-328-8996

VERMONT
Department of Housing and
  Community Affairs
Nancy Eldridge
Pavilion Building
Montpelier, VT 05602
Phone: 802-828-3217

261

Rural Vermont
Arthony Pollina
15 Barre Street
Montpelier, VT 05602
Phone: 802-223-7222

Vermont Affordable Housing
  Coalition
Kirby A. Dunn
P.O. Box 1603
Burlington, VT 05402
Phone: 802-863-6248

Vermont Coalition for the
  Homeless/Vermont Housing Now
Lucille Bonvouloir
P.O. Box 1616
Burlington, VT 05402
Phone: 802-864-7402

VIRGINIA
Peninsula Family Service
Faye C. Webb
1520 Aberdeen Road
Hampton, VA 23666
Phone: 804-838-1960

Rural Virgina, Inc.
Rick Cagan
P.O. Box 105
Richmond, VA 23201
Phone: 804-524-5853

Southwest Virginia Housing
  Coalition
Appalachian Office of Peace and
  Justice
Anthony Flaccavento
P.O. Box 660
St. Paul, VA 24283
Phone: 703-762-5050

Virgina Coalition for the Homeless
Sue M. Capers
7825 Cherokee Road
Richmond, VA 23225
Phone: 804-320-4577

Virginia Housing Coalition
John McCrimmon
C/o County Community Action
  Agency
P.O. Box H-K
Williamsburg, VA 23187
Phone: 804-729-9332

Virginia Department of Housing
  and Community Development
Robert J. Adams
205 North Fourth Street
Richmond, VA 23219
Phone: 804-786-5395

Travelers of Virginia
Willard Smith
515 East Main
Richmond, VA 23219
Phone: 804-643-0279

WASHINGTON
Emergency Housing Services
Department of Community
  Development
Corine Foster
9th and Columbia Building, MSGH-
  51
Olympia, WA 98504
Phone: 206-586-1363

Washington Coalition for Rural
  Housing
Kurt Creager
19021 90th Place, NE
Bothell, WA 98011
Phone: 206-296-8644

Washington Low-Income Housing
  Coalition
Ken Katahira
409 Maynard South
Seattle, WA 98104
Phone: 206-624-1802

Washington State Coalition for the
  Homeless
Maureen Howard
C/o Martin Luther King Ecumenical
  Ctr.
1424 Tacoma Avenue South, Suite
  A
Tacoma, WA 98402
Phone: 206-383-1585

WEST VIRGINIA
Office of Economic Opportunity
Community Development Division
Governor's Office of Community
  and Industrial Development
Joseph L. Barker
1204 Kanawha Boulevard East
Charleston, WV 25301
Phone: 304-348-4010

West Virginia Coalition for the
  Homeless
Chuck Hamsher
1205 Quarrier Street, 1st Floor
Charleston, WV 25301
Phone: 304-344-3970

WISCONSIN
Community Advocates
Ramon Wagner/Joseph Volk
4906 West Fond du Lac Avenue
Milwaukee, WI 53216
Phone: 414-449-4774

Department of Health and Social
  Services
Patricia Goodrich
1 West Wilson Street
P.O. Box 7850
Madison, WI 53707
Phone: 608-266-3681

Foundation for Rural Housing, Inc.
C. Thompson
4506 Regent Street
Madison, WI 53705
Phone: 608-238-3448

Governor's Interagency
  Coordinating Committee
Division of Economic Support
Judith Wilcox
P.O. Box 7935
Madison, WI 53707
Phone: 608-266-9388

WYOMING
Division of Community Programs
Department of Health and Social
  Services
Gary E. Maier
2300 Capitol Avenue
Cheyenne, WY 82002
Phone: 307-777-6779

NOTES

Preface

1. From *The Seed Trilogy* by Noah Snider.

Chapter 2   Who Are We?

1. Nationally, between 25 and 33 percent of homeless people are families with children. However, this figure varies considerably from city to city. In some areas as many as 65 percent of the homeless are reported to be families. Service providers almost always report that families are the fastest-growing segment of the homeless population. *Checklist for Success: Programs to Help the Hungry and Homeless,* prepared for the Emergency Food and Shelter Program by the National Alliance to End Homelessness, Spring 1990.
2. The office edition of *Webster's Dictionary.*

Chapter 6   The Ivory Tower

1. Thomas R. Malthus (1766–1834) father of the Malthusian theory, a doctrine that the increase in population is greater than the increase of subsistence, and unless birth numbers are controlled, poverty or war must serve as natural restriction of the increase.

Chapter 8   Life in the Garbage Can

1. Adapted from Lester R. Brown and William U. Chandler, et al, *State of the World* (Washington, DC: Norton & Norton, 1988).
2. Please buy and read the newest information published by Norton & Norton and distrituted by the Worldwatch Institute. Their address is: Worldwatch Institute, 1776 Massachusetts Ave. NW, Washington, DC 20036.

Chapter 9   Chasing the Same Dollar and Dream

1. Adapted from the supplement "Housing Is a Human Right!" published by the National Low-Income Housing Coalition, 1012 14th Street NW, #1500, Washington, DC 20005.
2. Paul A. Leonard is a policy analyst at the Center on Budget and

Policy Priorities. He directs the center's housing policy project and has authored a series of reports on housing conditions for the poor in major metropolitan areas. Cushing N. Dolbeare is a consultant on housing and public policy issues. She is the founder of the Low-Income Housing Information Service and National Low-Income Housing Coalition. She is the author of numerous studies on low-income housing needs and programs. Edward B. Lazere is a research assistant at the Center on Budget and Policy Priorities. His research focuses on affordable housing and related issues. All the information from both nonprofit organizations is available to the public for a small charge by writing to the *Center on Budget and Policy Priorities, 236 Massachusetts Avenue, NE, Suite 305, Washington, DC 20002* or to the *Low-Income Housing Information Service, 1012 14th Street, NW, Washington, DC 20005.*

Chapter 10   The Pac Man of Change

1. Thomas Macaulay, *Edinborough Review, 1800–1859,* "Review Southbey's Colloquies" (1830).
2. Friedrich Engels, from *The Industrial Proletariat* (1892).
3. Friedrich Engels, from *The Condition of the Working Class in England* (1845).
4. Ibid.
5. Charles Kingsley, from *Alton Locke* (1850).

Chapter 12   Rumor

1. From Book Two of *The Seed Trilogy* by Noah Snider.

Chapter 13   The Shepherds

1. Thomas Huxley, from "A Liberal Education: A Game of Chess," address delivered to the South London Working Men's College in 1868.

Chapter 19   The Meeting

1. You can write to the Adopt-a-Family Network Project, "Families Helping Families," Jan Johnson, Director, Community Center, 6250 NE Loop 820, Fort Worth, TX 76180.
2. Don Marquis, *Archy and Mehitabel* (New York: Doubleday, 1970 reprint).

ABOUT THE AUTHOR

Noah Snider, now an author and songwriter, was a husband, father, and a successful businessman who ended up homeless and alone. Snider no longer lives on the streets, but his years of homelessness gave him a deep compassion for the growing numbers of homeless people.